D0129590

Family Stress:

Coping
and Adaptation

Editors:
Hamilton I. McCubbin
Pauline G. Boss

A special issue of Family Relations
October 1980—Vol. 29, No. 4
National Council on Family Relations

PREFACE

Family Stress and Coping: Targets for Theory, Research, Counseling, and Education*

HAMILTON I. MCCUBBIN AND PAULINE GROSSENBACHER BOSS,
GUEST EDITORS**

Even under the most propitious circumstances, the family struggles with life's hardships as it attempts to fulfill its life span responsibility of socializing its members to become unique individuals as well as independent and responsible members of society. The growing body of research suggests that the family unit is "stressed" by a host of predictable and unpredictable life events such as parenthood, retirement and the loss of a family member, each of which has the capability of pulling the family unit together, moving the family unit to a higher order of functioning and effectiveness, or possibly of tearing the family unit apart. With increasing precision, researchers and counselors have been able to describe and document the nature and dynamics of family adjustment to such life events and change. These investigations also point to the commonsensical notion that families can be strengthened to defend themselves against the harmful effects of stress and that in times of extreme hardships, families would benefit from guidance and assistance in coping with stress.

Counselors and researchers exploring the intricacies of family behavior in response to stressful life events have generally focused on the psychological hardships and dysfunctional interpersonal behaviors. Predictably, we have tended to overlook the social context in which family coping and adjustment takes place. It has been widely assumed that the family was "at risk" due to the alleged absence of kinship and community supports. During the past decade we have witnessed the emergence of a wealth of investigations pointing to protective, buffering, *and* healing *elements within community life.*

The recent decade review on family stress and coping (McCubbin, Joy, Cauble, Comeau, Patterson & Needle, Nov. 1980) indicates that kinship systems are alive and well *and play a major role in supporting families under stress. Concomitantly, the community has been a major source of* social support *for families in crisis situations. This emphasis on the community and social resources for families under stress represents a major shift in inquiry from why families fail to why and how families succeed.*

Researchers and counselors have been so preoccupied with documenting the adverse effects of change and stress that they have generally overlooked the fact that some, if not most families are able to cope with stress, and if faced with a crisis, have the ability to recover. Without minimizing the difficulties and hardships of family life, we need to explore the circumstances and critical family and community resources which contribute to family coping and adaptation. This special issue represents our continued effort to highlight this important line of inquiry. By selecting articles which underscore theory, systematic research and which offer guidelines for and examples of clinical intervention, we, the editors, feel we have played a part in encouraging research and practice in this important domain of family stress and coping.

REFERENCE

McCubbin, H., Joy, C., Cauble, A., Comeau, J., Patterson, J., & Needle, R. Family stress and coping: A decade review. *Journal of Marriage and the Family,* Nov. 1980.

*This special issue would not have been possible without the support of select individuals and organizations. At the University of Minnesota—St. Paul, we would like to thank Dean William Hueg of the Institute of Agriculture, Forestry and Home Economics, Dr. Richard Sauer (Director) and Dr. Signe Betsinger (Assistant Director) of the Agricultural Experiment Station, and Dean Keith McFarland of the College of Home Economics who encouraged us and granted us the resources for this 18-month effort. At the University of Wisconsin—Madison, we would like to thank The Graduate School and Dean Elizabeth Simpson of the School of Family Resources and Consumer Sciences. We offer special thanks to Mrs. Diane Felicetta (Minnesota) and Mrs. Jane Haverkate Weier (Wisconsin) who attended to the details and ensured our communication across Universities. We thank our colleagues who served on the editorial board and who served as experts and special readers. We offer our deepest appreciation to Dr. James Walters and Dr. Lynda Henley Walters of Family Relations *who committed themselves to this special issue, created this unique opportunity for developing editors, shared their wisdom and experience, and guided us with their patience and understanding.*

**Hamilton I. McCubbin is Professor and Head, and Pauline Grossenbacher Boss is Associate Professor, Family Social Science Department, University of Minnesota, St. Paul, Minnesota 55108.

(Formerly *The Family Coordinator*)

Special Issue: Family Stress, Coping, and Adaptation
Hamilton I. McCubbin and Pauline G. Boss
Guest Editors

Volume 29, Number 4   October, 1980

CONTENTS

*The numbers in parentheses are the page numbers for the articles in the original volume from which this issue was reprinted.

Family Paradigm and Family Coping: A Proposal for Linking the Family's Intrinsic Adaptive Capacities To Its Responses To Stress*

DAVID REISS** AND MARY ELLEN OLIVERI***

Recently, there has been an increased interest in delineating the strategies by which families cope with stressful and challenging events and circumstances. This essay is an effort to explore the range and variety of such coping strategies. More important, it attempts to show how these strategies are related to one another and to more fundamental adaptive capacities of families; these capacities are manifest in the routines that are typical of the quiescent periods of the families' lives. The relationships we posit are shaped by a theory developing out of an extended series of laboratory and field studies in our center. Kuhn's concept of paradigm has been a helpful organizing metaphor for this theoretical work. It has led us to suspect that a family's adaptive capacities—both its everyday routines as well as its attempts to cope with unusual and stressful events—are shaped by its abiding conception of the social world in which it lives.

Careful, direct observational studies of families in their natural settings—their homes and communities—are indicating that large segments of family life are humdrum and routine. Although the routines of daily life doubtless serve important functions for families during stable times, occasional events and circumstances challenge the family's well-

*The work described in this paper was supported by DHEW Grant MH 26711.

**David Reiss is Director, Center for Family Research, and Professor, Department of Psychiatry and Behavioral Sciences, The George Washington University School of Medicine, 2300 Eye Street, N.W., Washington, D.C. 20037

***Mary Ellen Oliveri is Investigator, Center for Family Research, and Assistant Research Professor, Department of Psychiatry and Behavioral Sciences, George Washington University School of Medicine, 2300 Eye Street, N.W., Washington, D.C. 20037

(*Family Relations*, 1980, **29**, 431-444.)

formed habits. It is then that the family is called upon to exert some unusual effort: to observe, to experience, to define, to understand and to take some kind of special action so that it can return to the more orderly routines of its daily life. These sequences of experiences and actions, at times of challenge, are occasionally imaginative and inspired, and other times banal and tragic. All of them in their endless variety are coming to be known in our field by the somewhat prosaic term of "coping strategies."

This essay is an attempt to picture some of the variables of these strategies of coping with stress and to show how they derive from underlying intrinsic adaptive capacities of families that, while stable and enduring, may be little noticed during the more ordinary routines of everyday life. More specifically, our aim is to refine a model of family coping so that we may measure a family's intrinsic adaptive capacities at a quiescent period in its life, and use those measurements to predict the family's response to stress. Our efforts along these lines have proceeded through three phases. First, we have over many years developed a set of laboratory procedures which highlight variation in how families solve externally-given problems, and we have explored what underlying adaptive capacities are expressed by the various problem-solving styles we observe (Reiss, 1967, 1968, 1969, 1971b, 1971c). This phase of our work has been aided by a developing theory and set of methods which conceive of a broad variety of family problem-solving routines as shaped by an enduring conception each family holds about the fundamental nature of its social world and its place in that world (Reiss, 1971d). Although our theoretical work draws on several sources, Kuhn's (1970) concept of paradigm has been a particularly helpful organizing metaphor. A second phase has been the development of hypotheses about what sorts of coping strategies a family with a particular set of adaptive capacities would develop in the face of stress. Third, we test these predictions by comparing our laboratory findings with assessments of actual coping strategies families use in times of stress. The first of these phases has to some degree been accomplished and is summarized in the first part of this essay. The second phase is outlined in the main portion of this essay. The final phase is under active investigation in our laboratory now.

The Concept of the Family Paradigm

Family Problem Solving and Shared Constructs

For many years we have investigated several aspects of family problem solving. Initially, we used a well-controlled and precise series of laboratory methods, and our interest was in distinguishing different styles or patterns of problem solving. Indeed we found marked differences among families along three principal dimensions (Reiss, 1971d). First, families differed in the extent to which they could detect patterns and organization in the complex stimulus arrays with which we presented them as a group. Second, families differed in their degrees of coordina-

tion, cooperation, and agreement as they progressed through the many phases of our problems. Finally, families differed in their openness to new information: some families reached decisions early whereas others delayed closure as long as possible.

Our first question about these differences in problem solving style concerned their correlates in the actual lives of families, and several studies have suggested that there are some remarkably detailed parallels. For example, in a recent series of clinical studies we have been able to use families' problem-solving styles, measured in the laboratory, to make fine-grained predictions successfully about their patterns of adjustment to the psychiatric hospitalization of an adolescent member (Reiss, Costell, Jones, & Berkman, 1980). Also, in recent studies of nonclinical families, problem-solving styles have correlated with the patterns of relationships between families and their extended kin (Oliveri & Reiss, in press).

Since the problem-solving styles we were observing seemed to reflect more general modes of family adaptation, we wondered what factors or circumstances shaped and controlled them. We examined the most obvious variables to answer this question, but in our samples (we have now tested well over 400 families), social class, family structure, race and the religion of the family, as well as the intelligence, problem-solving skills, and perceptual styles of individual members, have had no relationship with the family group's problem-solving style. However, detailed observation of our families in the laboratory, and interviewing of them after the formal procedures had been administered, gave us our first clue about what did shape their problem-solving styles. It seemed that a specific family's problem-solving style arose less from its understanding of the problems we presented them, and much more from their perception of the research setting and the research team. For all families, the research setting is ambiguous and moderately stressful. Despite the careful oral and written instructions we give them before they come, and once again when they arrive, families really don't know why we are doing the research, what we expect of them, and how they are being assessed. Each family must come to its own conclusions on these matters. These conclusions, we have found, are formed early (often before the family arrives at our doorstep) and seem to determine all that comes afterwards.

For example, some families mistrust us from the outset. They feel we are giving them an insoluble puzzle whose *real* (although concealed) purpose is to humiliate them or strain the ties of one member to another. For them, the true problem is not to solve the logical puzzle we give them but rather to stick together to finish the puzzles and then, as quickly as possible, beat a hasty though decorous retreat. Hence, they show a particular "problem-solving style": very tight consensus, early closure and crude pattern recognition (they haven't really tried to look for patterns). In sharp contrast are families who trust us (whether or not we, in fact, deserve it). They assume right from the start we have given them a soluble puzzle and that we are being honest when we tell them "this is a study to learn more about how families solve problems." They go about their business cooperatively, efficiently, waiting for the maximum amount of data before making a final decision. Thus, they show another kind of "problem solving style": cooperative and effective search for patterns with delayed closure.

From the outset we doubed that these shared family perceptions of the situation resulted from anything we did, purposively or not (Robert Rosenthal, 1969, notwithstanding). First, the reactions of our families were so varied even though our approach to them was relatively uniform. Second, the beliefs about us seemed to be held with great and profound conviction. We began to feel that our laboratory problem-solving procedure had serendipitously uncovered, for each family, a pervasive orientation to the social environment. We reasoned that this orientation might be built into the family and condition the quality of its engagement with any social setting, particularly if the setting were at all ambiguous. This would be a good explanation not only for the variety of problem-solving styles we had observed in the laboratory but, more importantly, for the pin-point predictions regarding families' relationships with

social communities in their everyday worlds (e.g., the social community of the psychiatric hospital or of the extended family).

We have begun to look at this issue directly, and have been developing measures to assess the family's perception of a variety of communities and groups with which it comes into contact. For example, we have recently published a report exploring how a family perceives other families and again have shown surprising, but by now understandable, correlations between problem-solving style and these shared perceptions of other families (Reiss, Costell, Berkman, & Jones, in press). Our recent work has revealed, in each family, a rich and ordered set of beliefs about the social world. These beliefs seem sensibly connected to the ways families actually respond to and interact with their social world.

Our attention has now turned to exploring these shared beliefs, assumptions and orientations families hold. Since our evidence suggests that they are built-in and enduring components of family life, we have asked what function they serve. It was not enough to argue that they played a role in regulating the family's transactions with its social environment. We now want to know why families develop such shared beliefs and assumptions to perform such a function. Equally important, we want to know how such belief systems develop and what circumstances lead to major changes. This line of theorizing has been described in some detail elsewhere (Reiss, in press) along with evidence in support of it. We will only summarize our thinking here in preparation for our discussion of family stress and coping.

The Nature and Function of Shared Constructs

This line of theorizing has been supported and shaped by the ideas on individual psychology of Heider (1958) and Kelly (1955) and on social process by Berger and Luckman (1966). A beginning premise is that each individual must develop his own set of constructs of social phenomena, bound together with his theory of how the social world works. This personal system of ideas, opinions, hunches, assumptions, hypotheses and convictions is a constant guide to individuals in any novel situation. It shapes their hypotheses about that situation, their investigations and conclusions, and is a constant guide for their behavior. In our work on theory, we have added to these familiar notions some ideas about the individual's needs to share with others this task of developing personal theories. Indeed, we have argued with the assistance of thoughts from Berger and Luckman that lengthy, intimate, face-to-face relationships cannot go forward without a reconciliation, integration and shared development of the basic premises of these personal theories. In other words, when two or more individuals develop an intimate relationship, they engage in a process of reconciling the basic premises of their personal construct systems. Thus, a shared system of construing in a family reflects the progressive and crucial integration, over time, of the personal explanatory systems of each member. Conversely, the dissolution or splitting of families develops out of the disavowal of shared premises and personal constructs.

The concept of shared beliefs has been a little difficult to swallow for people who recognize how much disagreement and conflict are invariable components of family life. Our view is that the presence of conflict or disagreement itself does not necessarily mean these underlying shared beliefs are absent. Indeed, what family members often share at times of argument and dissension are beliefs about what is important to argue about and how such arguments may ultimately be resolved. For example, a husband and wife argue bitterly about whose responsibility it is to clean the children's toys from the sidewalk in front of their house. They accuse each other of risking criticism from their neighbors. The wife becomes more strident and the husband sulks away to clean up. We may say this couple, despite its argument, share at least two conceptions. First, both share an extreme sensitivity to the opinion of their neighbors. Second, they share an assumption that the most strident arguer must win out. Underlying, shared beliefs of this kind cannot easily be reported verbally by the family. Often, they must be inferred from observations of the family's behavior. Our own data are tentative

but do seem to support the idea that beliefs or orientations of this kind are truly shared (Reiss, 1971a; Reiss & Salzman, 1973). We also have reported some preliminary evidence that these shared beliefs are more evident in a family's non-verbal behavior than in its discussion (Reiss, 1970).

Our model acknowledges that there are, in all likelihood, several mechanisms by which shared constructs develop and change. Our main interest has been in the role of serious and disabling crisis in family life. We have seen in this circumstance, though rare in the life of an ordinary family, an opportunity to understand some of the fundamental aspects of the development and change of family constructs. Drawing on clinical experience and the recent theoretical work of Kantor and Lehr (1975) we have argued that in severe family crisis, whatever the cause, the family's typical mode of conceptualizing its position in the world becomes more clear, stark, simple. It loses its background position as a gentle coordinator of family affairs and becomes a conspicuous eminence with which no family member feels entirely comfortable. As the crisis becomes more severe, members start to disown this eminence which now seems oppressive. Dissolution of the family or a split of one member from the rest is imminent and often occurs.

At this point in the progressive decay of a family, a reorganization of their mode of construing their position in the world is often possible. In a clinical setting it may be influenced by a therapist; a religious family may draw on a priest or a clerical community. In any case, the recovery and reconstruction from extreme crisis can bring a new organization to family life and more importantly, for our purposes, to their typical mode of construing events. Surface manifestations of these shifts are seen in the way some families respond to the unanticipated death of a child, to a prolonged and disabling illness in an older member, to a move or a job loss. Crisis provides the raw material for a fundamental revision of its shared mode of construing the environment. The new system of constructs can become a point around which the family organizes. Consider, for example, a family that finds it can thrive following the death of a dominant grandmother who controlled the family through dire predictions of danger only she could thwart. A new set of concepts about the family's relationship to the social world can emerge through grief and crisis following grandmother's death. The family can develop an entirely new sense of its own potency. The important point here is that the force, persistence and pervasiveness of the new construct system comes from its initial and continuing role in providing family coherence after a time of crisis. We have argued that this force continues even after the crisis is no longer consciously remembered.

This crisis-oriented group dynamic, as we propose it, bears an interesting relationship to that described by T. S. Kuhn for scientific revolutions (Kuhn, 1970). His familiar formulation pictures, in effect, scientists as a quasi-social group whose behavior is shaped by a set of fundamental assumptions about the natural world. When these assumptions fail to account for new data, dissolution occurs, the community of scientists can no longer function as a smoothly working "group," and crisis arises. A clever new solution to existing problems serves as a continuing model or paradigm for the rebuilding of a new system of framing assumptions. Whatever difficulty Kuhn's ideas have encountered in the philosophy of science (Suppe, 1977) they have been a useful set of metaphors for our work. We now refer to the *family paradigm* as that new idea or approach, born in crisis, which serves as a background and orienting idea or perspective to the family's problem solving in daily life. A family paradigm serves as a stable disposition or orientation whenever the family must actively construe a new situation.

We do not have a clear idea, as yet, of the circumstances under which crisis produces a genuine change or "revolution" in family life. After crisis some families return to the old order whereas others undergo major transformations. Some hypotheses in this regard have been formulated elsewhere (Reiss, in press) but this matter is an important area for future investigation.

Dimensions of Family Paradigm

If our argument thus far is on the mark, then it follows that if we know the family's paradigm we should be able to predict a wide range of its responses to ambiguous and stressful events in its social world. We are just beginning to examine these possibilities in a series of related research programs. We are aided by two factors of immense practical importance. First, as we have already indicated, it appears possible to delineate, at least in part, these underlying orientations in family life by our laboratory problem-solving techniques. They serve in part as a group Rorschach: an ambiguous field on which the family can project its own assumptions. However, unlike the Rorschach, our procedures require the family to *act* rather than just talk. These actions are measurable by precise quantitative techniques. A second factor of practical importance is that a great deal of variation in problem-solving behavior, and we believe in the underlying paradigms that produce it, can be accounted for by three conceptually distinct dimensions. Thus, if we know a family's position along each of these three dimensions we should be able to successfully predict a great range of their responses to challenging social situations. It is the burden of this essay to specify these predictions. First, however, we must summarize our cardinal dimensions. The conceptualization and validation of these dimensions is based on work carried out in our own laboratory. Although the findings from this work are internally consistent, it must be emphasized that the findings themselves, and the interpretation we attach to them, need to be corroborated by other investigators in different settings.

Configuration

In our problem-solving tasks we recognize this dimension by the degree to which the family can discover the hidden or underlying patterns in the stimulus arrays we present them. Our data suggest that this problem-solving behavior reflects a fundamental conception, by the family, that the social world in which they live is ordered by a coherent set of principles which they can discover and master through exploration and interpretation (Reiss, 1971b; Reiss, in press, Reiss, et al., 1980). For example, families who recognize patterns in the laboratory problem-solving task also have well-worked out, ordered and subtle conceptions of other families they know (Reiss, et al, in press). Also, in our clinical studies, they are sensitive to subtle cues, particularly emotional ones, in developing their impressions of an in-patient treatment program to which their adolescent child has been admitted (Costell et al., in press). The sense of potential mastery over the social environment characterizing families high on configuration has also been revealed in the patterns of social network interactions of nonclinical families; configuration is positively associated with the degree of autonomy of individual family members in relation to the network of extended family (Oliveri & Reiss, in press). Elsewhere, we have proposed that families high or low on configuration can be recognized by observing their everyday household routines. For example, families high on configuration practice rituals which tie them firmly to wider social groups outside the home, such as the home celebration of ethnic rituals or the regular invitation of guests to dinner (Reiss, in press). They also arrange their household activities to clearly reflect an ordered and comprehensive grasp of the family's role in the community. For example, a child will be given space to study and a mother space to conduct meetings if her vocation or avocation requires it. In contrast, the rituals of low-configuration families reflect idiosyncratic ties to their own past and are incomprehensible and separate from the larger community. Their households are either an inchoate jumble or a frozen idealization of the past. An example of the latter is the family of a physician's widow who kept the deceased doctor's desk, medical equipment and books in place for over a decade after his death.

Coordination

We recognize this dimension by the care with which each member dovetails his problem-solving efforts with others in the family. This is more than a measure of simple agreement on the nature of the problem's solution. Our measurement of coordination is based on the degree to which members attend to the details of each other's problem-solving efforts. These problem-solving patterns reflect the family's belief that they, in fact, occupy the same experiential world, a world which operates in the same way for all of them. Beyond that, families high on this dimension see themselves as facing their social world as a group; they feel themselves to be a group, but even more important, feel the world treats them as a group. Thus, what happens to one will have implications for the rest. Our data do indeed suggest that families who are high on this dimension carefully compare and integrate their impressions about many aspects of their social world. For example, members in high-coordination families take care to develop similar views of the in-patient treatment program (Costell, Reiss, Berkman, & Jones, in press) and are precisely attuned to one another's efforts to explore and understand other families (Reiss, in press). It is also of interest that these families are embedded in nuclear families who are close and well connected; in these cases the wife's and husband's families often know and relate to one another (Oliveri & Reiss, in press). We have proposed that families high in coordination, as measured in the laboratory, also show a great deal of synchrony and coordination of planning and scheduling in their daily lives. The dimension of coordination is similar, in some respects, to the recently re-conceptualized dimension of cohesion as presented by Olson (1979). Our dimension focuses more specifically on the family's conception or belief about their experiential world. Unlike Olson, we do not regard either the extreme or moderate values on this dimension as adaptive or non-adaptive. As we will briefly review at the end of this essay, in our view family adaptiveness must take into account the family's own goals as well as the social setting in which it lives.

Closure

In our problem-solving situation, this dimension is measured by the degree to which families delay their final decisions until they have all the evidence they can obtain. Families who show delayed closure are rated high on this dimension. They have a strong engagement in the novelty and uniqueness of each new setting which they experience with a relative freshness and little preconception. Low-scoring families reach decisions early and stick with them. They seem dominated by the convictions and forms of their own past. They see the world as constantly reminiscent, as pre-figured and, at most, a modest reshuffling of past experience. In some cases they truly see the world through the eyes of their ancestors. (Olson's dimension of adaptability (1979) is similar in some respects). It is particularly interesting that, in our studies of social network, families with delayed closure are significantly invested in the largest number of extended family members. This is a reflection, we argue, of their thirst for access to maximum breadth and variety of input from the environment that assures continued openness of the family to new experiences (Oliveri & Reiss, in press). We have proposed that, in their own home, early-closure families will show a leisurely pacing of activities, what Kantor and Lehr have referred to as slow "clocking." A more frenetic pacing of events, rapid clocking, will be seen in delayed-closure families. The rituals of early-closure families will invoke the family's past. Consider for example the ritual where every Christmas night a family writes an account of the evening, round-robin style, and then reads the accounts of previous Christmases. In contrast, the rituals of the delayed-closure families will cut them off from the past. For example, a mother and father who have grown up in an orthodox Jewish family fail to celebrate Jewish holidays in their home but annually help their two children to hang Christmas stockings.

In repeated samples of clinic and non-clinic families we have seen that these dimensions are orthogonal. Thus a family may have any combination of high and low scores on all three.

Stress and the Family Paradigm

A Working Definition of Family Stress

In this essay, a preliminary attempt at theoretical synthesis, it seems wise to begin simply. Thus, we will want to consider only those events and circumstances that are relatively brief and circumscribed, lasting weeks or at most months, but not years. Further, we will want to focus on events or circumstances that happen to the family, such as neighborhood changes and physical illness, rather than events that happen within the family, such as marital separations and the birth of children. The latter internal, rather than external, stress events are every bit as important as the former for a general theory of family stress and coping. However, they are particularly difficult conundrums since they are simultaneously stressful events and, in all likelihood, responses to stress. This dual role is easy to see for such an obvious internal event as marital separation. More subtly, La Rossa (1977) has shown quite convincingly how conceiving and bearing children can also be a strategy by which couples cope with preexisting stress. It must be acknowledged, however, that it is no easy matter to distinguish internal and external events. Neighborhood changes, such as a new road or a significant demographic shift, may be relatively beyond the control of the family and hence qualify as truly external. Physical illness, on the other hand, is another matter. Numerous studies have shown that physical illness in one or more member may be part of the family's effort to cope with some other stress, chronic or acute, in their lives. Nonetheless, we will focus on those events and circumstances that seem primarily or substantially to be external.

The next problem concerns some definition of what kinds of external events or circumstances may be regarded as stressful for families. Equally important, for our purposes, is to conceive of a way of judging the magnitude of stress that inheres in the event. Hill (1965) has proposed two factors which interact to establish the stressfulness of an event and the magnitude of that stress. The first is the objective hardships for a particular family which accompany the event. Second is the definition the family makes of the event: how stressful this event seems to them. From our perspective this second factor, the definitional process, is part of the family's *response* to the event; it does not inhere, in any sense, in the stressful qualities of the event itself. Indeed, we will try to show, in the last portion of this essay, that the full range of a family's response to a stressful event can be shown to be related to these definitional processes, not only as their definitional processes are activated at times of stress but as they operate to regulate the routine transactions of a family with its outer world.

Hill's first factor, the actual hardships associated with an event, is not an entirely satisfactory way of judging the magnitude of stress in an event. Hardships do not arrive objectively and unvarnished at the family's boundary for them to define and respond to. Hardships, of whatever magnitude, are transformed by the culture (Hill recognized this process as "cultural definition"). For example, in Navajo society, physical illness is regarded as a failure of fit between the ill person and supernatural forces; it becomes the community's responsibility, under the guidance of the shaman, to provide healing through a reestablishment of harmony between the ill person and the supernatural (Kluckhohn, 1958). All the objective hardships accompanying illness may be identical for a Navajo family and a neighboring Anglo family, but the meaning to the average family within each culture will be different. The Anglo family will see illness as its unique burden to bear, the Navajo as a burden to be shared with its community. It is useful, then, to distinguish conceptually between two aspects of stress. First, the magnitude of a stressful event is determined by the interaction of hardship and cultural definition. Second, the family's definitional processes constitute the core of all the coping responses which follow. Cultural definition shapes the magnitude of the stress; family definition shapes the style of the response.

It is now a practical matter to determine the "cultural definition" of stressful events. Quite unintentionally, the tradition of life events research begun by Holmes and Rahe (1967) has given us some preliminary tools. When these researchers ask a group of judges to rate the "magnitude of stress" inherent in a set of events they are, in effect, asking them to read their own culture. They are asking: "In your culture how much stress or lifechange will this event produce in the average person?" In the most careful study to date, for example, Dohrenwend, Krasnoff, Askenasy, and Dohrenwend (1978) found significant and interpretable differences between Black, Puerto Rican,

and White subcultures in New York City. Our question, however, is somewhat different from investigators in the life events tradition. We want to know, for any particular culture, what events are regarded as stressful for the average *family*. We believe the most sensible approach here requires two steps. The first is to interview a sample of families representative of a particular subculture; in this interview of the whole family as a group the aim is to determine what recent events have significantly altered or disrupted the family's usual routines. The next step is to recruit a second representative sample of families, from the same subculture, and ask each family to work as a group to rate the events, which were provided by the first sample, for the stress or magnitude of change those events will induce in the average family in their community, and for the "externality" of those events. We are already engaged in a study of this kind and have found some intriguing results. For example, families are regularly reporting to us when we interview the family group the importance of neighborhood changes to them. They have included changes such as demographic ones, alterations in the age or race of neighbors, and spatial changes, such as the construction of new highways with consequent changes in traffic patterns and access routes. No events of this kind appear on any of the standard life events lists, constructed for individuals.

Now that we have working concepts and methods to determine the magnitude of stressful events, our interest will focus on events of *moderate* severity. As we have explained elsewhere, severe stress may overwhelm any semblance of family organization. The family's set of beliefs, organized by its central paradigm, may be shattered. Its coping strategies may be determined as much by the nature of the support it receives from the surrounding community (church, neighborhood, therapists, extended family) as from its pre-existing patterns. Thus, it is more difficult to predict from a knowledge of the family's paradigm how it will respond to severe stress. Moderate stress on the other hand will, more often than not, be encompassable by the family paradigm. Here a knowledge of the family's paradigm can help us predict, organize, and understand the family's repertoire of coping strategies.

Stages of a Family's Response to Moderate Stress

It is important to distinguish different phases or stages of a family's responses to moderate stress, since different coping strategies are likely to be employed during different phases. We have drawn on two promising sources. The first has been Joan Aldous' (1971) adaptation of the problem-solving perspectives originally developed by **John Dewey (1910) and applied to individuals** and families by Brim (1962). This approach views the family's response to any significant problem or stress as a quasi-logical, rational process in which options are developed and explored, and decisions are made based on these options. Aldous lists the following six stages:

1. identification and definition of the problem
2. collection of information about the problem
3. production of alternative solutions
4. deciding among alternatives
5. taking action to solve the problem
6. evaluation of action taken

Although useful, this system of stages implies a stark rationality to family process. It needs to be brought closer to actual sequences in family life. Concepts drawn from work phases in small task groups are useful here. A good source is the work of Chris Argyris who has been a leader in conceptualizing adaptive work in these groups (1965a, 1965b). Borrowing freely from his work, we may revise the specific stages of a family's response to a stressful event as follows:

1. definition of the event; delineating it as a problem or as a routine occurrence; accepting or rejecting group or individual responsibility for response
2. information seeking; encouragement or discouragement of individual explorations
3. self organization, role allocation, selection or confirmation of competent or incompetent leadership in the group
4. trial solutions, risk taking
5. decision-making; consensus or dissension
6. self-evaluation; sense of group confidence; *élan*
7. commitment or failure of commitment to group decision

There are still problems with this scheme. As Weick (1971) and others have pointed out, any notion of a family's response to a stressful or problematic event must recognize particular features of family life. For example, the stages of a family response may interpenetrate, be skipped entirely, or not follow in an easily-recognizable sequence. Thus, it seems reasonable, at the very least, to combine the stages derived from Aldous and Argyris. Further, it seems best to regard these stages as three conceptual vantage points for examining a family's response to a stressful event rather than considering them as sequential phases which follow one another in regular or predictable order. Somewhat arbitrarily, we have combined the Aldous-Argyris phases as follows:

1. definition of the events and search for additional information
2. initial response and trial solutions
3. final decisions or closing position and family's commitment to this

We regard these as three forms of family process: definition, trial action, and commitment to decision. *They may occur in any order or simultaneously.* As an example of how the order may be reversed, consider the Jones family's response to a new family, the Smiths, who moved in next door. The family who had lived in the house, before the Smiths moved in, was friendly and open. Accordingly, the Jones' first response to the Smiths was on the entirely implicit and unstated assumption that, like the old neighbors, they would be open and friendly as well. However, their first interactions (initial response and trial solution) are unhappy; they are rebuffed by the Smiths. The Jones family begins to develop a shared sense that they have difficult neighbors who must be avoided or closely watched (closing position). Only then do they begin to recognize, after taking trial action and assuming a closing position, that they have defined a difficult problem.

Dimension of Paradigm and Coping Strategies

Let us now consider the relationship between our three cardinal dimensions of paradigm—configuration, coordination and closure—and the three aspects of the family's response to stressful events. Our hypotheses are summarized in Table 1. We have reasoned that each of the three dimensions should relate to each of the three aspects of the family's response to stress.

Configuration, as we have defined it in many contexts, refers to a sense of mastery in the family. Families high on this dimension feel they can gain control in a novel or challenging environment through investigation and understanding. Thus, their definition of a problematic or stressful event is organized around a concept that as a family they can do something in response. In effect, the outcome of solution is, at least in part, their responsibility. Argyris has referred to this as "owning up." Families low on this dimension feel their future is in the hands of fate. Stressful events enhance their sense of being victimized. Rather than owning up, they disown or disavow responsibility. Some of these families will have faith in an abiding and providing destiny; others will feel pessimistic and victimized. In terms of initial responses and trial solutions, families high on configuration should be oriented toward investigation, information gathering and in general exploration and use of people and resources outside the family. Probably there are few instances where families entertain a specific, clearly-articulated hypothesis; nonetheless, high-configuration families during this phase probably have some implicit idea or question which is modified, sharpened, or answered with increasing information and experience. When the high-configuration family reaches a decision, a solution or a closing position, there is some pride, sense of accomplishment, or tangible growth. In contrast, a low-configuration family does not sense any connection between its own response to the problem, the outcome, and its own characteristics as a group. If things have gone well the family feels fortunate; destiny has smiled. If the outcome or closing position is some-

how negative or disappointing, the family's sense of victimization is enhanced.

Coordination refers to solidarity in family organization. Solidarity, then, should be the hallmark of the adaptive or coping style of high-coordination families. These families should often define any problem as one that somehow involves or concerns the whole family. Stressful events in the environment are often experienced as happening to the family as a unitary group rather than to a particular individual. As a result, information and/or feelings about these events are quickly shared. Low-coordination families, in contrast, rarely perceive stress events as happening to the family. Rather they perceive events as befalling individuals only; as a consequence, information about the event is exchanged slowly, if at all. The initial responses and trial solutions of high-coordination families are carefully dove-tailed. People work in recognizable relationships to one another, role allocation is clear and individuals pay attention to what others do and find out. In low-coordination families individuals act on their own; in some families they do so in lonely isolation, and in others in endless struggle and competition. When they finally reach a closing position or decision, high-coordination families forge a genuine agreement. All members remain committed to this position until or unless they forge a new consensus on a new position. In low-coordination families, an apparent consensus will turn out to be forced on the group by a single individual. Quite often the family cannot or does not reach any consensus, or the status of their agreement is unclear.

Closure refers to the role of tradition in the family's attempt to cope with the here-and-now. High-closure (which means delayed-closure) families emphasize the here-and-now; the immediacy of current experience is the major determinant of what they believe and how they act. Families low on closure are oriented toward their past. Over long periods, family traditions and perspectives play an enormous role in their efforts to interpret the present. Over shorter periods, the family cannot tolerate uncertainty; they reach decisions quickly and stand by them rather than remain open to fresh experience and ideas. This

Table 1
Hypothesized Influence of Family Paradigm Dimensions on the Three Aspects of the Family's Response to Stressful Events

Paradigm Dimensions		Definition of the Event and Search for Additional Information	Phases of Family Coping	
			Initial Responses and Trial Solutions	Final Decision or Closing Position and Family's Commitment to This
Configuration: Mastery	High:	1. Owning up — Family takes responsibility for event and/or coping	2. Exploration — Family's initial responses are designed to seek information and outside resources, or are in response to information and outside support	3. Response to outcome — The family is proud of accomplishment, or feels it has learned something of value in failure
	Low:	Family feels victimized and blames outside forces	Initial reactions are unrelated to information or explanation	The family feels fortunate if successful or victimized if not
Coordination: Solidarity	High:	4. Family Identity — Readily perceived as family issue; information exchanged quickly	5. Organization or response — Organized, integrated response by all family members; roles clear	6. Consensus on decision — Decision was reached with clear consensus and family remains committed to it
	Low:	Slowly or not perceived as family issue; information exchanged slowly; events are seen as happening to individual members	Individuals act on own; overt or covert conflict possible	The consensus was forced on the family by a single individual; the status of agreement unclear, or no consensus is reached
Closure: Openness	High: (Delayed)	7. Reference to the past — Focuses on current experiences; past family history unimportant	8. Novelty of responses — First responses include trying something new; individual experiences, intuitions, and guesses are encouraged	9. Self-evaluation — As a result of coping, family alters conception of itself in some way
	Low:	Past determines current perception and action; little interest in raw experience; more interest in convention or tradition	First responses mostly typical or familiar	As a result of coping, family confirms conception of itself

stance toward experience influences families in all three phases of their coping with stressful events. With respect to problem definition, high-closure families value and search for immediate data. The nature of the problem is often left somewhat up in the air; clarification is expected in time, but not necessarily fashioned immediately. The family does not have a rich sense of its own past and a sense of family convention. The initial responses and trial solutions in high-closure families are often novel and intuitive. The family encourages the members to take risks, and to be responsive to idiosyncratic and uncanny experiences. Low-closure families try to routinize experience (Aldous has provided a laboratory study of this form of routinization in family life [Aldous et al., 1974]). The family's initial responses and trial solutions are conservative, drawing on a repertoire of established or traditional behaviors and attitudes in the family. After they come to a closing position, high-closure families will alter the conception of themselves in some way. The decision or closing position will be reached relatively slowly and some aspects or phases of the family's response to the problem should clearly precede the closing position. In low-closure families, the final decision confirms rather than alters the family's conception of itself. Often the decision or closing position is reached early or may even be the family's first recognizable response. In low-closure families the problem definition and trial solutions are shaped by an abiding conception of what the closing position or decision is or should be.

Table 1 identifies nine different tasks of family coping beginning with 1, "owning up," which is the acceptance or rejection of family responsibility for responding to the stressful event; the table ends with 9, the family's evaluation of its own response. The numbering is meant for ease of reference; we do not mean to imply that the coping process is in any sense sequential according to this numbering system. Families may begin almost anywhere, skip some steps, and end almost anywhere else. Within each task are two contrasting coping strategies. Thus, within task 1 a family may either acknowledge responsibility for dealing with the stress or disown that re-

sponsibility. If a family's paradigm is located high on the configuration dimension, we would predict that it would, in most circumstances, own up to its responsibility to meet or deal with the stressful event. Also, a high-configuration family should, during the time when the family makes its initial response (second column), actively explore its environment for useful information, people, and resources. Finally, when at 2 closing position high-configuration families should feel pride in accomplishment, or learn from failure. Likewise, a family's position on the coordination dimension should predict which of the coping strategies it will pick in the task areas: (4) family identity, (5) organization of response, and (6) consensus on decision. A family's position on the closure dimension should predict which of the pair it will pick in: (7) reference to the past, (8) novelty of response, and (9) self-evaluation. We should be able to predict which of these 18 coping strategies any particular family will use based on its typical problem-solving patterns as measured in our laboratory and are currently engaged in a series of investigations to explore just this point.

It is helpful to consider, however briefly, the similarity between the concepts represented in Table 1 and other work on family stress and coping. First consider, in more general perspective, the contents of the three main columns. The coping strategies we list under "definition of the event" are similar to what Hill (1965) has called by the same name. Hill evidently regarded family definitional processes as conceptually and temporally prior to the family's active coping responses to the stressful situation. We see definitional process as more action oriented, as initiating a series of family actions in response to stress, as continuing throughout the family's response to stress, and as ending only when closure is complete (which, in some families, it may never be). Indeed, we see definitional and action processes as intertwined throughout the family's response to and efforts to cope with stress; we do not separate off, as does Hill, the "definition of the event" as a distinct conceptual component. To our knowledge the sequences of action and experience outlined in the last column, "closing position," are ordinarily not viewed as coping strategies by other investigators. In our view, however, the process by which closure is reached, and even more important, the process integrating the family's final resolution in the continuing stream of its life and development, are as critical in coping as the other strategies deployed during other phases of their response. Boss' study of families of servicemen missing in action suggests that some families may never reach a closing position (Boss, 1977). Many of her families could not accept the father's status years after he was reported missing. They continued to act as if he were alive and were thus unable to bring to closure their response to his loss. Her data suggest that, paradoxically, it may be our early-closure families who stand in greatest risk of this form of failed closure. Their inability to make major shifts and the importance to them of maintaining tradition, may make them unable to reach closure in times of grief and give up someone or something that has been treasured

On a more microscopic level some of the strategies we are proposing are similar to coping strategies described by McCubbin (1979) and Boss (1977) for wives of absent husbands. For example, our "exploration" seems a prototype of what they call Establishing Independence and Self-Sufficiency. McCubbin and Boss describe the latter as the wife's acquisition of skills, experience, and training to deal with the objective hardships entailed by her absent husband. They describe another strategy, "Maintaining the Past and Dependence on Religion." This seems similar to, in some respects, each of the lower strategies in cells 7, 8, and 9 of our table. Finally, their strategy of "Maintaining Family Integration and Structure" is similar to the strategy of organizing the family, described in the upper portion of cell 5.

Hill, McCubbin, and Boss, as well as other scholars in this field, have attempted to define strategies that are most adaptive. We, quite emphatically, do not. More specifically, we do not suggest that the strategy labeled "high" within any of the nine cells in Table 1 is more effective or adaptive than the strategy labeled "low." For example, it is likely that the average Navajo family would not "own up"

to its responsibility to bring relief to an ill member but would, in effect, disown such responsibility in the service of joining in communal healing rights. The question of the adaptiveness of coping strategies must take into account the family's own objectives and the nature of the social community in which it lives. In our fledgling science of family stress and coping we may be rushing to judgment, on very slender evidence, concerning which strategies are "best."

Our aim in this paper has been to emphasize the extraordinary variety of coping strategies families employ in response to stress. We have tried to show how these strategies may be related to an enduring structure of beliefs, convictions, and assumptions the family holds about its social world. Kuhn's concept of paradigm, used as a metaphor, helps us understand how these shared beliefs shape family action.

REFERENCES

Aldous, J. A framework for the analysis of family problem solving. In J. Aldous, T. Condon, R. Hill, M. Straus, & I. Tallman (Eds.), *Family problem solving: A symposium on theoretical, methodological and substantive concerns.* Hinsdale, Ill.: Dryden, 1971.

Argyris, C. Explorations in interpersonal competence—I. *Journal of Applied Behavioral Science,* 1965 1, 58-83.

Argyris, C. Explorations in interpersonal competence—II. *Journal of Applied Behavioral Science,* 1965, 1, 147-177.

Berger, P. L., & Luckman, T. *The social construction of reality.* New York: Doubleday, 1966.

Boss, P. A clarification of the concept of psychological father presence in families experiencing ambiguity of boundary. *Journal of Marriage and the Family,* 1977, 39, 141-151.

Costell, R., Reiss, D., Berkman, H., & Jones, C. The family meets the hospital: Predicting the family's perception of the treatment program from its problem-solving style. *Archives of General Psychiatry,* in press.

Dewey, J. *How we think.* New York: D. C. Heath, 1910.

Dohrenwend, B. S., Krasnoff, L., Askenasy, A. R., & Dohrenwend, B. P. Exemplification of a method for scaling life events: The PERI life events scale. *Journal of Health and Social Behavior,* 1978, 19, 205-229.

Heider, F. *The psychology of interpersonal relations.* New York: Wiley, 1958.

Hill, R. Genetic features of families under stress. In H. J. Parad (Ed.) *Crisis intervention.* New York: Family Service Association of America, 1965.

Holmes, T. H., & Rahe, R. H. The social readjustment rating scale. *Journal of Psychosomatic Research,* 1967, 11, 213-218.

Kantor, D., & Lehr, W. *Inside the family*. San Francisco: Jossey-Bass, 1975.

Kelly, G. *The psychology of personal constructs*. New York: Norton, 1955.

Kluckhohn, C., & Leighton, D. *The Navajo*. Cambridge: Harvard University Press, 1958.

Kuhn, T. S. *The structure of scientific revolutions*. Chicago: University of Chicago Press, 1970.

LaRossa, R. *Conflict and power in marriage*. Beverly Hills: Sage, 1977.

McCubbin, H. I. Integrating coping behavior in family stress theory. *Journal of Marriage and the Family*. 1979, **41**, 237-244.

Oliveri, M. E., & Reiss, D. The structure of families' ties to their kin: The shaping role of social constructions. *Journal of Marriage and the Family,* in press.

Olson, D. D., Sprenkle, D. H., & Russell, C. S. Circumplex model of marital and family systems: I. Cohesion and adaptability dimensions, family types and clinical applications. *Family Process*, 1979, **18**, 3-28.

Reiss, D. Individual thinking and family interaction II: A study of pattern recognition and hypothesis testing in families of normals, character disorders and schizophrenics. *Journal of Psychiatric Research*, 1967, **5**, 193-211.

Reiss, D. Individual thinking and family interaction III: An experimental study of categorization performance in families of normals, character disorders and schizophrenics. *Journal of Nervous and Mental Disease*, 1968, **146**, 384-403.

Reiss, D. Individual thinking and family interaction IV: A study of information exchange in families of normals, those with character disorders and schizophrenics. *Journal of Nervous and Mental Disease*, 1969, **149**, 473-490.

Reiss, D. Individual thinking and family interaction V: Proposals for the contrasting character of experiential sensitivity and expressive form in families. *Journal of Nervous and Mental Disease*, 1970, **151**, 187-202.

Reiss, D. Intimacy and problem solving: An automated procedure for testing a theory of consensual experience in families. *Archives of General Psychiatry*, 1971, **22**, 442-455 (a).

Reiss, D. Varieties of consensual experience I: A theory for relating family interaction to individual thinking. *Family Process*, 1971, **10**, 1-28 (b).

Reiss, D. Varieties of consensual experience II: Dimensions of a family's experience of its environment. *Family Process*, 1971, **10**, 28-35 (c).

Reiss, D. Varieties of consensual experience III: Contrasts between families of normals, delinquents and schizophrenics. *Journal of Nervous and Mental Disease*, 1971, **152**, 73-95 (d).

Reiss, D. *The family's construction of reality*. Cambridge: Harvard University Press, in press.

Reiss, D., Costell, R., Jones, C., & Berkman, H. The family meets the hospital: A laboratory forecast of the encounter. *Archives of General Psychiatry*, 1980, **37**, 141-154.

Reiss, D., Costell, R., Berkman, H., & Jones, C. How one family perceives another: The relationship between social constructions and problem solving competence. *Family Process*, in press.

Reiss, D., & Salzman, C. Resilience of family process: Effect of secobarbital. *Archives of General Psychiatry*, 1973, **28**, 425-433.

Rosenthal, R. Interpersonal expectations: Effects of the experimenter's hypothesis. In R. Rosenthal & R. Rosnow (Eds.), *Artifact in behavioral research*. New York: Academic Press, 1969.

Suppe, F. Exemplars, theories and disciplinary matrices. In F. Suppe (Ed.), *The structure of scientific theories* (Second Edition). Urbana: University Illinois Press, 1977.

Wieck, K. E. Group processes, family processes and problem solving. In J. Aldous, T. Condor, R. Hill, M. Straus, & I. Tallman (Eds.) *Family problem solving: A symposium on theoretical, methodological and substantive concerns*. Hinsdale, IL: Dryden Press, 1971.

Normative Family Stress: Family Boundary Changes Across the Life-Span

PAULINE G. BOSS*

Normative stress in families results whenever components are added to or subtracted from a family system. From birth to death, family boundaries change and remain ambiguous during the process of reorganization after acquisition or loss of a member. The family's perception of who is inside or outside the family system is significantly related to the interaction within that system as well as between that system and the outside world. It is proposed that due to the process of family boundary maintenance, there is little similarity in family structures across time: family structures are constantly changing to facilitate the accomplishment of functions while maintaining family boundaries.

All families, functional and dysfunctional, experience stress—that is, change at various times throughout the family life cycle. However, the question remains as to *why* some families recover from the stress of change and, in fact, become stronger, whereas other families cannot cope and are caught in a downward spiral toward increasing dysfunction.

Issues related to this question were addressed decades ago in the contexts of non-normative crises encountered by families: Angell (1939) and Cavan (1938) on effects of the depression; DuVall (1948), Hill (1949), and Boulding (1950) on the effects of separation and reunion. In the 1970s a number of studies were conducted at the Center for Prisoner of War Studies in San Diego on the effects of military separation (for a review, see McCubbin, Hunter, and Dahl, 1976).

Normative Family Stress and Family Boundaries

Normative life-span stress for the family has been studied much less extensively.

Rhona Rapoport's work (1963) represents a classic in that sparse literature. Though her research centered on the stress of change resulting from "getting married," she focused theoretically on other critical transition points in normal family development: the birth of the first child, children going to school for the first time, death of a spouse, or adolescents leaving home (Rapoport, 1963). These she called "points-of-no-return" which lead either to resolution and growth or to maladaptation and subsequent deterioration of the system. She wrote:

> It is postulated that the way these normal "crisis" or status transitions are handled or coped with, will affect outcome—both in terms of the mental health of the individuals, and in terms of the enduring family relationship (Rapoport, 1963, p. 69).

Later Stierlin (1972) referred to family types and the adolescent's struggle to move out of the family system. If the dominant family type is binding and closed, the adolescent's attempt to unbind himself will be crisis-producing for the family, at least for a time. Stierlin sees this struggle for independence as functional for parents as well as adolescents and illustrates this point with the analogy of Martin Luther who forced the sixteenth century church to reform and strengthen itself "while

*Pauline Boss is Associate Professor, Child and Family Studies Program, University of Wisconsin, Madison, WI 53706.

(*Family Relations*, 1980, 29, 445-450.)

he, in separating himself from it, bore the onus of rebel . . . " (Stierlin, 1972, p. 174).

More recently, Kantor and Lehr (1975) addressed the issue of the dimensions of family space or boundaries. They defined boundaries as " . . . all the interface rings that constitute the totality of family process interactions . . . " and stated:

> Families that adopt the closed-type homeostatic ideal define their boundaries in terms of the fixed constancy feedback patterns. . . . Families that seek the random ideal define their boundaries in terms of variety loops rather than constancy loops. . . . Disequilibrium is the random homeostatic ideal. Families that adopt an open homeostatic ideal opt for a mixture of equilibrium and disequilibrium. . . . Open family boundaries are defined in terms of a combination of constancy and variety loop patterns, employed to maximize the potential for a joint negotiation of distance regulation issues at interface (Kantor & Lehr, 1975, pp. 116-117).

Although Kantor and Lehr's boundary types are not classified as either enabling or disabling, Boss proposes that a high degree of boundary ambiguity in any family system may cause dysfunction (Boss, 1975, Note 1; 1977, 1980). If a family member is perceived as psychologically present, but is, in reality, physically absent for a long time, the family boundary is ambiguous and cannot be maintained. The reverse also manifests boundary ambiguity: physical presence with psychological absence, as in some intact families where a parent is consistently preoccupied with outside work (Boss, McCubbin, & Lester, 1979). Operationalization is based on whether or not roles are still being assigned to the absent person and whether or not the absent member is still perceived as present. Thus the premise is based on role theory and symbolic interaction.

This premise of boundary ambiguity plus the works of Kantor and Lehr reflect the influence of earlier works by Piaget and Inhelder (1956), who investigated space as a central aspect of individual perception and cognition. Using this spatial metaphor from early developmentalists, Kantor and Lehr also focused on structuralism for family boundary maintenance as the family responds to everyday life.

> At each stage of development in a family's life cycle, new distance-regulation crises appear, stimulating new images and re-emphasizing older ones. The development of family and individual strategies at each stage continues to be dependent on the interaction of family and individual image hierarchies . . . (Kantor & Lehr, 1975, p. 249).

Therefore, in Kantor and Lehr's terms the perception of family boundary (who is inside or outside the family sytem) is a distance-regulation or space-bounding issue. But even before Kantor and Lehr, family therapists proposed the critical nature of both real and perceived family boundaries. Boszormenyi-Nagy and Spark (1973, p. 84) referred to boundaries between the family and the larger world formed by "invisible loyalties" such as family values. From a more microscopic perspective, Minuchin (1974) used boundaries within family sub-systems in clinical assessment of family functioning. He believed that for proper family functioning, the boundaries of subsystems must be clear.

> [Boundaries] must be defined well enough to allow subsystem members to carry out their functions without undue interference, but they must allow contact between the members of the subsystem and others. The composition of subsystems organized around family functions is not nearly as significant as the clarity of system boundaries. A parental subsystem that includes a grandmother or a parental child can function quite well, so long as lines of responsibility and authority are clearly drawn (Minuchin, 1974, p. 54).

Concomitantly, Minuchin (1974) referred to "diffuse boundaries" (p. 61) as indicators of dysfunctional families. For example diffuse boundaries are found in "enmeshed" families where mother and children are in coalition again the father-husband. In such families, boundaries between the generations, both real and symbolic, remain ambiguous.

Accommodation to Family Stress

Based on the perspective of family therapists and earlier developmentalists and on the initial testing by this author of the boundary ambiguity propositions, it is proposed that individual and family life span perceptions of who is inside or outside the family system are significantly related to the interaction within that system and between that system and the outside world. The specific theoretical proposition is that *the greater the boundary ambiguity at various developmental and normative junctures throughout the family life-cycle, the higher the family and individual dysfunction*. Resolution of the ambiguity is necessary before the family system can reorganize and move on toward new functioning at a lower level of stress. Non-resolution of boundary ambiguity holds the family at a higher stress level by blocking the regenerative power to reorganize and develop new levels of organization. Boundaries of the system cannot be maintained, so the viability of the system is blurred. Dysfunction results.

Change in Family Boundaries

Obviously, some families resolve the stress of membership change much more quickly than do others. For example, roles and tasks may be quickly reassigned when a new baby joins a family. The father takes over the cooking; grandmother or father or a friend takes over the housework temporarily. The theoretical proposition refers operationally to task accomplishment through role performances (function) within the family structure across time. That is, boundaries are maintained after the birth of a baby by a major shifting of roles

and tasks within the family system. Furthermore, interaction of the family with the outside world may be altered: grandmother or a professional support person temporarily becomes active within the system while the new mother temporarily may not be employed outside the home. The latter alone is a major boundary change for many new mothers who are accustomed to daily interaction with colleagues or friends in their outside work world. The task of redefining her family roles after having a new baby is complicated for an employed woman when boundaries remain unclear—in this case, when she isn't sure if she's in or out of the family with respect to her roles and perceptions. She may want to be out in the work world, but she may feel she should be with her new baby, or vice versa. Until she and her family clarify how she is in and how she is out, both perceptually and physically, the family system cannot fully reorganize after the impact of acquiring a new member. Needless to say, the same clarity is necessary to redefine the new father's role.

To emphasize the recurrence and complexity of such situations of change in family systems across time, some examples of Change in Family Boundaries Over the Life-Span are presented in Figure 1. The major assumptions in this model is that *family system boundaries will change over the life-span*. Furthermore, boundary changes resulting from adding and/or losing family members cannot be predicted normatively for diverse American families beyond initial pairing and

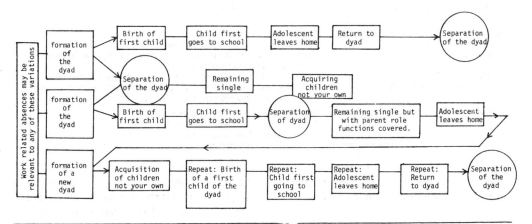

Figure 1. Selective examples of changes in family boundaries over the life-span.

Table 1
Selected References to Illustrate Normative Life-Span Boundary Changes

Type of Life-Span Family Boundary Changes	Boundary Stressors Related to Physical and Psychological Membership in the System
Formation of the dyad Rapoport (1963)	*acquisition of a mate *acquisition of in-laws *realignment with family of orientation *incorporating or rejecting former friendships
Birth of the first child LeMasters, 1957 Russell, 1974 Pridham & Hansen, 1977	*acquisition of a new member *possible separation from extra-familial work world *if so, loss of working colleagues, etc.
Children first going to school Anderson, 1976 Klein & Ross, 1958	*separation of child from the family system to the world of school *acquisition of child's teacher, friends, and peers, i.e., acceptance of them as part of the child's world
Job-related parent/spouse absence or presence Hill, 1949 Boulding, 1950 Boss, 1975, 1980; Note 1 McCubbin et al., 1976 Boss, McCubbin, Lester, 1979 Hooper, J. O., 1979	*fluctuating acquisition *and* separation due to extra-familial role, i.e., military service, routine absence of the corporate executive etc. Stress results from repeated exit and re-entry of the member. Also includes job changes such as return of mother to college or work after she's been a full-time home-maker or retirement of father from work back into the home.
Adolescent children leaving home Stierlin, 1974 Boss & Whitaker, 1979	*separation of adolescent from the family system to his peers, school or job system *acquisition of the adolescent's peers and intimates/same and opposite sex
Taking in child(ren) not your own or blending children from different dyads Duberman, 1975 Visher & Visher, 1978, 1979	*acquisition of another's offspring into the family system, i.e., stepchildren, grandchildren, other nonrelated children.
Loss of a spouse (through death, divorce, etc.) Parkes, 1972 Lopata, 1973, 1979 Bohannan, 1970 Wallerstein & Kelly, Studies from 1974 through 1977 Weiss, 1975 Hetherington, 1971, 1976 Boss & Whitaker, 1979	*separation of mate from the dyad, therefore dissolution of the marital dyad. Note: In case of divorce, the dyad may continue and function on other levels, such as co-parenting, etc.
Loss of parent(s) Sheehy, 1976 Silverstone & Hyman, 1976 Levinson, 1978	*separation of child from parent(s) (child may likely be an adult)
Formation of a new dyad: remarriage Bernard, 1956 Messinger, 1976 Westoff, 1977 Whiteside, 1978 Roosevelt & Lofas, 1976	*acquistion of a new mate *acquisition of a new set of in-laws *realignment with family of orientation and former in-laws, children of former marriage, etc. *incorporating or rejecting former friendships, former spouses etc., former spouse may still be in partnership with a member of the new dyad regarding parenting.
Remaining single Stein, 1976	*realignment with family of orientation *if previously married, realignment with former in-laws *acquisition of friends, intimates, colleagues, etc.

final separation. Hence, various family structural patterns may be exhibited as families progress throughout the life cycle.

Variability in Family Structures for Boundary Maintenance

With an obvious focus on normative function more than on normative structure, it is suggested that there may be no universals in family structural boundaries beyond the original formation of the boundary and its eventual dissolution through family separation. Between these two stages, it is variance more than universality that allows for coping and functional adaptation across the life-span. Varied structures across *and* among families may support the accomplishment of functions that are necessary for family survival and growth over time. In other words, there may indeed be more than one way for families to reach the same end goal (von Bertalanffy, 1968; pp. 40, 132; Buckley, 1967; Hill, 1971).

The Black American family is an excellent example of adaptive boundary maintenance in the face of severe stress from both inside and outside the family. Such families survived only because of adaptations to the normative family structure, as the television epic *Roots* so clearly illustrated. The Haley family added and exited people as they needed regardless of societal norms or biological destiny. There was no doubt that Chicken George was still the father and husband in his family and that he still performed the necessary functions for his family even though he remained up North for many years. The family boundary stretched, because of necessity, to retain him as a viable member of the system. Indeed, he actively performed the role of provider and purchaser of freedom for the rest of his family system. It was precisely such boundary elasticity that permitted this Black family to perceive his membership within the system despite great physical distance.

To provide examples of the types of boundary changes families appear to encounter in their everyday life over time, selected representative research is noted in Table 1. The boundary changes listed are derived from the classic Rapoport (1963) article, but with these revisions: first, because the "formation of the dyad" is not always synonymous with "marriage," the former term is used. Second, because the "death of a spouse" is not the only recognized way to break up a dyad, "loss of a spouse," which can include death, divorce, or desertion, is used in Table 1. Third, the "acquisition of children not your own" is added because of the frequency of this phenomenon today in remarried or blended families and, traditionally, in the Black American subculture. Fourth, "formation of a new dyad" is added because of the high rate of remarriage today. Finally, "work-related absence" is

added to Table 1 because it occurs in so many variations of American families today.

Summary

If it can be assumed that family structural adaptations have been made for the survival of the organism, then these adaptations must be recognized and documented before scientists can proceed toward valid explanation of why some families can cope with the stress of normative membership change whereas others cannot.

Stress continues in any family until membership can be clarified and the system reorganized regarding (a) who performs what roles and tasks, and (b) how family members perceive the absent member. Challenges to the family's capacity for boundary maintenance come not only from outside forces, but also from normal developmental maturation throughout the life cycle. Such challenges are met by families by varying their structure to maintain functions. Recognizing and investigating variability in structure for boundary maintenance offers one promising approach to study the original question of why some families can cope with everyday life stresses whereas others cannot.

REFERENCE NOTE

1. Boss, P. G. *Psychological father absence and presence: A theoretical formulation for an investigation into family systems interaction.* Unpublished doctoral dissertation, University of Wisconsin, Madison, August, 1975.

REFERENCES

Anderson, L. S. When a child begins school. *Children Today,* August 1976, 16-19.

Angell, R. C. *The family encounters the depression.* New York: Scribner's & Sons, 1936.

Bernard, J. *Remarriage.* New York: Holt, Rinehart, and Winston, 1956.

Bohannan, P. *Divorce and after.* Doubleday, 1970.

Boss, P. G. A clarification of the concept of psychological father presence in families experiencing ambiguity of boundary. *Journal of Marriage and the Family,* 1977, **39,** 141-151.

Boss, P. G., The relationship of psychological father presence, wife's personal qualities and wife/family dysfunction in families of missing fathers. *Journal of Marriage and the Family,* 1980, **42,** 541-549.

Boss, P. G., McCubbin, H. I., & Lester, G. The corporate executive wife's coping patterns in response to routine husband-father absence. *Family Process,* March 1979, **18,** 79-86.

Boss, P. G., & Whitaker, C. Dialogue on separation. *The Family Coordinator*, 1979, **28**, 391-398.

Boszormenyi-Nagy, I., & Spark, G. M. *Invisible loyalties*. New York: Harper & Row, 1973.

Boulding, E. Family adjustment to war separation and reunion. *Annals of the American Academy of Political and Social Science*, 1950, **272**, 59-68.

Buckley, W. *Sociology and modern systems theory*. Englewood Cliffs, NJ: Prentice-Hall, 1967.

Cavan, R. S., & Ranck, K. H. *The family and the depression*. Chicago: University of Chicago Press, 1938.

Duberman, L. *The reconstituted family: A study of remarried couples and their children*. Chicago: Nelson-Hall, 1975.

DuVall, E. M. Loneliness and the serviceman's wife. *Marriage and Family Living*, August, 1943, 77-82.

Hetherington, E. M., & Deur, J. The effects of father absence on child development. *Young Children*, 1971, **26**, 233-248.

Hetherington, E. M., Cox, M., & Cox, R. Divorced fathers. *The Family Coordinator*, 1976, **25**, 417-428.

Hill, R. *Families under stress*. Connecticut: Greenwood Press, 1949.

Hill, R. Modern systems theory and the family: A confrontation. *Social Science Information*, 1971, **72**, 7-26.

Hooper, J. O. My wife, the student. *The Family Coordinator*, 1979, **28**, 459-464.

Kantor, O., & Lehr, W. *Inside the family*. San Francisco: Jossey-Bass, 1975.

Klein, D. C., & Ross, A. Kindergarten entry: A study of role transition. In M. Krugman (Eds.), *Orthopsychiatry and the school*. New York: American Orthopsychiatric Association, 1958.

LeMasters, E. E. Parenthood as crisis. *Marriage and Family Living*, 1957, **29**, 352-355.

Levinson, D. J. *The seasons of a man's life*. New York: Ballantine Books, 1978.

Lopata, H. I. *Widowhood in an American City*. Cambridge, MA: Schenkman, 1973.

Lopata, H. I. *Women as widows*. New York: Elsevier, 1979.

McCubbin, H., Dahl, B., & Hunter, E. Research in the military family: A review. In H. McCubbin, B. Dahl, & E. Hunter (Eds.), *Families in the military system*. Beverly Hills: Sage, 1976.

Messinger, L. Remarriage between divorced people with children from previous marriages. *Journal of Marriage and Family Counseling*, 1976, **2**, 193-200.

Minuchin, S. *Families and family therapy*. Cambridge, MA: Harvard University Press.

Parad, H. J. (Ed.) *Crisis intervention: Selected readings*. New York: Family Service Association of America, 1965.

Parkes, C. M. *Bereavement: Studies of grief in adult life*. New York: International Universities Press, Inc., 1972.

Piaget, J., & Inhelder, B. *The child's conception of space*. London: Routledge & Kegan Paul, 1956.

Pridham, K. F., Hansen, M., & Conrad, H. H. Anticipatory care as problem-solving in family medicine and nursing. *Journal of Family Practice*, 1977, **4**, 1077-1081.

Rapoport, R. Normal crises, family structure, and mental health. *Family Process*, 1963, **2**.

Roosevelt, R., & Lofas, J. *Living in step: A remarriage manual for parents and children*. New York: McGraw-Hill, 1976.

Russell, C. Transition to parenthood: Problems and gratifications. *Journal of Marriage and the Family*, 1974, 294-301.

Silverstone, B., & Hyman, H. *You and your aging parents*. New York: Patheon, 1976.

Sheehy, G. *Passages: Predictable crises of adult life*. New York: Dutton, 1976.

Stein, P. *Single*. Englewood Cliffs, NJ: Prentice-Hall, 1976.

Stierlin, H. *Separating parents and adolescents*. New York: Quadrangle, 1974.

Visher, E., & Visher, J. Common problems of step parents and their spouses. *American Journal of Orthopsychiatry*, April, 1978, **48**(2), 252-262.

Visher, E., & Visher, J. *Stepfamilies: A guide to working with step-parents and step-children*. New York: Brunner-Mazel, 1979.

von Bertalanffy, L. *General systems theory* (revised edition). New York: George Brazilley, 1968.

Wallerstein, J. S., & Kelly, J. B. The effects of parental divorce: The adolescent experience. In E. J. Anthony & C. Koupernik (Eds.), *The child and his family: Children at psychiatric risk III*. New York: Wiley, 1974.

Wallerstein, J. S., & Kelly, J. B. The effects of parental divorce: Experiences of the preschool child. *American Academy of Child Psychiatry*, 1975, **14**(4), 600-616.

Wallerstein, J. S., & Kelly, J. B. The effects of parental divorce: Experiences of the child in early latency. *American Journal of Orthopsychiatry*, 1976, **46**, 20-32. (a)

Wallerstein, J. S., & Kelly, J. B. The effects of parental divorce: Experiences of the child in later latency. *American Journal of Orthopsychiatry*, 1976, **46**, 256-269. (b)

Wallerstein, J. S., & Kelly, J. B. Divorce counseling: A community service for families in the midst of divorce. *American Journal of Orthopsychiatry*, 1977, **47**, 4-22 (a)

Wallerstein, J. S., & Kelly, J. B. Brief intervention with children in divorcing families. *American Journal of Orthopsychiatry*, 1977, **47**, 23-37. (b)

Weiss, R. *Marital separation*. New York: Basic Books, 1975.

Westoff, L. A. *The second time around: Remarriage in America*. New York: Viking, 1977.

Whiteside, M., & Auerbach, L. Can the daughter of my father's new wife be my sister? Families of remarriage in family therapy. *Journal of Divorce*, 1978, **1**, 271-283.

Normative Stress and Young Families: Adaptation and Development

COLLEEN S. BELL, JAMES E. JOHNSON,
ANN V. MCGILLICUDDY-DELISI, AND IRVING E. SIGEL*

This paper represents a departure from the usual identification of stress as related to critical events in family development by focusing upon number and spacing of children as perpetrators of normative stress. The effects of these family structural characteristics on children's cognitive development, marital satisfaction and parent-child relations are summarized and a typology of normative stress based on level of family impact is offered. Growth-enhancing aspects of stress are suggested in the context of the family as a system of mutual influences.

In the family literature, adaptive processes under crisis conditions related to critical events have been studied a great deal (Hill, 1958), but less is known about family functioning over time under conditions of normal stress.[1] For example, families cannot escape dealing with an inflationary economy and energy problems. Young families may find themselves in the situation where the normal stresses associated with family responsibilities and trying to make it in an occupation are each at high levels. Unfortunately, these major adult developmental tasks are not staggered in time for most people. Concurrently, many adults in young families encounter for the first time the stress associated with aging grandparents and parents. Later stages of family development may bring a continuation of these and the possible addition of new stressors (e.g., midlife career stress and parenting older children). A lifespan perspective on these normative changes is presented by Boss (Note 1).

As changing numbers of family members press on resources of space, time, energy, and materials, and as the interactional complexity of the family increases, what are the stresses? How is the family affected? What coping strategies are there for successful adaptation and development? Although the immediate situation and individuals' perceptions of social conditions are seen as major determinants of family dynamics (with family structural characteristics as peripheral), the purpose of this paper is to integrate structural and interactional analysis. Although few would claim that sheer number and spacing of children determines family relations, family structure can be seen as important.

This paper is a review of research concerning the impact of family size and spacing on child development, marital satisfaction, and parent-child relationships. The literature is discussed within the context of a conceptual model of the family as a system of mutual influences (McGillicuddy-DeLisi, Sigel, & Johnson, 1979). The premise of this paper is that the intensity of stress may be modulated within the system to *enhance* growth and development.

Effects on Child Development

Family size has been shown to be negatively related to intellectual achievement in a

---

*Colleen Bell, Specialist, and James E. Johnson, Assistant Professor, are affiliated with the School of Family Resources and Consumer Sciences, 1300 Linden Drive, Madison, WI 53706. Ann McGillicuddy-DeLisi and Irving E. Sigel are affiliated with the Center for Assessment and Research in Human Development, Princeton, NJ 08540.

[1]Normative stress excludes stress associated with circumstances such as terminal illness, hospitalization, atypical children or other unusual conditions.

(*Family Relations*, 1980, **29**, 453-458.)

number of studies; e.g., Anastasi (1956) and Wray (1971). Children from large families tend to perform more poorly on indices of intelligence and academic ability than children from smaller families. The inverse relation between family size and intelligence has been reported even with the effects of social class adjusted (Douglas, 1964; Nisbet & Entwistle, 1966). On the other hand, some research has shown social class to be a relevant factor. For instance, Anastasi (1959) found the effect of family size on I.Q. score less pronounced in upper income groups.

Belmont and Marolla (1973) also found an inverse relation between family size and I.Q. Controlling for birth order, the influence of family size on intelligence was strongest for working class families, and less marked for white-collar families. Family size was not significantly related to I.Q. in farm families.

Zajonc and Marcus (1975) have proposed a confluence model to explain the effects of family size and birth order on intelligence. In this model, family size is a suppressing factor; i.e., each additional child in the family is seen as diluting the intellectual environment of the home. The greater the age differences, the less damaging the effects of family size. The model used by Zajonc and Markus (1975) to explain the Belmont and Marolla (1973) finding included a factor for the spacing of children in the family. Large spacing was held to be beneficial to younger children in the family and detrimental to the older children, whereas small spacing was less detrimental to the older child but harmful to the younger child. The rationale rests on the belief that it is desirable for the child to be able to teach younger siblings, but undesirable to be taught by a sibling.

Evidence contrary to the Zajonc confluence model comes from studies by McCall and Johnson (1972) and McCutcheon (1977), among others. Recently Galbraith & Smith (Note 2) criticized Zajonc for using between-family data to make within-family inferences. These researchers presented new within-family data that showed essentially a zero correlation between spacing and academic achievement. Nevertheless, continued interest in family configuration is illustrated by a recent book by Marjoribanks (1979) in which the thesis is

developed that structural variables such as family size and spacing may not only mediate learning opportunities in the home but also produce independent effects through the social meaning ascribed to such factors both within families and in society.

The impact of family configuration factors goes beyond the realm of intellectual functioning. With foci ranging from achievement motivation (Rosen, 1961; Elder, 1962) to independence and responsibility (Bossard & Boll, 1955; Rosen, 1961), scores of studies have generally reported that firstborn children stand apart from laterborns in having greater levels of achievement motivation and independence (Sampson, 1965).

In conclusion, understanding children's growth and development in relation to family structure must include birth order and social class as moderating variables together with acknowledgment of the dynamic reciprocal interaction between the child and environment.

Effects on the Marital Dyad

A great deal of research has been done showing that the number of children in the family is related to lower marital morale (Bossard & Boll, 1956; Burgess & Cottrell, 1939; Christensen & Philbuck, 1952; Lang, 1932; Reed, 1948). Bossard and Boll (1956), in their classic study of 100 large families, concluded that compared to those in smaller families, parents with six or more children were more fixed in their roles, had less satisfying marital communication, and were less egalitarian. A U-shaped curve relating the number of children with marital satisfaction also has been reported (Nye & Hoffman, 1963; Nye, Carlson, & Garrett, 1970; Thornton, 1977). Thornton (1977) found that women with large families or with no children were the most likely to experience marital disruption. From all of the above studies, statements of cause and effect cannot be made.

An integration of structural and interactional levels of analysis in family research is needed in order to better understand how normative stress operates within families. Rollins and Galligan (1978), in an extensive review chapter, stated: "The impact on the marital relationship of number and spacing of children as well as the arrival of a child seems to depend upon specific circumstances within the family" (p. 80). Reinforcing this sentiment, Renee (1970) suggested that having difficult children may especially relate to marital dissatisfaction and Russell (1974) noted the positive as well as negative aspects of having children.

Child spacing (time interval from the beginning of a marriage to the first child and then all following children) also has received considerable research attention. Christensen (1968) proposed a "value-behavior discrepancy" (or lack of it) to account for marital satisfaction or dissatisfaction. Although Reed's (1948) findings supported Christensen's hypothesis, Farber and Blackman (1956) failed to find success in controlling the birth of children to be a crucial factor in marital adjustment. Freedman and Coombs (1966) pointed out that close spacing may have some advantages over larger intervals in that siblings closer in age can offer more mutual companionship and women are able to reenter the labor market earlier. Nevertheless, couples usually report a greater dissatisfaction with close spacing.

Miller (1975), in a paper critical of the child density variable (ratio of number of children to years of marriage), found no relation between child spacing or density and marital satisfaction. Miller argued that in multivariate analyses, the length of marriage and the number of children should be entered as separate factors. Figley (1973) also found no evidence relating child density to marital satisfaction or communication. On the other hand, Hurley and Palonen (1967) found a significant inverse relation between marital adjustment and child density.

One difficulty associated with integrating family and child areas of research is illustrated by the divergence that exists in the definition of the variable *child spacing*. In the family literature reported above, *child spacing* refers to the interval from time of marriage to first and subsequent births. On the other hand, in the Zajonc confluence model noted earlier, *child spacing* refers only to interval between births as an index of the family environment affecting cognitive development. Family researchers seem to focus on the marital subsystem whereas developmental and educational psychologists focus on children. Just as family researchers (e.g., Campbell, 1970) have attended to the interval from marriage to the first child as an important structural variable for family research, perhaps child development researchers should ask what relevance this variable has for the development of children. Likewise, family researchers may try redefining child spacing omitting the interval from marriage to the first child and analyzing the family environment using sibling density as a structural variable. The generation of new ideas for research could result from such blending of perspectives across disciplines.

Effects on Parent-Child Relations

Life in the family is viewed as varying in part because of differences in family size and child spacing. As previously noted, it is recognized that such structural variables may have more than a peripheral role in accounting for variance in family and individual behavior (cf. Marjoribanks, 1979). In addition, the effects of structural variables, as mediated by family environments, impact family relationships. How the parent-child subsystem is affected by these structural variables is the question to which we now turn.

In a previous section it was noted that according to some (e.g., Zajonc & Markus, 1975), small families with large spacing tend to produce children with higher intelligence as well as more independent and achievement-oriented offspring (Bossard & Boll, 1955; Rosen, 1961). The nature of the parent-child interactions that may mediate such effects are suggested by a number of investigations.

Marjoribanks, Walberg, and Bargen (1975) used the inverse of sibling density as a variable in connection with achievement on the basis that parental attention becomes divided as more children are added to the family. Stress related to the number and spacing of children influences learning environments. Furthermore, the learning environments that result vary for each child depending upon his or her position in the family, which, in turn, produces differential cognitive and social consequences for the child.

Nye et al. (1970) found a linear increase in the use of corporal punishment with family size and Bartow (1961) reported a correlation between family size and the number of rules mothers expected children to follow although the number of rules diminished in families of five or more. Elder and Bowerman (1963) and Bossard and Boll (1956) found fathers to be more involved in child management and discipline as family size increased. Douglas (1964) found that parental interest in children's school work declined with increased family size in both middle and lower class samples. In summarizing this literature, Terhune and Pilie (1974) stated that as family size increases, the amount of parental attention and the quality of maternal care tend to decrease: parents show less interest in their children's school progress, family tensions increase, parent-child closeness decreases (except for later-born children), and family management by parents tends to become more authoritarian. Increasing family size and sibling density creates more demands on the parents' finite time and energies. For example, Knox and Wilson (1978) interviewed mothers of one and two children and found that, with the second child, mothers were more tired at the end of the day and had less time for their husbands. Deacon and Firebaugh (1975) found that the number and ages of children affected the amount of time spent on housework and in community participation.

The Harvard Stress and Families Project (Zelkowitz, Saunders, Longfellow, & Belle, Note 3) has found that single mothers and mothers with three or more children under 16 years living at home have the same pattern of high subjective stress with respect to behavior toward children: less nurturance, fewer friendly responses to children, and a more dominating style of interaction. However, these same mothers also were more compliant and exhibited more frequent prosocial behavior. The Stress and Families Project is studying linkages among stress, maternal depression, and the effects on children.

In all of the research reviewed in this paper, criticisms abound with respect to the rather crude measures used. Moreover, it is obvious that other variables (e.g., social class and birth order effects) must be taken into account. As yet, cause and effect questions have not been answered. Some of the older studies may have been confounded by cohort effects and findings may no longer apply. Continued longitudinal and indepth studies are needed to examine the family in transition in a changing world.

Discussion

The previous overview of research included selective examples of configuration-related stress effects on family relationships and individual development. For purposes of analysis, these effects can be conceptualized as operating on three general levels.

Levels of Stress

The first level may be described best as the *intrapsychic level.* Normative stress within young families influences all members of the family as individuals. For example, Nye et al. (1970) concluded that children from large families often feel neglected and rejected by parents. Likewise, parents are affected by internal conflicts between competing desires that become amplified with increases in family size and sibling density. Moreover, a lack of agreement between personal expectations for family life and resultant actuality with respect to the timing and number of births can engender disappointment and unhappiness in parents. Perhaps the difference between one's ideal age for becoming a parent and the actual age contributes to intrapsychic stress.

A second level is the *interpersonal level.* Because physical resources such as time, money, human energy, and space are finite in availability, decisions and planning are needed for their allocation. Pressure on the family is caused by a lack of mesh or balance between any two people's personal beliefs, values, and expectations. Interpersonal conflicts increase in frequency as the interactional networks become more complex as brought on by growing family size and density.

The final level can be labeled *systemic stress* and represents the composite stress in the family. Tension or conflict between any two members necessarily influences all family members. Again, as the structure of the family increases in complexity, the strain within the system grows. This pressure is continuous and unavoidable.

Stress impacts the family system at all three of these levels simultaneously and each level feeds into the next. The intrapsychic stress of an individual may contribute to interpersonal conflicts which in turn, both feed back into the intrapsychic level as well as influence the system as a whole. The reciprocity in family relationships creates opportunity for mutual support and facilitates family coping, adaptation, and development.

Coping, Adaptation and Development

Young families can cope with normal stress associated with the number and spacing of children by using resources internal as well as external to the family. A large proportion of behaviors effective in easing family stress due to number and spacing of children are internally focused. For example, democratic division of labor can be a mechanism for apportioning work and responsibilities more equitably. Increased communication facilitates managerial efficiency. In addition, new parents adjust by accepting postponement of personal goals and by prioritizing family, work, friends, and leisure. Also, by conserving energy through combining and integrating two or more of the above areas of one's life space, more than one need can be satisfied at a time. Concomitant with these coping devices, parents can benefit from using external supports such as community day care and parent education programs.

These coping strategies imply change in levels of stress. Their use has potential both for alleviating and introducing stress at intrapsychic, interpersonal and systemic levels. This illustrates the continuous nature of adaptation, development and reciprocity within the family as well as between the family and its environment. Motion elicits motion.

For example, an older child may assume some caregiving responsibility for younger siblings during times when parents are under stress. This experience is potentially both negative and positive for the child. Negative outcomes have been suggested in the Zajonc confluence model in which sibling density can be thought of as the source of stress which adversely affects children's cognitive development. At the same time, however, benefits may result in that the situation may foster independence and prosocial skills in the older sibling. Moderate stress can be a motivating force for growth and development.

The internal stresses in families are specific to life stage and family configuration. These are givens that define the constraints on behavior and influence the daily patterns as well as long term beliefs, attitudes, and values of the individual members. As a family unit develops, the constraints imposed by the original configuration evolve and present new stresses. The process is one of perpetual striving for resolution. The potential for growth in individuals, subsystems and the whole system is continuous. One might view maintenance and enhancement, stability and change, adaptation and development, stress and tranquility as mutually dependent states whose interpenetration dialectically propel family development.

REFERENCE NOTES

1. Boss, P. G. *Normative family stress: Family boundary changes across the lifespan.* Paper presented at the Research and Theory Section, National Council on Family Relations Annual Meeting, Boston, Massachusetts, August, 1979.
2. Galbraith, R. & Smith, J. *Sibling spacing and academic achievement: A within-family perspective.* Paper presented at the Society for Research in Child Development, San Francisco, March, 1979.
3. Zelkowitz, P., Saunders, E., Longfellow, C., & Belle, D. *Stress and depression: Their impact on the mother-child relationships.* Paper presented at the Biennial Meeting of the Society for Research in Child Development, San Francisco, March 15-18, 1979.

REFERENCES

Anastasi, A. Intelligence and family size. *Pyschological Bulletin*, 1956, **53**, 187-209.
Anastasi, A. Differentiating effect of intelligence and social status. *Eugenics Quarterly*, 1959, **6**, 84-91.
Bartow, J. Family size as related to child-rearing practices. *Dissertation Abstracts*, 1961, **22**, 558.
Belmont, L. & Marolla, F. Birth order, family size, and intelligence. *Science*, 1973, **182**, 1096-1101.
Bossard, J., & Boll, E. Personality roles in the large family. *Child Development*, 1955, **26**, 71-78.
Bossard, J., & Boll, E. *The large family system: An original study in the sociology of family behavior.* Philadelphia: University of Pennsylvania Press, 1956.

Burgess, E., & Cottrell, L. *Predicting success or failure in marriage*. New York: Prentice-Hall, 1939.

Christensen, H. Children in the family: Relationship of number and spacing to marital success. *Journal of Marriage and the Family*, 1968, **30**, 283-289.

Christensen, H. & Philbuck, R. Family size as a factor in marital adjustments of college couples. *American Sociological Review*, 1952, **17**, 306-312.

Deacon, R., & Firebaugh, F. *Home management: Context and concepts*. Boston: Houghton Mifflin, 1975.

Douglas, J. W. B. *The home and the school*. London: Macgibbon & Kee, 1964.

Elder, G. H., Jr. Family structure: The effects of size of family, sex composition and ordinal position on academic motivation and achievement. In *Adolescent achievement and mobility aspirations*. Chapel Hill, NC: Institute for Research in Social Science, 1962.

Elder, G., & Bowerman, C. Family structure and childrearing patterns: The effect of family size and sex composition. *American Sociological Review*, 1963, **28**, 891-905.

Farber, B., & Blackman, L. Marital role tension and number and sex of children. *American Sociological Review*, 1956, **21**, 596-601.

Figley, C. Child density and the marital relationship. *Journal of Marriage and the Family*, 1973, **35**, 272-282.

Freedman, R., & Coombs, L. Childspacing and family economic position. *American Sociological Review*, 1966, **31**, 631-648.

Hill, R. Social stresses on the family: Generic features of families under stress. *Social Casework*, 1958, **39**, 139-150.

Hurley, J., & Palonen, D. Marital satisfaction and child density among university student parents. *Journal of Marriage and the Family*, 1967, **29**, 483-484.

Knox, D., & Wilson, K. The difference between having one and two children. *The Family Coordinator*, 1978, **27**, 23-35.

Lang, R. D. *The study of ratings of marital adjustment*. Unpublished Masters thesis, University of Chicago, 1932.

Marjoribanks, K. *Families and their learning environments*. London: Routledge & Kegan Paul, 1979.

Marjoribanks, K., Walbert, H., & Bargen, M. Mental abilities: Sibling constellation and social class correlates. *British Journal of Social and Clinical Psychology*, 1975, **14**, 109-116.

Miller, B. Child density, marital satisfaction, and commentionalization: A research note. *Journal of Marriage and the Family*, 1975, **37**, 345-347.

McCall, J., & Johnson, O. The independence of intelligence from family size and birth order. *The Journal of Genetic Psychology*, 1972, **121**, 207-213.

McCutcheon, L. Dumber by the dozen? Not necessarily! *Psychological Reports*, 1977, **40**, 109-110.

McGillicuddy-DeLisi, A. V., Sigel, I. E., & Johnson, J. E. The family as a system of mutual influences: Parental beliefs, distancing behaviors, and children's representational thinking. In M. Lewis & L. Rosenblum (Eds.), *The child and its family*. New York: Plenum, 1979.

Nisbet, J. D., & Entwistle, N. J. Intelligence and family size, 1949-1965. *British Journal of Educational Psychology*, 1966, **37**, 188.

Nye, F. I., Carlson, J., & Garrett, G. Family size, interaction, affect and stress. *Journal of Marriage and the Family*, 1970, **32**, 216-226.

Nye, F. I., & Hoffman, L. *The employed mother in America*. Chicago: Rand McNally, 1963.

Reed, R. B. Social and psychological factors affecting fertility. The interrelationship of marital adjustment, fertility control, and the size of family. *The Milbank Memorial Fund Quarterly*, 1948, **25**, 383-425.

Renee, K. S. Correlates of dissatisfaction in marriage. *Journal of Marriage and the Family*, 1970, **32**, 54-67.

Rollins, B., & Galligan, R. The developing child and marital satisfaction. In R. Lerner & G. Spanier (Eds.), *Child influences on marital and family interaction: A lifespan perspective*. New York: Academic Press, 1978.

Rosen, B. C. Family structure and achievement motivation. *American Sociological Review*, 1961, **26**, 574-585.

Russell, C. Transition to parenthood: Problems and gratifications. *Journal of Marriage and the Family*, 1974, **36**, 294-302.

Sampson, E. E. The study of ordinal position: Antecedents and outcomes. In B. Maher (Ed.), *Progress in experimental personality research* (Vol. 2). New York: Academic Press, 1965.

Terhune, K. W., & Pilie, R. J. *A review of the actual and expected consequences of family size*. Department of Health, Education and Welfare Publication (NIH) 76-779. Washington, DC: U.S. Government Printing Office, 1974.

Thornton, A. Children and marital stability. *Journal of Marriage and the Family*, 1977, **39**, 531-540.

Wray, J. D. Population pressure on families: Family size and child spacing. *Reports on Population/Family Planning*, 1971, No. 9.

Zajonc, R., & Markus, G. Birth order and intellectual development. *Psychological Review*, 1975, **82**, 74-88.

Normal Stresses During the Transition To Parenthood*

BRENT C. MILLER AND DONNA L. SOLLIE**

The transition to parenthood is discussed as a normal developmental event. Longitudinal data, before and after the first child, show that both personal and marital stresses increase, especially among new mothers, after the first baby is born. Feelings of personal well being among new parents are higher soon after the baby is born than later; well being of both mothers and fathers declines by the time the baby is seven or eight months old. Parental reports of adaptation are compared with normal coping strategies suggested in the literature.

Some events in life are fairly predictable; they occur at about the same time and in the same order for most people. This is not to say that everyone goes through precisely the same sequence of life events, but there is a series of normative experiences. Such normal or developmental events, and their attendant problems, can be anticipated.

For a large majority of married adults one of the sharpest expected changes is the transition to parenthood. Although pregnancy is a harbinger, the roles and tasks of parenting are acquired abruptly. As soon as the first infant is born, and certainly by the time parents go home from the hospital, they *have* parental roles—there are social expectations about what they should do. By comparison, later normative changes during the parental career

occur much more gradually as children become toddlers, school children, teenagers, and then leave home. There is, then, a point in time when parental roles are abruptly acquired, but there is also a more gradual transition into the skills and routines of parenting. Although the transition to parenthood is considered a "critical role transition *point*," it is also a *phase* or span of time (Aldous, 1978).

Previous Studies

Based on Hill's (1949) conceptualization that accession, or adding a family member, would constitute a sharp change for which old patterns were inadequate, LeMasters (1957) conducted the first study of parenthood as a "crisis." He found, as did Dyer (1963), that a majority of middle-class parents experienced "extensive or severe" crisis as defined above. Both of these studies can be faulted for small unrepresentative samples, and the LeMasters study for probable experimenter effects, (Rosenthal, 1966) because he helped the couples decide how much crisis they had experienced.

The term "crisis" has also been criticized because the transition to parenthood is generally considered to be a normal event. Because of this, Rapoport (1963) suggested the term "normal crisis," and Rossi (1968) advocated

*Appreciation is expressed to the office of Graduate Studies and Research at the University of Tennessee, Knoxville, for supporting the larger study on which this paper is based, and to the College of Family Life at Utah State University for supporting the analyses.

**Brent C. Miller is Assistant Professor, Department of Family and Human Development, Utah State University, Logan, Utah, 84322, and Donna L. Sollie is Assistant Professor, Department of Home and Family Life, Texas Tech University, Lubbock, Texas 79409.

(*Family Relations*, 1980, **29**, 459-465.)

dropping references to crisis altogether: "There is an uncomfortable incongruity in speaking of any crisis as normal. If the transition is achieved and if a successful reintegration . . . occurs, then crisis is a misnomer" (p. 28). After Rossi's classic essay, the use of the term crisis dropped off, but comparisons with earlier studies continued to be based on amounts of "crisis" experienced.

Hobbs (1965, 1968) and Jacoby (1969) reported much lower levels of crisis experienced by new parents than either LeMasters or Dyer had found. More recent studies (Russell, 1974; Hobbs & Wimbish, 1977; Hobbs & Cole, 1976) have arrived at similar conclusions. Part of the discrepancy between the earlier and later studies seems to be due to focusing on different aspects of the transition; recent studies have focused more on *reactions* to changes (feelings and attitudes) rather than on the *changes* (behavior patterns) themselves. The Hobbs checklist, for example, asks questions about how "bothered" parents were about various problems of new parents; only small amounts of crisis have been found when operationalized in this way. It would probably be accurate to say that the behavioral changes accompanying new parenthood are typically extensive, but most new parents are only slightly or mildly bothered by these changes, and a large number report gratifications arising from first parenthood as well (Russell, 1974).

Social desirability is a problem when changes or reactions during the transition to parenthood are assessed in the usual way. When the researcher connects children and problems by asking the new parents to tell how bothered they are, or how much things have changed, a nagging doubt arises about how truthful parents will be. Because of the strongly pronatalist and romantic view of children in American society (LeMasters, 1974), it is difficult for new parents to objectively answer questions about how children changed their lives. Consequently, there is some question about the validity of their self reports.

Another general criticism of most transition to parenthood research is that is has usually been conducted after the fact. When changes and their accompanying stresses are to be studied, inferential validity is stronger if subjects are assessed both before and after the first child. With before and after measures, changes do not have to be recalled or estimated by the new parents—they can be calculated by the researcher directly. In one longitudinal study of this kind, Feldman (1971) found declining marital satisfaction between 5 months of pregnancy and 5 months postpartum, especially among couples who had the most companionate relationships before parenthood. Ryder (1973), who used a different measure of marital satisfaction, did not find significant decreases in husband or wife scores; he did report, however, that new mothers reported more lovesickness (a feeling that their husbands were not paying enough attention to them) after their baby had been born.

Taking this information into account, the present research was designed to: (a) study the same couples as they *changed* over time; (b) measure *stresses* during the transition more directly; and (c) avoid *socially desirable* responses by not overtly connecting children with the new parents' evaluations of their personal and marital feelings. Based on the previous studies, it was expected that stresses would increase after having a baby, more so among mothers than fathers.

Methods

Sample and Design

The 120 couples who began the present study were recruited from one of three different hospital-based parenthood preparation classes in Knoxville, Tennessee. Couples volunteered to participate after hearing a brief overview of what would be required; they were not randomly selected. The majority of couples had middle-class occupations, incomes, and lifestyles. Both husband and wife in 109 couples completed and returned questionnaires at three points in time: first, when the wife was in midpregnancy; second, when the baby was about five to six weeks old; and finally, when the baby was between six and eight months old. Eleven couples were lost from the sample because of such diverse reasons as divorce, disinterest, and moving without forwarding addresses.

The longitudinal design of the present study made it possible to objectively describe changes in stresses that occurred during the transition to parenthood, rather than relying on the remembered or recalled experiences of new parents studied retrospectively. Couples were studied twice after becoming parents because of the baby honeymoon idea expressed by Feldman (as cited in Hobbs, 1968). When babies were only five to six weeks old, few and/or slight changes were expected, but changes were expected to be more pronounced by the time babies were eight months old.

Measures

At all three points in time, measures of personal well-being, personal stress, and marital stress were included in the questionnaires along with many other measures not reported here. The measures of personal well being and personal stress came from a national survey of the quality of American life (Campbell, Converse, & Rodgers, 1976). Before and twice after having their first child, husbands and wives rated how they felt about their present lives on nine semantic differential adjective pairs, such as boring-interesting, enjoyable-miserable, and so on. When factor analyzed in the present study, seven of these nine items were very strongly associated with each other as Campbell et al. found. These seven items were used in a summated scale to measure *personal well being*. The two remaining items were highly intercorrelated, but less related to the other seven items. These two semantic differential items "easy-hard," and "tied down-free" were summed to create a scale of *personal stress* for husbands and wives at each of the three points in time.

The measure of *marital stress* was previously developed by Pearlin (1975). Respondents indicated the degree to which they felt bothered, bored, tense, frustrated, unhappy, worried, and neglected in their day-to-day marriage relationship. These items formed a unidimensional scale when factor analyzed, with an alpha reliability coefficient of .87. Because none of the dependent measures were overtly linked to the fact that subjects had become parents between time 1 and time 2, the data reported here should be less affected by social desirability than the retrospective transition to parenthood data.

Results and Discussion

The personal well being, personal stress, and marital stress mean scores of new mothers and fathers are shown in Table 1. Differences between row means were tested with paired or correlated t-tests.

Nine of the 18 t-tests showed significant differences, but only two of these differences were between the pregnancy and one-month postpartum measures. Both new mothers and fathers reported higher scores on personal stress items ("hard-easy" and "tied down-free") after they had become parents. The magnitude of these changes is especially interesting; wives' personal stress scores dur-

Table 1.
Changes in Personal Well-Being, Personal Stress, and Marital
Stress During the Transition to Parenthood+

Parents Well-Being	Time 1 6 Months Pregnant	Time 2 Baby 1 Month	Time 3 Baby 8 Months
Mothers			
Personal Well-Being	30.57	31.20***	30.01
Personal Stress	4.52***	5.99	6.19***
Marital Stress	9.50	9.97*	10.53***
Fathers			
Personal Well-Being	30.69	30.77**	29.80***
Personal Stress	5.19**	5.64	5.69***
Marital Stress	9.55	9.26	9.76

+Row means which are significantly different have asterisks between them. Asterisks after the 8 months column (Time 3) refer to the comparison of Time 1 (pregnancy) and Time 3 (8 months) mean scores.

*Paired t-test, difference between means $p < .05$
**Paired t-test, difference between means $p < .01$.
***Paired t-test, difference between means $p < .001$.

ing pregnancy were lower than their husbands' scores, but new mothers ended up with higher personal stress scores than their husbands. The fact that seven of the nine significant differences were between one month and eight months postpartum, and pregnancy and eight months postpartum, provides some support for the notion of the "baby honeymoon" in the early postpartum period.

Personal well being scores of new mothers were lower at time 3 than at time 2, and personal well being for fathers was lower at time 3 than during the pregnancy observation or when the baby was about one month old. The most interesting sex difference in the changes were evident on the marital stress scale. New mothers reported higher stress in their marriages after the baby had been born than before, and even higher marital stress by the time the baby was about eight months old. New fathers' marital stress scores, by contrast, remained essentially the same across the year of the study. These data coincide with Ryder's (1973) finding that new mothers were more likely than fathers to report that their spouses were not paying enough attention to them.

Although we should be cautious about generalizing from volunteer samples, the agreement of these findings with previous research suggests that the typical new parenthood experience probably includes a slight to modest decline in personal well being and some increase in personal stress over the first year or so of parenting. New mothers feel these changes more keenly than fathers, and wives are more likely than husbands to view their marriages as changing in a negative way. The changes noted above were statistically significant (not likely to be due to chance) in the present study, but it must be pointed out that they were not huge changes. Even in the moderate changes of these new parents, however, a number of coping strategies seem to be brought into play.

Adaptation to Stress

Preparation for parenthood through reading, attending classes, or caring for infants probably increases the prospective parent's feelings of preparedness and self-confidence, but no amount of preparation and rehearsal can fully simulate the constant and immediate needs of an infant. The sometimes overwhelming demands of new parenthood usually result in some degree of personal and marital stress (Sollie & Miller, 1980). So, the question of how new parents cope is especially appropriate.

McCubbin, Boss, and Wilson (Note 1) noted that successful adaptation to stress involves at least two major kinds of family resources. The first of these includes the internal resources of the family, such as adaptability and integration. The second includes coping strategies that can strengthen the organization and functioning of the family, including the utilization of community and social supports. McCubbin (1979) has also emphasized the need for interpersonal support systems, noting that families have the capacity to organize a variety of supports to respond to stresses in adaptive ways.

Although the parents in this study were not directly asked to identify coping behaviors that they used, they were asked to write an open-ended response about the positive and negative aspects of having a baby in their lives. Several strategies that they relied on were evident in their replies.

Adaptability appeared as a major strategy utilized by these first-time parents in coping with the stresses they experienced. For example, a theme that appeared frequently in their comments was the change from an orderly, predictable life to a relatively disorderly and unpredictable one. As one father said, *"I certainly don't try to keep rigid schedules anymore! And I'm becoming a more flexible person."* A new mother wrote,

> *One of the hardest adjustments for me was the unpredictibleness of my day. I couldn't be sure of anything—that I would be able to take a nap after her next feeding, that I would have time to clean the house on a certain day, that I would have time to fix supper, etc.*

Other coping strategies of new parents which reflect adaptability included learning patience, becoming more organized, and becoming more flexible.

Integration of the family was also evident in the responses of these first-time parents, especially in the emphasis by some respondents on parenthood as a shared responsibility. Another example of integration was the attempt to continue some activities that were engaged in before the birth of the child—that is, to maintain a sense of continuity, and to recognize the importance of the husband-wife relationship. Husband-wife discussions of feelings were utilized by some couples during this period. One wife wrote of her husband, *"He's been very understanding of my feelings and doubts and because we're very open with each other I can express a lot of what I feel, which helps."* Many respondents indicated that the child brought them closer together, increased their interdependence, and expanded their feelings of unity and cohesion. In this sense, integration of the family is a coping resource that may be present before the birth of the child, but which can increase afterward. Husband-wife integration could be enhanced through discussing each spouse's expectations of their own and the other's roles after the birth of the child. Fein (1976) found that husband-wife negotiation of roles was an important factor in the adjustment of first-time fathers.

Other coping strategies seemed to be directed toward strengthening individual responses to some of the stresses experienced. These included utilizing social supports and looking to the future. For example, support from neighbors and friends in the form of advice, information, and caretaking was reported as being helpful. Taking time away from the baby was also beneficial, both during day and at night. One husband noted that a positive aspect of parenthood was *"My being able to help with the baby, giving my wife time to herself—therefore giving myself personal satisfaction."* This statement also reflects family integration. Just realizing that ambivalent feelings are also experienced by others can be reassuring. One mother said, *"Because an infant is so demanding, there are days when one wishes the baby did not exist. Knowing these feelings are normal, however, makes coping with the day-to-day routine possible."*

Looking to the future was also a personal coping strategy. One mother commented, *"Most of the time I realize that she will get better as time goes on. This isn't as hard during the day, but at night I find I can't deal with her as objectively."* Another mother who missed her teaching career wrote, *"I have applied to do some teaching on a homebound basis and just knowing that I might soon be working has lifted my spirits."* A father expressed some of his negative thoughts about the present and hopes for the future as follows: *"Care of the baby has been somewhat tiring for both of us. I expect my thoughts to become positive again after the baby grows some more, becomes more predictable, and can be played with."*

One aspect of motherhood that appeared to be stress-producing did not seem to have any ready solutions—the problem of balancing motherhood and a career. This dilemma was identified over 20 years ago in LeMasters' (1957) classic study of parenthood as crisis. Although only a small number of the women in this sample were strongly career-oriented, this issue is becoming increasingly salient as more and more women make career commitments outside the home. The comments of some mothers expressed their doubts and the lack of easy answers to this dilemma. One mother said,

My baby is a new individual in my life whom I love dearly, but at this point I am not personally fulfilled in simply being a mother. I am finding it difficult to cope with the boredom and lack of intellectual stimulation in my life. I gave up my career in teaching because I felt it would be unfair to take my baby to a daycare center or babysitter. I'm very undecided as to what I should do.

Another mother wrote, *"Like many new mothers I am faced with hard decisions about the future of my career since my baby was born. I am full of doubts, and I'm uncertain how to maintain my career and raise my child satisfactorily."* When a mother does interrupt her career, she may experience both intellectual and social voids in her life. Additionally, she may feel tied down and find it difficult to adjust to the changes in the husband-wife roles in her marriage. Lamb (1978) noted that a change from egalitarian roles to more stereotyped roles could be a cause of stress for some couples, and it would seem especially likely to be stressful for career-minded but homebound mothers.

Conclusions and Recommendations

When babies in this study were just over a month old, changes in their parents' personal and marital stress were less evident than when babies were eight months old, providing some evidence for Feldman's notion of a baby honeymoon. Perceived personal stress (feelings of being tied down and that life is hard rather than easy) increased significantly for both mothers and fathers during the transition to parenthood, but among mothers more than fathers. Marital stress remained essentially unchanged among fathers over the course of the study, but perceptions of marital stress increased among new mothers between the time when babies were one month and eight months old.

These average or typical patterns reflect relatively small changes in total scores, and they also hide the few couples for whom the transition to parenthood was a very difficult experience as well as those whose personal lives and marriages improved. The unusual couples, whose lives and marriages more markedly deteriorated or improved during the transition to parenthood, are those who it seems especially important to learn more about, so that new parenthood problems could be prevented, better treated, or at least better understood.

Considered as a normal developmental event in the individual and family life cycle, the birth of the first child can be both a source of stress and an event to test the family's coping strategies. That is, the baby can cause certain stresses arising from lack of sleep, tiredness, less time for self and spouse, and feelings of overwhelming responsibility and being tied down. At the same time though, the baby can provide a sense of fulfillment, new meaning in life, and can strengthen the bond between husband and wife, thus contributing to a sense of family cohesiveness (Sollie & Miller, 1980). This cohesiveness or integration is one of the intrafamily resources identified by McCubbin, Boss and Wilson (Note 1) which facilitates adaptation to stress.

Families not only rely on their own internal resources, but they also develop coping strategies by utilizing community and social supports. In addition to relying on extended family or friends during the transition to parenthood, many new parents are taking advantage of preparenthood classes offered by local hospitals, community agencies, and other organizations. Unfortunately, most of these classes are really prenatal or childbirth preparation classes which fall short in helping prospective parents *after* the child is born. New parents are probably in greater need of information and support during the months after their baby is born than during the months leading up to delivery.

Although there are logistical problems in bringing new parents together, it would seem that postparenthood classes have a relatively untapped potential for providing support systems after the birth of the child (Cowan, Cowan, Coie, & Coie, 1978). Such classes could teach basic skills, provide an opportunity for observing others with their infants, provide an outlet for expressing feelings, and an opportunity to share ideas, experiences, and problems of adjusting to parenthood. Since the negotiation and resolution of marital and parental roles may be an important factor in adjusting to parenthood (Fein, 1976), husband and wife integration might also be enhanced by discussing role expectations after the baby is born.

It is our general impression that romantic conceptions about having children are declining in our culture. People seem to be more realistic about the impacts children have on parents and marriage. This realization, in and of itself, might be another way of better coping with the stress of parenting. Knowledge about the probable effects of children, both positive and negative, and a less romantic definition of infants, might help new parents cope more easily with the usual stresses that accompany this normal life event.

REFERENCE NOTE

1. McCubbin, H. I., Boss, P. G., & Wilson, L. R. *Developments in family stress theory: Implications for family impact analysis.* Paper presented at the Preconference Theory and Methodology workshop of the National Council on Family Relations, Philadelphia, PA, October, 1978.

REFERENCES

Aldous, J. *Family careers: Developmental change in families*. New York: Wiley, 1978.

Campbell, A., Converse, P., & Rodgers, W. *The quality of American life*. New York: Russell Sage, 1976.

Cowan, C. P., Cowan, P. A., Coie, L., & Coie, J. D. Becoming a family: The impact of a first child's birth on a couple's relationship. In W. B. Miller, & L. F. Newman (Eds.), *The first child and family formation*. Chapel Hill, NC: Carolina Population Center, 1978.

Dyer, E. D. Parenthood as crisis: A restudy. *Marriage and Family Living*, 1963, **25**, 196-201.

Fein, R. A. Men's entrance to parenthood. *The Family Coordinator*, 1976, **25**, 341-350.

Feldman, H. The effects of children on the family. In Andree Michel (Ed.), *Family issues of employed women in Europe and America*. Leiden: E. J. Brill, 1971.

Hill, R. *Families under stress*. New York: Harper, 1949.

Hobbs, D. F., Jr. Parenthood as crisis: A third study. *Journal of Marriage and the Family*, 1965, **27**, 367-372.

Hobbs, D. F., Jr. Transition to parenthood: A replication and an extension. *Journal of Marriage and the Family*, 1968, **30**, 413-417.

Hobbs, D. F., Jr., & Cole, S. P. Transition to parenthood: A decade replication. *Journal of Marriage and the Family*, 1976, **38**, 723-731.

Hobbs, D. F., Jr., & Wimbish, J. M. Transition to parenthood by Black couples. *Journal of Marriage and the Family*, 1977, **39**, 677-689.

Jacoby, A. P. Transition to parenthood: A reassessment. *Journal of Marriage and the Family*, 1969, **31**, 720-727.

Lamb, M. E. Influence of the child on marital quality and family interaction during the prenatal, perinatal, and infancy periods. In R. M. Lerner & G. B. Spanier (Eds.), *Child influences on marital and family interaction: A lifespan perspective*. New York: Academic Press, 1978.

LeMasters, E. E. Parenthood as crisis. *Marriage and Family Living*, 1957, **19**, 352-355.

McCubbin, H. I. Integrating coping behavior in family stress theory. *Journal of Marriage and the Family*, 1979, **41**, 237-244.

Pearlin, L. I. Status inequality and stress in marriage. *American Sociological Review*, 1975, **40** (June), 344-357.

Rapoport, R. Normal crises, family structure, and mental health. *Family Process*, 1963, **2**, 68-80.

Rossi, A. S. Transition to parenthood. *Journal of Marriage and the Family*, 1968, **30**, 26-39.

Rosenthal, R. *Experimenter effects in behavioral research*. New York: Appleton-Century-Crofts, 1966.

Russell, C. S. Transition to parenthood: Problems and gratifications. *Journal of Marriage and the Family*, 1974, **36**, 294-302.

Ryder, R. G. Longitudinal data relating marriage satisfaction and having a child. *Journal of Marriage and the Family*, 1973, **35**, 604-607.

Sollie, D. L., & Miller, B. C. The transition to parenthood as a critical time for building family strengths. In N. Stinnett, B. Chesser, J. DeFrain, & P. Knaub (Eds.), *Family Strengths: Positive Models for Family Life*. Lincoln, NE: University of Nebraska Press, 1980.

PURPOSES OF NCFR

The National Council on Family Relations is an international non-profit educational and resource organization dedicated to the strengthening of marriage and the family. The goals of the NCFR are to enable professional practitioners, academicians, and interested laypersons to: work together on the establishment of professional standards in the field; promote and coordinate educational efforts; encourage research about the family; encourage the development of community services for families; stimulate sound, coherent governmental policies pertaining to family issues; provide information regarding training centers; and share pertinent information with professional colleagues and organizations working with families.

BENEFITS OF MEMBERSHIP

* **Choice of two NCFR Journals**
    The *Journal of Marriage and the Family*, emphasizing significant advances in family research
    Family Relations, a journal of applied aspects of family and child studies
    The *Journal of Family History*, carrying studies in Family, Kinship, and Demography
* **Reduced subscription to the third journal**
* **A quarterly newsletter** describing Council affairs, carrying employment information, and a calendar of special events
* **An established Annual Meeting,** where:
    Members may meet leading professionals in the family field
    Stimulating plenary sessions and Section meetings are offered
    New books and films may be viewed
* **Membership in a state or provincial Affiliated Council on Family Relations**
* **Section membership.** Members may join one or more Sections. The *Family Therapy Section* is concerned with the training of marriage and family therapists, and issues connected with therapy practice . . . The *Family Action Section* is the action arm of the NCFR. Some of its work centers around preparing position papers on legislative issues affecting families. Its Focus Groups are in the areas of aging, middle age, family health, family law, marriage enrichment, single parent families, and remarriage . . . The *Education Section's* activities include sharing information on effective family life education teaching methods and materials, helping in the coordination of education—research—practical experiences, offering information on new programs and processes, developing strategies for evaluating educational programs, and promoting interchange between teachers . . . The *International Section* is interested in international family-related issues, in international collaborative projects, and with enriching NCFR programs with international content . . . The *Research and Theory Section* is interested in all aspects of family research and theory building. Each year this Section holds a pre-NCFR Annual Meeting workshop on theory development and methods . . . The *Ethnic Minorities Section* is committed to increasing minority representation in the NCFR and to facilitating communication between minority members.
* **The Family Resource and Referral Center (FR&RC)**
    A national online (public access) computerized bibliographic database representing the family field. (NCFR members are offered a 10% discount on custom searches.)

Write for an invitational membership brochure:

National Council on Family Relations
1219 University Avenue Southeast
Minneapolis, Minnesota 55414

Child's School Entry: A Stressful Event in the Lives of Fathers*

ELLEN HOCK, PATRICK C. MCKENRY, MICHAEL D. HOCK,
SANTO TRIOLO, AND LUAN STEWART**

A child's school entry, viewed as a normal transition point in the family life cycle, was considered as a source of stress for fathers. Forty fathers of children entering school were interviewed. Fathers' anxiety concerning school entrance, sadness about separation, and duration of sadness were assessed. Findings suggest that most fathers do experience some anxiety related to this event, and that their anxiety and sadness are related to the level of anxiety felt by their wives, their socioeconomic status, and their confidence that schooling would be a quality experience for their child. Mother work status was not related to any component of father stress.

Certain naturally-occurring events generate transient changes in established life patterns of individuals. Rapoport (1963) suggests that family members experience the normal crisis of transition during predictable, "normal" transition points in the family life cycle—the birth of a child, children entering school, children leaving home. When an event is normal and expected but potentially stressful, it can be viewed as a normative crisis because members of the family may experience anxiety, may acquire new roles, or may find it neces-

*Preparation of this manuscript was supported, in part, by the Ohio Agricultural Research and Development Center (H-615 and H-644).

**Ellen Hock is Associate Professor, Departments of Family Relations and Human Development and Pediatrics, The Ohio State University and the Ohio Agricultural Research and Development Center, Columbus, Ohio 43210. Patrick C. McKenry is Assistant Professor, Department of Family Relations, and Human Development, The Ohio State University and the Ohio Agricultural Research and Development Center. Michael D. Hock is Lecturer, School of Public Administration, The Ohio State University and Director of Public Management Programs, Graduate School of Administration, Capital University, Columbus, Ohio. Santo Triolo and Luan Stewart are Graduate Research Associates, Department of Family Relations and Human Development, The Ohio State University.

(*Family Relations*, 1980, **29**, 467-472.)

sary to modify existing roles. One developmental transition of potential significance is a child's entrance into the public school system.

Considering the near-universal nature of school entry and its potential impact on family life, studies of child school entry are unexpectedly rare. This event in family life can be studied using concepts of role change of family members and separation of children from parents. We approach this event to describe stress during this transition on the father of a child. Existing studies focus on the child's adjustment, ignoring impact on either parent. Hill and Rodgers (1964) suggested that "considerable insight into family dynamics could be gained by more intensive study of families during this period of initial extensive contact outside the home on the part of children" (p. 195).

The child entering school acquires the new role of pupil, and also establishes a link between the family and another important social institution. The structural characteristics of this transition are akin to Hill's (1949) stress category of dismemberment. As defined by Hill, dismemberment creates a situation wherein the "amputated" family member's roles must be reallocated, with an ensuing period of confusion and uncertainty.

On entry into the educational system, occupants of the child position—children—become deeply involved in relationships outside the family system; this demands change in role patterns within the family system (Ferguson & Freeark, Note 1). To the extent that family role changes impede the functioning of the family in its affectional and emotion-satisfying performances, such a developmental transition can be stress or crisis producing.

In addition to school entry demanding new roles for the child and other family members, the developmental transition of school entry represents a significant separation event between parents and child and may stimulate strong parental emotional responses of anxiety, sadness, or depression. Conversations with parents of 5-year-olds about to enter school reinforced our belief that school entry was a potent affect-inducing event. Parents we questioned reported that as the start of school drew close they felt they were "losing their babies." Parents reported worry and sadness because their children would be all alone, and because they as parents would not be there to protect and help them.

In addition to sadness associated with "loss" of a child, another distinctive feature of school entry is that parents may feel they are losing control over the lives of their children. Parents may perceive the school community (peers, older children, teachers, and principals) as having more influence over their children than parents have.

Social scientists, family life educators, clinicians, and parents have begun a long-overdue assessment of the problems and possibilities of relationships between *fathers* and children. Increasing numbers of men are reaching out for more sustaining relationships with the young in their lives. The expressive role of father is increasingly being viewed as a major factor in adult well-being (Fein, 1978). Yet only in the last decade have researchers begun to look carefully at the relationships men establish with their young children. Although novels and popular magazines have presented personal accounts, there has been little systematic exploration of the fathering experience (Fein, 1978). deLissovoy (1976) has noted the need for research on the feelings and attitudes of fathers.

The father, at this developmental stage of child school entry, often is portrayed as indifferent, or wanting to turn his awkward "in-between" child over to the school, teacher, and others for training (Hawkins, 1974). Researchers long have assumed that men are less affected by a child's experience—fathers presumably experience little emotional impact as a result of their children's behavior.

Maternal employment could contribute to any stress the father experiences as a result of school separation because the mother's job may increase his responsibilities for child care as well as reducing the amount of personal care he receives. Two recent studies reached entirely different conclusions on the impact of wife-mother employment on father stress (cf. Burke & Weir, 1976; Staines, Pleck, Shepark, & O'Connor, 1978). The contradictory findings of these two studies indicate that additional research is needed to clarify the issue (Booth, 1979).

In this study, we wished to explore the nature of father feelings at the time his child entered school. We desired both to extend knowledge of the fathering experience and to look at the nature and some correlates of stress that fathers experienced during this developmental transition for the family. As a result, we focused our exploratory investigation on several broad questions:

1. What is the nature of selected father emotions at the start of his child's school experience? Is the father anxious or not about his child's start to school? Does the father report feelings of sadness at his child's leaving? If so, how long do those feelings persist?

2. Which parallel emotions does the mother report? What is the congruence of mother and father feelings when the child starts school?

3. Which father attributes and family features are associated with differences in father emotions when the child starts school—especially father's closeness to his child, his beliefs about the quality of school experience for his child, and social class?

4. Are there differences in the emotions of fathers who have wives in paid work and fathers who have wives who are not in the labor force?

Methods

Subjects

Fathers in this study were members of families that had participated in a larger, longitudinal study of mother-father-infant interaction from the time of infant birth, with births occuring between November, 1973 and February, 1974. At the time of school entry of the children in this longitudinal study (fall of 1979), fathers of the longitudinal study families were contacted by telephone to determine their willingness to participate in this study. The potential study population was composed of 50 fathers; of those, 40 agreed to participate and were interviewed.

The original, longitudinal study was begun in 1973. The sample was composed of matched pairs of mothers and infants with one-half of the mothers planning to work and one-half planning to stay at home to rear their infant during the first year of infant life. Later, many of these mothers chose to work. (See Hock, 1976, for details of sample selection.) Five years later, at the time of this study, one-half of the mothers in these families were working more than 20 hours a week outside the home.

Thus, this sample of fathers is composed of 20 men with wives in the paid labor force and 20 with wives not in the labor force. The 40 fathers had a mean age of approximately 34 years, and all were in paid employment. Ninety-five percent were white, and the fathers tended to be "middle class" (with a mean of 32.75 on the Hollingshead/Redlich Two-Factor Index). All responding fathers were married at the time of the interviews.

The children of these fathers were an average of 5½ years of age at the time of this study; 50% of the subject children were boys; 65% of the subject children were first-born; and 17% of the subject children were only children.

Data Collection and Analysis

Data collection began within five days of the time the child started school and ended within four weeks. Fathers were questioned about the first "real" day of school when their child spent time at school without either parent. Variables in the study included father feelings at school beginning (anxiety, sadness, and duration of sadness), father involvement with his child ("closeness" and extent of father-child activities), and father confidence about the quality of school experience for his child. In addition, parallel variables were considered for the mother regarding anxiety, sadness, and duration of sadness at the time of school beginning. Finally, some demographic features of the family were studied: family socioeconomic status and mother work status.

Data were collected by telephone interview of fathers; other study data were acquired from previously-conducted telephone interviews of mothers. Fathers were interviewed by trained interviewers at a date and time fathers specified to be convenient. The telephone interview, containing closed- and open-ended questions, required an average of 15 minutes to complete. All fathers consenting to participate completed the interview. Data were also available on the spouses of all study participants.

Certain of the study variables were created by interviewer rating of father responses. These variables and interrater reliability of ratings were father sadness ($r = .94$) and duration of father sadness ($r = 1.00$). Table 1 contains the variables of this study, explanation of variables, example questions, the source of data, and extreme points of the rating scales.

Because we wished to explore associations between certain feelings of fathers and other father attributes and features of family life, Pearsonian correlational analysis was chosen with .05 as the level of statistical significance. In the following sections of this report, all significant correlations between study variables are presented.

Findings and Discussion

The study findings appear to confirm the notion that school entry is a unique, distinctive, stress-provoking event for *both* mothers and fathers. Over 50% of the fathers reported feeling anxious about their child's entry into school (25% of the fathers reported "a lot" of anxiety; 28% reported "some"; 47% reported none). More than 50% of the mothers reported the same feelings of anxiety, almost in

Table 1
Father Emotions When the Child Started School:
Variables, Explanations, Example Questions and Responses

Variable and Explanation	Example Telephone Interview Question(s)	Scale, Source of Data and Extremes
A. Dependent Variables:		
1. Father Anxiety (degree to which father is anxious about his child starting school)	"Before school started, did *you* personally feel anxious about having (your child) start school?"	1 = none; 2 = some; 3 = a lot. (Father report)
2. Father Sadness (affect and intensity of sadness, crying, and feeling of loss about his child starting school)	"On the first 'real' day of school (when your child spent the time at school without you), did you feel sad after your child left for school? Cry or feel depressed?"	1 = no sadness; 9 = much grieving, intense sadness. (Interviewer rating of instance of most intense affect)
3. Duration of Father Sadness (period of time father sadness persisted)	". . . (H)ow long did the feeling persist?" "How did you feel a week or so later?"	1 = no sadness; 9 = week or more. (Interviewer rating of duration of most intense affect)
B. Independent Variables:		
1. Father Closeness to Child (degree of closeness father feels to his child)	"Some parents are close to their children; others are not. Do you have a . . . close relationship with your 5-year-old?"	1 = very close; 3 = not very close. (Father report)
2. Extent of Father Activities with Child (number of specific, diverse activities engaged in by father with child)	"Do you regularly shop for your child's clothes or shoes?", and others specified and appropriate to 5-year-old children.	0 = none; 12 = maximum of specified activities (Father report)
3. Father Confidence of Positive School Experience (degree to which father believes school and teacher will provide a good learning experience for his child)	". . . (T)hink about how confident you are that the school and teacher will provide a quality or good learning experience for (your child). Please rate your feelings on a scale of one to ten. . . ."	1 = unsure of quality learning experience; 10 = extremely sure of quality learning experience. (Father report)
4. Mother's Present Work Status (whether or not mother is doing paid work outside the home more than 20 hours a week)	(Derived from data collected from mother)	1 = mother in paid work; 2 = mother not in labor force.
5. Mother Anxiety	(Mother feelings about her child starting school; derived from data collected from mother, where questioning is identical to that of father depicted under independent variables 1, 2, and 3 above)	(Same as for father depicted under independent variables 1, 2, and 3 above)
6. Mother Sadness		
7. Duration of Mother Sadness		

the same proportion as fathers (22% of the mothers reported "a lot" of anxiety; 40% reported "some"; 38% reported none). These findings support Hill's (1949) and Rapoport's (1963) suggestions that a normal expectable transition point for families, such as school entry of a child, involves feelings of anxiety, stress, or a crisis for members of involved families.

There was a significant correlation among the three dependent measures of stress—anxiety, sadness, and duration of sadness. Father anxiety regarding his child's school entry was positively related to his sadness at the time ($r = .38$) and the duration of that sadness ($r = .36$). Fathers who were anxious about their child starting school were more likely to experience sadness on the child's first day of school and to experience that sadness for a longer period of time than fathers who were less anxious. Furthermore, intensity of the sadness experienced by fathers was positively related to the duration of that sadness ($r = .91$).

The more confident a father was about the good quality of the school experience for his child, the less sadness he felt ($r = -.40$). So, fathers who experienced sadness about separation also had low confidence that the school would provide a quality experience for their children.

Father closeness to his child was not related to father stress experienced at the beginning of the child's school experience. But the father's closeness to his child was positively related to his confidence that the school would provide a good quality experience for his child ($r = .36$); fathers who believed school would be a good quality experience were close to their children. And father closeness to his child was significantly related to the total number of activities in which father and child were engaged together ($r = .37$).

Interestingly, mother's work status was not related to any component of father stress at his child's school entry. This finding appears consistent with Booth's (1979) contention that a wife's employment does not contribute to any stress experienced by her husband.

The married pairs of mothers and fathers in this study appeared to have consistent views and emotions at the time of their child's school entry. Examination of the data on mothers in these families provided a more complete understanding of father stress in this period. Mother anxiety at her child's entry was positively related to father's anxiety ($r = .35$) and father's sadness ($r = .30$). These similar views about anxiety and sadness reported by both parents in a marital dyad suggest that communication between mothers and fathers may be the basis of feelings in each partner about a normal, developmental transition point. Fathers may have been reacting as much to mothers' emotional states and

views—or vice-versa—as to the actual school entry of the child. Thus, the importance of studying the family as a system of interrelated positions in further study of events such as child school entry is obvious. As noted by Larson (1974),

... to ignore the variant perceptions of family structure and process creates a sterile and simplistic view of family phenomena. Intrafamily diversity should not be an artifact of our analytical schemes. (p. 136)

The stress fathers reported at their child's school entry was significantly related to family socioeconomic status. Fathers who were lower in socioeconomic status were more anxious ($r = -.67$), more often sad ($r = -.30$), and experienced sadness for a longer time ($r = -.32$). These findings deserve exploration.

The finding that father stress is related negatively to socioeconomic status is consistent with Hill's (1949) thoughts that lower socioeconomic status families have fewer resources (financial and psychological) to deal with stressful events and that lower socioeconomic status families are more prone to stress as a result. As well, lower status families have been thought to be relatively more alienated from societal institutions (such as school systems) than families of higher status, being more distrustful and feeling powerless (Irelan, 1966). Thus, it seems possible that socioeconomic status could affect the definition of the "stressor event" of school entry (using Hill's [1949] ABC = X paradigm). Lower status fathers may feel more strongly the "loss" of their child to an unfamiliar, "alien" institution or may feel that the child will be influenced by an institution over which the father can have no control.

Lower status mothers appear to experience the same anxiety. Mothers' anxiety, like fathers' anxiety, was negatively related to family socioeconomic status ($r = -.35$). Such findings as these underscore the importance of examining the family as a system of interrelated positions rather than looking merely at relations between one parent and his or her child (as has been done often in mother-child studies).

The findings of this exploratory study have some important implications for family service practitioners, educators, and further research activities. Fathers, as well as mothers, clearly exhibit a range of emotional reactions to the event of a child's school entry. The sensitivities of both men and women to such an event should be noted by practitioners and studied by researchers. Particularly, educators may need to confront father concerns over a child's school entry because fathers who are sad at child school entry may also have little confidence that schooling will be a quality experience for their child. As well, educators may find anxiety exhibited and interpreted differently by lower status fathers than other fathers. Sensitive treatment of fathers' concerns may improve father participation in his child's education and father involvement in the governance of schools.

REFERENCE NOTE

1. Ferguson, L. R., & Freeark, K. *School entry: Transition for mother and child*. Paper presented at the annual meeting of the Society for Research in Child Development, San Francisco, 1979.

REFERENCES

Booth, A. Does wives' employment cause stress for husbands? *The Family Coordinator*, 1979, **28**, 445-449.

Burke, R., & Weir, T. Relationship of wives' employment status to husband, wife, and pair satisfaction and performance. *Journal of Marriage and the Family*, 1976, **38**, 279-287.

deLissovoy, V. Comments on "The keeping of fathers of America." *The Family Coordinator*, 1976, **25**, 393-396.

Fein, R. A. Research on fathering: Social policy and an emergent perspective. *Journal of Social Issues*, 1978, **34**, 122-136.

Hawkins, L. F. Child rearing interests of fathers of first grade children. *Home Economics Research Journal*, 1974, **25**, 393-396.

Hill, R. *Families under stress*. New York: Harper, 1949.

Hill, R., & Rodgers, R. H. The developmental approach. In H. T. Christensen (Ed.), *Handbook of marriage and the family*. New York: Rand McNally, 1964.

Hock, E. *Alternative approaches to child rearing and their effects on the mother-infant relationship* (ED 122943). Urbana, IL: Educational Resources Information Center/Early Childhood Education, 1976.

Irelan, L. M. *Low-income life styles*. Washington, DC: U.S. Government Printing Office, 1966.

Larson, L. E. System and subsystem perception of family roles. *Journal of Marriage and the Family*, 1974, **36**, 123-138.

Rapoport, R. Normal crises, family structure, and mental health. *Family Process*, 1963, **2** (1), 68-80.

Staines, G., Pleck, J., Shepark, L., & O'Connor, P. Wives' employment status and marital adjustment, *Psychology of Women Quarterly*, 1978, **3**, 90-120.

Dual-Career Family Stress and Coping: A Literature Review

DENISE A. SKINNER*

The literature concerning dual-career family stress and coping is reviewed. Sources of dual-career strain are delineated, and the coping patterns employed by couples in managing the stress are summarized. Although acknowledging stressful aspects of dual-career living, it was found that most participants defined their lifestyle positively. Achieving a balance between the advantages and disadvantages of the lifestyle appears to be the overriding concern of most dual-career couples. Some implications for family practitioners are discussed.

A significant influence on contemporary family living is the increasing rate of female participation in the labor force. Examination of Department of Labor statistics reveals that the married woman is the key source of this growth and helps explain the growing interest in dual-career families reflected in both the professional and popular literature. Although it is difficult to assess the number of married *career* women in the work force, it seems reasonable to assume that the percentage for this group is positively related to the general increase in labor force participation rates of women (Hopkins & White, 1978). As more and more women seek increased education and training, along with an increased demand for skilled labor and a greater awareness of sex-role equality, the dual-career lifestyle is likely to increase in prevalence and acceptability (Rapoport & Rapoport, 1976).

A significant feature of the dual-career lifestyle is that it produces considerable stress and strain. The often competing demands of the occupational structure and those of a rich family life present a number of challenges for dual-career family members. Much of the literature implies that the stress is inherent in a dual-career lifestyle. However, some of the constraints of the lifestyle might be explained by the fact that it is a relatively new and minority pattern. In coping with the pressures of this variant pattern, dual-career couples have been forced to come up with individual solutions as no institutionalized supports exist (Holmstrom, 1973).

The research on dual-career families has been primarily descriptive in nature and has focused on women. Rapoport and Rapoport, who coined the term "dual-career family" in 1969, were pioneers in the study of the impact of career and family on each other. Their research was followed shortly thereafter by other definitive studies on the dual-career lifestyle (Epstein, 1971; Holmstrom, 1973; Garland, 1972; Poloma, 1972). More recent dual-career research has focused heavily on the stresses of the lifestyle and on the management of the strains by the participants (Rapoport & Rapoport, 1978).

The purpose of this literature review is to delineate the sources of dual-career strain and summarize the coping patterns employed

*Denise A. Skinner is Assistant Professor, Department of Human Development, Family Relations, and Community Educational Services, University of Wisconsin-Stout, Menomonie, WI, and a doctoral candidate in the Department of Family Social Science, University of Minnesota, St. Paul, MN.

(*Family Relations*, 1980, **29**, 473-480.)

by dual-career couples in managing stress. Hopefully, this summary will benefit family practitioners as they assist individuals in making adaptive lifestyle choices as well as aid dual-career participants in effective stress-reduction and in developing coping strategies.

The Etiology of Dual-Career Stress

Rapoport and Rapoport (1978) in reviewing the 1960's studies of dual-career families have noted that the stresses of this pattern have been differently conceptualized by various researchers. "The concepts include *dilemmas* (such as) overload, . . . network, identity; *conflicts* between earlier and later norms . . . , *barriers* of domestic isolation, sex-role prejudices . . . , and *problems* such as the wife finding an appropriate job . . . " (p. 5).

Although there is a considerable degree of variation in dual-career stress, there are also common patterns. In the review that follows, an adaptation of the Rapoports' (1971) delineation of strains confronting dual-career families will be used as an organizing framework in highlighting these common patterns reported in the literature. Although interactive and cyclical in nature, strains have been classified as primarily (a) internal: arising within the family; or (b) external: the result of conflict of the dual-career family and other societal structures (Bebbington, 1973).

Internal Strain

Overload issues. The problem of work and role overload is a common source of strain for dual-career families (Epstein, 1971; Garland, 1972, Heckman, Bryson, & Bryson, 1977; Holmstrom, 1973; Poloma, 1972; Rapoport & Rapoport, 1976; St. John-Parsons, 1978). When each individual is engaged in an active work role and active family roles, the total volume of activities is considerably increased over what a conventional family experiences (Portner, Note 1). In dual-career families this can result in overload, with household tasks generally handled as overtime.

The feelings of overload and the degree of strain experienced varied for couples in the Rapoports' study (1976). The Rapoports suggested that overload was affected by four conditions, which were, in part, self-imposed:

(a) the degree to which having children and a family life (as distinct from simply being married) was salient; (b) the degree to which the couple aspired to a high standard of domestic living; (c) the degree to which there was satisfactory reapportionment of tasks; and (d) the degree to which the social-psychological overload compounded the physical overloads (pp. 302-305).

There was a positive relationship between the conditions in items (a), (b), and (d) above, and the degree of strain experienced. Satisfactory reapportionment of tasks was a coping strategy that helped alleviate strain.

Identity issues. The identity dilemma for dual-career participants is the result of discontinuity between early gender-role socialization and current wishes or practices (Rapoport & Rapoport, 1976). The essence of masculinity in our culture is still centered on successful experiences in the work role, and femininity is still centered on the domestic scene (Heckman, Bryson, & Bryson, 1977; Holmstrom, 1973). The internalized "shoulds" regarding these traditional male and female roles conflict with the more androgynous roles attempted by many dual-career couples, resulting in tension and strain.

Bernard, (1974) focusing on professional women, observed that intrapersonal integration of work and domestic roles and the personality characteristics associated with each, does *not* constitute the "psychological work" of the career mother. Rather, the major difficulty, according to Bernard, is that the woman *alone* is the one who must achieve this identity integration.

Role-cycling issues. The dilemma of role-cycling, identified by Rapoport and Rapoport (1976), refers to attempts by the dual-career couple to mesh their different individual career cycles with the cycle of their family. Bebbington (1973) noted that role cycling, unlike other sources of strain, has a developmental pattern. Both employment and family careers have transition points at which there is a restructuring of roles which become sources of "normative" stress.

Dual-career couples attempt to avoid additional strain by staggering the career and family cycles such that transition points are not occurring at the same time. Many couples establish themselves occupationally before having children for this reason (Bebbington, 1973; Holmstrom, 1973; Rapoport & Rapoport, 1976). Stress may also result when the developmental sequence of one spouse's career conflicts with that of the other (Bebbington, 1973). The structural and attitudinal barriers of the occupational world, yet to be discussed, further contribute to the difficulty in role-cycling for many dual-career couples.

Family characteristics. Holmstrom (1973) identified the isolation of the modern nuclear family as a barrier to having two careers in one family. The difficulty of childrearing apart from relatives or other such extended support systems is a source of strain.

The presence or absence of children as well as the stage of the family life cycle seems to affect the complexity of the dual career lifestyle (Holmstrom, 1973, Rapoport & Rapoport, 1976). Heckman, et al. (1977) found that it was the older professional couples and those who had not had children who saw the lifestyle as advantageous. The demands of childrearing, *particularly the problems asssociated with finding satisfactory childcare arrangements*, are a source of strain for younger dual-career couples, especially for the women (Bryson, Bryson, & Johnson, 1978; Gove & Geerken, 1977; Holmstrom, 1973; Orden & Bradburn, 1969; Rapoport & Rapoport, 1971; St. John-Parsons, 1978). In relation to this, a child-free lifestyle has been noted by Movius (1976) as a career-facilitating strategy for women.

External Strains

Normative issues. Despite changing social norms, the dual-career lifestyle still runs counter to traditional family norms of our culture. Rapoport and Rapoport (1976) have explained that although intellectually the dual-career pattern is approved, internalized values from early socialization are still strong and produce tension, anxiety, and guilt. Pivotal points such as career transitions or the birth of a child can activate these normative dilemmas.

One of the more frequently cited problems by dual-career professionals is the expectation on the part of others that the dual-career husband and wife behave in traditional male/female roles (Heckman, et al., 1977). This is consistent with the earlier findings of Epstein

(1971) who indicated that dual-career individuals experienced guilt because they were not conforming to the socially approved work-family structure. Furthermore, the women often had to deal with the implied or overt social controls placed on them by their children according to Epstein's study.

Occupational structure. Holmstrom (1973, p. 517) has commented on the inflexibility of professions noting that "pressures for geographic mobility, the status inconsistencies of professional women because the professions are dominated by men, and the pressure for fulltime and continuous careers" are a source of strain for dual-career couples.

The demand for geographical mobility and its effect on dual-career couples noted earlier by Holmstrom (1973) was also examined by Duncan and Perrucci (1976). They found that the egalitarian orientation toward decision-making promoted in dual-career living was not carried out in job moves with the wives experiencing more of the stress. However, Wallston, Foster, and Berger (1978) using simulated job-seeking situations, found many professional couples attempting egalitarian or nontraditional job-seeking patterns. These authors have suggested that institutional constraints are in part responsible for highly traditional actual job decisions.

Finally, the demands of particular professions for single-minded continuous commitment, for other family members' needs to be subordinated to the job, and for a "support person" (typically the wife) to be available for entertaining, etc., are a source of stress for dual-career couples. The "two-person career" (Papanek, 1973) which depends heavily on an auxiliary support partner is incompatible with the dual-career orientation, according to Hunt and Hunt (1977). Handy (1978) in a study of executive men found that the dual-career relationship was infrequent and difficult when the husband was in such a "greedy occupation."

Social network dilemmas. Maintaining relationships outside the immediate family is a problem for dual-career members for a variety of reasons. The general dilemma exists because of the overload strain discussed earlier, which creates limitations on the availability of time to interact with friends and relatives (Portner, Note 1).

Rapoport and Rapoport (1976) found that the dual-career couples whom they studied reported problems in sustaining the kinds of interaction that their more conventional relatives and friends wanted. Not only was there less time for socializing, but, also, kin were at times asked by the dual-career couples to help out which sometimes produced tension. St. John-Parsons (1978) reported that kin relationships deteriorated when dual-career couples could not meet some of the expected social obligations. The husbands in his study experienced the greater loss as ties to their families of orientation lessened.

The study by St. John-Parsons (1978) revealed that none of the dual-career families maintained extensive social relationships. According to the author, "a salient reason for their social dilemma was their sense of responsibility for and devotion to their children" (p. 40).

Impact of strain

The sources of strain delineated above suggest that dual-career families are vulnerable to a high degree of stress. However, family stress literature has indicated that the family's definition of the situation is an important component influencing the impact of various strains on the family (Burr, 1973). Bebbington (1973) has differentiated between the following two kinds of stress which can co-exist or operate separately in a given lifestyle: "(a) that deriving from an unsatisfactory resolution of conflict as between ideals and behavior; and (b) that deriving from intrinsic properties of the lifestyle, though ideals and behaviors may be consistent" (p. 535). Bebbington has suggested that dual-career participants do not seem to find the principle of "stress minimization" operative with regard to the second type of stress, but rather, accept an orientation of "stress-optimization" in interpreting inherent lifestyle stresses. Dual-career couples have accepted a high degree of the second type of stress as their solution to the dilemma of avoiding the discontinuity stress of the first type, according to Bebbington. They come to view their problems as having both positive as well as negative components and of a more routine than unusual nature.

The cumulative effect of various strains arising from occupational and familial role transitions can be estimated as "transitional density" (Bain, 1978). Bain has hypothesized that the stress experienced and the coping ability of a family in a particular transition is proportional to the stress generated by the transitional density. Applied to dual-career families this idea is specifically related to the particular family characteristics and the multiple role cycling strains previously discussed. The degree of stress experienced from other sources of strain (e.g., overload) may be compounded for a given family by the strain of their family life cycle stage or the newness of the dual-career pattern for them.

Marital Relationship

A considerable portion of the dual career literature focuses on the marital adjustment, happiness, or satisfaction of dual-career couples implying that the stress inherent in the lifestyle has an impact on the marital relationship. In Orden and Bradburn's (1969) study of working wives and marital happiness, they found that a woman's choice of employment (vs. full-time homemaking) strained the marriage only when there were preschool children in the family. They concluded that the woman's decision to work is associated with a high balance between satisfactions and strains for both partners.

Bailyn (1970) found that an all-consuming attitude toward career was associated with lowered marital satisfaction. Overinvolvement in one's career can result in strain on the marriage, according to Ridley (1973) who found marital adjustment highest when the husband was "medium" and the wife was "low" on job involvement. He concluded that tension in the marital relationship may occur when either partner becomes so highly involved in a job that family obligations are excluded. Occupational practices such as discriminatory sex-role attitudes can also heighten the stress in the dual-career marital relationship (Holmstrom, 1973; Rosen, Jerdee, & Prestwich, 1975). Finally, Richardson (1979) examined the hypothesis that marital stress would be attendant if working wives had higher occupational prestige than their husbands. He found no support for this hypothesis and suggested that its "mythic content" may be sustained, in part, because it is congruent with conventional sex-role orientations.

Rice (1979), focusing on personality patterns, noted the following psychological characteristics as typical of dual-career individuals:

A strong need for achievement, reliance on an extrinsic reward system (promotion, spouse recognition of efforts), hesitancy in making sustained interpersonal commitments, and vulnerability to self-esteem injury through dependency frustrations and fear of failure (p. 47).

The adaptive aspects of, for instance, high achievement may facilitate career advancement for both partners and contribute positively to marital adjustment, or high achievement needs may contribute to competitiveness in the pair.

Sex Differences

An overwhelming proportion of the literature reports that the impact of dual-career stress is felt most by women. Bernard (1974) has noted that a man can combine a professional career and parenting more easily than a woman can because less is expected of the man with regard to familial responsibilities.

Overload strain is a significant issue for dual-career women. Heckman et al. (1977), in assessing problem areas for dual-career couples, found that the women reported more problems in more areas than did men, and that many of the comments about problem areas by husbands were issues that had indirectly affected them because the issue had directly affected their wives. These researchers reported that several women in their study made significant concessions with regard to their careers because of family demands. They concluded that the continued existence of role conflict and overload strain are often at the expense of the woman's personal identity and career aspirations.

Occupationally, it has been the woman more often who takes the risks, sacrifices more, and compromises career ambitions in attempting to make the dual-career pattern operative (Epstein, 1971; Holmstrom, 1973; Poloma, 1972). Interestingly, however, some studies have reported that dual-career wives are more productive than other females in their respective professions (Bryson, Bryson, Licht, & Licht, 1976; Martin, Berry, & Jacobsen, 1975). One might conclude, as the Rapoports (1978) have done, that the wives were simultaneously exploited and facilitated.

Life for the dual-career male is not without its periods of stress, although the impact of various strains does not appear to be as significant as that reported for women. Garland (1972) reported that dual-career males felt strain in attempting to find free time, but overall, noted the advantages of the lifestyle. The findings of Burke and Weir (1976) do not provide as positive a report for dual-career men, however. While working wives were found to be more satisfied with life, marriage, and job than nonworking wives, husbands of working wives were less satisfied and performed less effectively than husbands of nonworking wives. Burke and Weir indicated that the greater stress experienced by the dual-career husband may be due, in part, to him losing part of his "active support system" when the wife commits herself to a career outside the home, and also to his assuming roles (e.g. housekeeping) which have not been valued as highly in our culture.

Using more sophisticated methodology, Booth (1977) replicated the Burke and Weir study and reported different conclusions. He found very little difference between working and nonworking wives, and reported that the wife's employment had little effect on the stress experienced by the husband. Furthermore, Booth concluded that the dual-career husband may be experiencing less stress than his conventional counterpart as the added income and personal fulfillment of the wife outweigh temporary problems in adjusting to the lifestyle.

Children

Dual-career couples may increase the degree of strain they themselves experience in an attempt to prevent the lifestyle from creating strain for their children. As was noted earlier in the study by St. John-Parsons (1978), some of the social strains the couples experienced was due to their sense of responsibility to their children. There is no evidence to suggest that the dual-career lifestyle, in and of itself, is stressful for children. What may be more significant for the children is the degree of stress experienced by the parents which may indirectly affect the children. In her study of maternal employment Hoffman (1974) concluded that,

> . . . the working mother who obtains satisfaction from her work, who has adequate arrangements so that her dual role does not involve undue strain, and who does not feel so guilty that she overcompensates is likely to do quite well and, under certain conditions, better than the nonworking mother (p. 142).

Coping Strategies

Just as the type and degree of strain experienced varies for dual-career families, so do the strategies employed for managing the stress. As was mentioned earlier in this paper, Bebbington (1973) suggested that "stress optimization," the acknowledging of dual-career stress as inevitable and preferable to the stress of alternative lifestyles available, is an orientation of many dual-career couples. Defining their situation as such may serve as a resource in successful adaptation to the stress. Dual-career couples also employ stress-mitigating strategies. These coping behaviors are aimed at maintaining or strengthening the family system and at securing support from sources external to the family.

Coping Behavior Within the Family System

Poloma (1972) outlined four tension-management techniques used by the dual-career women in her study. They reduced dissonance by defining their dual-career patterns as favorable or advantageous to them and their families when compared to other alternatives available. For instance, the career mother noted that she was a happier mother and wife because she worked outside the home than she would be if she were a fulltime homemaker. Secondly, they established priorities among and within their roles. The salient roles are familial ones and if a conflict situation occurs between family and career demands, the family needs come first. A third strategy employed was that of compartmentalizing work and family roles as much as pos-

sible. Leaving actual work and work-related problems at the office would be one way to segregate one's work and family roles. Finally, the women in Poloma's study managed strain by compromising career aspirations to meet other role demands.

Compromise is a common coping strategy noted in much of the dual-career literature as a way of reducing stress and making the lifestyle manageable. Women, in particular, compromise career goals if there are competing role demands (Bernard, 1974; Epstein, 1971; Heckman et al., 1977; Holmstrom, 1973). However, men in dual-careers make career sacrifices also, e.g., compromising advancement opportunities in an attempt to reduce role-conflict.

Prioritizing and compromising are coping strategies employed not only to deal with conflicts between roles but also in resolving competing demands within roles. Domestic overload, for instance, may be managed by deliberately lowering standards. One compromises ideal household standards because of constraints on time and energy in achieving them. Structurally, the domestic overload dilemma can also be managed within the family system by reorganizing who does what, with the husband and children taking on more of what traditionally has been the woman's responsibility. In these instances dual-career families are *actively* employing coping behaviors within the family aimed at strengthening its functioning and, thus, reducing the family's vulnerability to stress (McCubbin, 1979).

Some dual-career individuals take a more reactive orientation toward stress, and cope by attempting to manage and improve their behavior to better satisfy all of the lifestyle's demands. Holmstrom (1973) reported that the couples in her study adhered to organized schedules and that the women, in particular, were very conscious of how they allocated their time and effort. Flexibility and control over one's schedule are highly valued by career persons in attempting to meet overload and time pressures.

Finally, the presence of what Burke and Weir (1976) have labelled a helping component in the marital relationship can serve a stress-mitigating function within the dual-career family. Qualities such as open communication, empathy, emotional reassurance, support and sensitivity to the other's feelings, characterize this therapeutic role; the presence of these qualities would serve to strengthen the relationship. Related to this, Rapoport and Rapoport (1978) reported that couples established "tension lines," "points beyond which individuals feel they cannot be pushed except at risk to themselves or the relationship" (p. 6). Couples organized their family lives with sensitivity to these tension lines.

Coping Behaviors Involving External Support Systems

Dual-career couples also employ coping strategies aimed at securing support outside the family to help reduce stress. Holmstrom (1973) reported that couples were quite willing to use money to help resolve overload strain. Hiring help, especially for childcare, is a common expense in this lifestyle. Couples also buy time in various other ways such as hiring outside help to do domestic work and purchasing labor- and time-saving devices.

Outside support in terms of friendships were also important to the couples in the Rapoports' study (1976). The dual-career couples formed friendships on a couple basis, associating with other career couples. "Friendships, while gratifying, are also demanding, and in many of the couples there was a relatively explicit emphasis on the mutual service aspects of the relationship as well as the recreational aspect" (Rapoport, p. 316). Thus, establishing friendships with couples like themselves helped to validate the lifestyle for these dual-career couples and provided a reciprocal support structure.

The literature suggests that dual-career couples are increasingly interested in negotiating work arrangements which will reduce or remove some of this lifestyle's stress. Flexible scheduling, job sharing, and split-location employment are used by some dual-career couples as coping mechanisms to reduce the family's vulnerability to overload stress.

Finally, most of the researchers noted that achieving a balance between the disadvantages and advantages of the lifestyle was the overriding concern of dual-career couples.

Although noting the numerous strains associated with the lifestyle, dual-career couples were equally aware of the gains—things like personal fulfillment, increased standard of living, pride in each other's accomplishments, etc. The goal for most dual-career couples, then, is to ". . . plan how to manage the meshing of their two lives so as to achieve an equitable balance of strains and gains" (Rapoport and Rapoport, 1976, p. 298).

Implications for Practitioners

Increasingly, people are choosing dual-career living, a trend that will, no doubt, continue in the future. This has several implications for family life practitioners, particularly given the stress associated with the lifestyle. Certain changes seem necessary in facilitating dual-career living but these changes must occur by concerted efforts at many levels (Rapoport & Rapoport, 1976).

Individuals opting for the dual-career lifestyle, or any other family form for that matter, would benefit from knowledge of the issues central to that lifestyle's functioning. As Rapoport and Rapoport (1976) suggested ". . . the dissemination of a detailed knowledge of a range of lifestyles like the dual-career families will increase the potential for satisfactory choice of options in future" (p. 21). Such an education would enlarge traditional conceptions about men's and women's occupational and familial roles recognizing that different individuals would then have greater opportunities for making adaptive lifestyle choices.

Practitioners in marriage and family therapy may increasingly work with dual-career couples as their numbers increase and as the strains of the lifestyle remain. Rice (1979) has reported that competition, issues of power, and difficulty with the support structure are three common problem areas in dual-career marriages. He has suggested that "the guiding principle in therapy with dual-career couples is to help the partners achieve or restore a sense of equity in the marital relationship" (p. 103). Group-support sessions are suggested by Hopkins and White (1978) as a helpful therapeutic strategy with dual-career couples. Common-problem groups and groups of couples at differing life-cycle stages can provide a supportive structure for mutual sharing of concerns and coping skills. The goal of both preventive and remedial approaches should be to help couples assess their needs, increase interpersonal competencies, and deal constructively with the stress they experience (Rapoport & Rapoport, 1976).

Each family life professional has the opportunity to serve as a spokesperson for societal and institutional changes which would positively affect the functioning of dual-career families. Societal changes which would increase the quantity and quality of all kinds of services (educational, domestic, child-care, etc.) would strengthen the dual career lifestyle. Institutional changes which would increase the flexibility of the occupational structure would also aid significantly in reducing or eliminating some of the stress associated with the lifestyle. Flexible scheduling, increased availability of part-time employment, on-site day care facilities and maternity and paternity leaves are some of the occupational changes advocated to enable individuals to combine work and family roles with less strain. Assuming an advocacy role on behalf of the dual-career lifestyle involves initiating and supporting social policies which promote equity and pluralism (Rapoport & Rapoport, 1976). A society where these values prevail would enhance not only the dual-career lifestyle, but would serve to strengthen family life in general.

REFERENCE NOTE

1. Portner, J. Impact of work on the family. Minneapolis: Minnesota Council on Family Relations, 1219 University Avenue SE, 55414, 1978, 13-15.

REFERENCES

Bailyn, L. Career and family orientations of husbands and wives in relation to marital happiness. *Human Relations*, 1970, **23**(2), 97-113.

Bain, A. The capacity of families to cope with transitions: A theoretical essay. *Human Relations*, 1978, **31**, 675-688.

Bebbington, A. C. The function of stress in the establishment of the dual-career family. *Journal of Marriage and the Family*, 1973, **35**, 530-537.

Bernard, J. *The future of motherhood*. New York: Penguin, 1974.

Bird, C. *The two-paycheck marriage*. New York: Rawson, Wade, 1979.

Booth, A. wife's employment and husband's stress: A replication and refutation. *Journal of Marriage and the Family*, 1977, **39**, 645-50.

Bryson, R., Bryson, J., Licht, M., & Licht, B. The professional pair: Husband and wife psychologists. *American Psychologist*. 1976, **31**(1), 10-16.

Bryson, R., Bryson, J. B., & Johnson, M. F. Family size, satisfaction, and productivity in dual-career couples. In J. B. Bryson, & R. Bryson (Eds.), *Dual-career couples*. New York: Human Sciences, 1978.

Burke, R. J., & Weir, T. Relationship of wives' employment status to husband, wife and pair satisfaction and performance. *Journal of Marriage and the Family*, 1976, **38**, 279-287.

Burke, R. J., & Weir, T. Marital helping relationships: The moderators between stress and well-being. *Journal of Psychology*, 1977, **95**, 121-130.

Burr, A. *Theory construction and the sociology of the family*. New York: Wiley, 1977.

Duncan, R. P., & Perrucci, C. Dual occupation families and migration. *American Sociological Review*, 1976, **41**, 252-261.

Epstein, C. D., Law partners and marital partners: Strains and solutions in the dual-career family enterprise. *Human Relations*, 1971, **24**, 549-563.

Fogarty, M. P., Rapoport, R., & Rapoport, R. N. *Sex, career and family*. Beverly Hills: Sage, 1971.

Garland, N. T. The better half? The male in the dual profession family. In C. Safilios-Rothschild (Ed.), *Toward a sociology of women*. Lexington, MA: Xerox, 1972.

Gove, W. R., & Geerken, M. R. The effect of children and employment on the mental health of married men and women. *Social Forces*, 1977, **56**, 66-76.

Handy, C. Going against the grain: Working couples and greed occupations. In R. Rapoport & R. N. Rapoport (Eds.), *Working couples*. New York: Harper & Row, 1978.

Heckman, N. A., Bryson, R., & Bryson, J. Problems of professional couples: A content analysis. *Journal of Marriage and the Family*. 1977, **39**, 323-330.

Hoffman, L. W. Effects on child. In L. W. Hoffman & F. I. Nye (Eds.), *Working mothers*. San Francisco: Jossey-Bass, 1974.

Holmstrom, L. L. *The two-career family*. Cambridge, MA: Schenkman, 1973.

Hopkins, J., & White, P. The dual-career couple: Constraints and supports. *The Family Coordinator*, 1978, **27**, 253-259.

Hunt, J. G., & Hunt, L. L. Dilemmas and contradictions of status: The case of the dual-career family. *Social Problems*, 1977, **24**, 407-416.

Martin, T. W., Berry, K. J., & Jacobsen, R. B. The impact of dual-career marriages on female professional careers: An empirical test of a Parsonian hypothesis. *Journal of Marriage and the Family*, 1975, **37**, 734-742.

McCubbin, H. Integrating coping behavior in family stress theory. *Journal of Marriage and the Family*, 1979, **41**, 237-244.

Movius, M. Voluntary childlessness—The ultimate liberation. *The Family Coordinator*, 1976, **25**, 57-62.

Orden, S. R., & Bradburn, N. M. Working wives and marriage happiness. *American Journal of Sociology*, 1969, **74**, 382-407.

Papanek, H. Men, women and work: Reflections of the two-person career. *American Journal of Sociology*, 1973, **78**, 852-872.

Poloma, M. M. Role conflict and the married professional woman. In C. Safilios-Rothschild (Ed.), *Toward a sociology of women*. Lexington, MA: Xerox, 1972.

Poloma, M. M., & Garland, T. The married professional woman: A study of the tolerance of domestication. *Journal of Marriage and the Family*, 1971, **33**, 531-540.

Rapoport, R., & Rapoport, R. N. *Dual-career families*. Harmondsworth, England: Penguin, 1971.

Rapoport, R., & Rapoport, R. N. *Dual-career families re-examined*. New York: Harper & Row, 1976.

Rapoport, R., & Rapoport, R. N. (Eds.), *Working couples*. New York: Harper & Row, 1978.

Rapoport, R. N., & Rapoport, R. Dual-career families: Progress and prospects. *Marriage and Family Review*, 1978, **1**(5), 1-12.

Rice, D. *Dual-career marriage: Conflict and treatment*. New York: Free Press, 1979.

Richardson, J. G. Wife occupational superiority and marital troubles: An examination of the hypothesis. *Journal of Marriage and the Family*, 1979, **41**, 63-72.

Ridley, C. A. Exploring the impact of work satisfaction and involvement on marital interaction when both partners are employed. *Journal of Marriage and the Family*, 1973, **35**, 229-237.

Roland, A., & Harris, B. *Career and motherhood: Struggles for a new identity*. New York: Human Sciences, 1979.

St. John-Parsons, D. Continuous dual-career families: A case study. In J. B. Bryson & R. Bryson (Eds.), *Dual-career couples*. New York: Human Sciences, 1978.

Wallston, B. S., Foster, M. A., & Berger, M. I will follow him: Myth, reality, or forced choice—Job seeking experiences of dual-career couples. In J. B. Bryson & R. Bryson (Eds.), *Dual-career couples*. New York: Human Sciences, 1978.

PRESIDENTS OF THE NATIONAL COUNCIL ON FAMILY RELATIONS

Wesley R. Burr (1981-82)
Kate B. Garner (1980-81)
Ira L. Reiss (1979-80)
Paul C. Glick (1978-79)
Gerhard Neubeck (1977-78)
William C. Nichols, Jr. (1976-77)
Carlfred B. Broderick (1975-76)
Richard K. Kerckhoff (1974-75)
Leland J. Axelson (1973-74)
Murray A. Straus (1972-73)
Eleanore B. Luckey (1971-72)
Gerald R. Leslie (1970-71)
Richard N. Hey (1969-70)
Elizabeth S. Force (1968-69)
William F. Kenkel (1967-68)
William M. Smith, Jr. (1966-67)
F. Ivan Nye (1965-66)
Clark E. Vincent (1964-65)
Blaine R. Porter (1963-64)
Wallace C. Fulton (1962-63)
David R. Mace (1961-62)
Harold T. Christensen (1960-61)
Aaron L. Rutledge (1959-60)
Henry A. Bowman (1958-59) Deceased
Mildred I. Morgan (1957-58) Deceased
David B. Treat (1957)
Judson T. Landis (1956)
Gladys H. Groves (1955) Deceased
Dorothy T. Dyer (1954) Deceased
Robert G. Foster (ca. 1952-53) Deceased
John O. Grady (ca. 1951-52) Deceased
Nadina Kavinoky (ca. 1950-51) Deceased
Ernest G. Osborne (ca. 1948-50) Deceased
Lawrence K. Frank (ca. 1946-48) Deceased
Sidney E. Goldstein (ca. 1944-46) Deceased
Ernest W. Burgess (ca. 1942-44) Deceased
Ernest R. Groves (ca. 1940-42) Deceased
Adolph Meyer (ca. 1939-40) Deceased
Paul Sayre (ca. 1938-39) Deceased

Role Strain and Depression in Two-Job Families*

PAT M. KEITH AND ROBERT B. SCHAFER**

This study of 135 two-job families was an examination of factors associated with work-family role strain and depression. Analysis of separate interviews with husbands and wives indicated that, in general, time demands, both in the workplace and home, and stage in the life cycle influenced the role strain of both sexes and factors 'ffecting depression varied for men and women. Role strain, feelings of deprivation t home, comparative deprivation in work, and involvement in "feminine" household tasks were linked to male depression. Women were depressed if they evaluated their financial situation negatively and perceived their husband as an inadequate provider. It was concluded that both sexes may be somewhat disadvantaged by traditional attitudes toward the role of provider. In.plications for counseling are offered.

Two themes in popular and social science literature either directly or by implication focus on problems that occur when men and women try to allocate time between work and family. In earlier literature, involvement of men in work was reflected in the somewhat stereotypic profile of the husband so intensely involved and committed to his work that his family suffered from his psychological and physical absence and emotional neglect (Seidenberg, 1973). But with an increase in working couples, recent concern has been directed to factors associated with work-family stress experienced by women (Berkove, 1979; Hopkins & White, 1978). However, with some exceptions (e.g., Burke & Weir, 1976; Booth, 1979), conditions that may foster the stress of husbands in two-job famil-

ies have been neglected. Increasingly both men and women will spend most of their working years and will rear their children in two-career families.

Time Spent at Work

Although demanding careers are believed to shape events in the family, and time pressures are presumably instrumental in producing some of the role strain in the two-career family, the relation between stress and the time spent at work by both spouses rarely has been studied. In general, research on the influence of work time on family interaction has been neglected (Clark, Nye, & Gecas, 1978). A study of husbands' work time, however, did not support the assumption that there is competition between occupational and marital roles for men (Clark et al., 1978). Husbands' work time, for example, did not reduce their participation in most family roles. What needs to be examined is how the amount of time spent at work is reflected in the well-being of both men and women in the two-job family.

Evaluation of Work and Family

Despite i.s increasing prevalence, the two-job family is still a somewhat innovative form

*This research was supported by the Science and Education Administration of the United States Department of Agriculture under Grant No. 5901-0410-8-0096-0 from the Competitive Research Grants Office.

**Pat M. Keith is Professor, Department of Sociology, and Robert B. Schafer is Professor, Department of Sociology, Iowa State University, Ames, IA 50011.

(*Family Relations*, 1980, **29**, 483-488.)

and a new experience for many. In periods of role transition and change, individuals may engage in more questioning and assessment of their activities than later when patterns are well established. Consequently, perceptions of how well individuals and their spouses are managing various family roles may be especially important. Social psychological theory and research support the assumption that subjective evaluations of life are salient in determining human behavior and attitudes (Campbell, Converse, & Rodgers, 1976). Individual conceptions of reality are derived from interaction with others (Berger & Luckman, 1966), and whether persons evaluate their role as worker and their family situation positively or negatively may be based, in part, on how they feel they compared with others in their age group. Reference groups establish expectations and "appropriate" behavior as well as provide the framework within which to compare and evaluate individual situations with those of others. The objectives of this research were to examine individuals' comparative evaluations of their work-family situations with single career families and to examine assessments of their own and their spouses' competency in the role of provider in relation to role strain and depression. In addition, two family characteristics, i.e., number of children in household and spouses' division of labor will be considered.

Children

There is reason to expect that the number of children at home will be reflected in work-family role strain and depression in two-career families. Children create many demands on time, especially for women. Indeed, the presence of children has been shown to be associated with satisfaction derived from specific roles in that women with more children living at home experience greater disenchantment with homemaking (Pearlin, 1975). As the number of children increases, women in two-career families are more dissatisfied with the amount of time they have for domestic and avocational activities although their husbands' satisfaction with available time is not associated with the number of children (Bryson & Bryson, 1978). In an examination of stress and mental health using a more repre-

sentative sample of men and women, Gove and Geerken (1977) concluded that "having children in the household generally contributes to poor mental health" (p. 75). Although Gove and Geerken (1977) took the employment status of women into account in examining mental health and family characteristics, they did not control for the employment status of wives of the men who were studied. Thus, it was not possible to assess the impact of children on the well-being of both spouses in two-career families. We will investigate the influence of number of children at home on parental well-being.

Household Work

One mode of adaptation to role overload experienced by wives in two-job families is for husbands to become more involved in household tasks. Although most responsibilities for running the home apparently are still assumed by women (Keith & Brubaker, 1979), we need to know how spouses fare when role sharing or reversals do occur. There is some evidence that attempts to alleviate role overload of women may generate conflict. Wives, for example, may feel guilty when husbands help. As one wife noted, "When he does dishes, I always feel that he instead might be making a great scientific discovery." Or wives may have standards that husbands and others do not meet, or husbands may fail to do the tasks as soon as wives want tasks done.

Furthermore, it has been posited that husbands of employed women may be disadvantaged by a decline in emotional support and physical care usually received from wives, and husbands may lose self-esteem when they perform "feminine" tasks that are usually lower in status than activities connected with their work outside the home (Burke & Weir, 1976). Although Booth (1979) evaluated a portion of Burke and Weir's hypothesis concerning the impact of female employment on husbands' stress, he did not test their suggestion regarding the negative impact of performance of "feminine" tasks on the well-being of men. Because men usually experience more difficulty and conflict than women in performing cross-sex tasks, we might expect that men would be disadvantaged by their involvement in more "feminine" household tasks. In this research, we considered husbands' and wives' performance of "masculine" and "feminine" household tasks in relation to work-family role strain and depression.

Procedures

Sample

Data were analyzed from a sample of 135 two-job families in which both spouses were interviewed as a part of a study of nutrition and family life. The sampling and screening procedures were designed by the Statistical Laboratory at Iowa State University. Respondents, who were randomly selected from communities ranging in size from less than 10,000 to 50,000 or larger, were interviewed by trained interviewers.

Families varied from those in which the wife was under 45 and there was a child under 6 to those in which both spouses were over 60, and there were no children in the home. Women ranged in age from 20 to 68 with a mean age of 42 whereas men ranged in age from 24 to 73 with an average age of 44.

Seven percent of the respondents had less than 12 years of education while 37% were high school graduates. Thirty percent had some college, and one fourth were college graduates including some with graduate degrees. Seven percent had family incomes of less than $12,000 per year. Thirty-one percent had incomes between $12,000-20,000 while 62% had family incomes of $20,000 or more.

Measures

Work-family role strain was measured by the frequency (Never [1] to Very often [5]) with which respondents felt bothered by four situations: feeling that their job outside the home may interfere with their family life; feeling that family life may interfere with the job outside the home; thinking that the amount of work they have to do may interfere with how well it gets done; and feeling that others in the family will not do household tasks as well as they would do them. Data were coded so that a high score indicated higher work-family strain.

Depression was measured by eleven items that have been used in a number of studies and are published elsewhere (Pearlin, 1975;

Pearlin & Johnson, 1977). Respondents indicated the frequency (Never [1] to Very Often [5]) with which they experienced symptoms such as "lack of enthusiasm for doing anything," "poor appetite," "feeling hopeless about the future," and "having thoughts about ending your life." A high score reflected high depression.

Respondents reported the number of hours per week they worked at their primary job and hours spent at any additional jobs. Total hours per week spent at work were used in the analysis. To perform separate analyses for men and women, spouses' hours per week worked were coded for each respondent. Men worked an average of 48 hours per week whereas women worked an average of 32 hours per week.

Respondents reported the number of children who were living at home. The number of children living at home ranged from 0 to 7.

Persons indicated how well they and their spouses individually performed the provider role. Response categories ranged from "Much below average" (1) to "Much above average" (5). Both men and women compared their present financial situation and their work outside the home to that of other people of the same age and sex. For example, "Compare your present financial situation with that of other people of the same age and sex. Do you feel you are much worse off (1) . . . much better off (5)."

Two measures were used to assess general evaluations of life in relation to the impact of female employment in the two-job family. Women compared their general life situation with that of women who were full-time homemakers. Response categories ranged from "Much worse off" (1) to "Much better off" (5). Using the same response categories, men compared their situation with that of men whose wives were full-time homemakers.

Respondents indicated who usually did each of six tasks in their family (Husband always [1] . . . Wife always [5]). Responses to three tasks were combined to form an index of "masculine" activities: home repairs, handling finances, and lawn/yard work. Three tasks were combined to form a "feminine" activities index: laundry, dishwashing, and grocery shopping.

A multiple regression procedure was used to consider the relative influence of work time, age, family characteristics, and evaluation of family and provider roles on work-family strain and depression. Standardized regression coefficients (b) indicate the influence of each independent variable on role strain and depression with all other variables, in effect, held constant. Separate analyses were performed for men and women.

Results

Work-Family Role Strain

Women in two-job families experienced significantly more work-family role strain than men ($t = 3.47$; $p < .001$). Women were especially bothered that their job interfered with their family and that the amount of work they had to do interfered with how well it was done. Supporting suggestions in the literature, women were much more worried than men about the quality of others' performance of household tasks. Only 16% of the women compared with 43% of the men never worried about how well other persons would complete household tasks.

Given the tremendous demands confronted by women who were trying to manage jobs and households, we might have expected that they would perceive family obligations as interfering with job performance. But 45% of the women and 50% of the men said they were never bothered by their family obligations and responsibilities interfering with their work. However, slightly more men (12%) than women (11%) were sometimes troubled by their family responsibilities intruding on their work.

The family and personal factors affecting role strain were much the same for men and women (see Table 1). Hours per week spent at work was the most important variable in explaining work-family strain. Men and women who spent more time at work had higher strain although the relation was stronger for men ($r = .33$) than for women ($r = .17$).

Men and women who were younger and had more children at home experienced greater work-family strain than older persons with fewer or no children at home. Although age and the number of children at home were correlated, they also had independent effects on work-family strain.

As their spouses spent more time at work, the level of strain expressed by women increased ($r = .16$). But the amount of time their wives spent in the labor force was not significantly associated with the strain experienced by the husbands. To a degree this may reflect the dominant position of the male work role in the family. In some families, a condition of wives' employment may be that it does not inconvenience the husband.

Table 1
Summary of Multiple Regressions for Work-Family Role Strain and
Depression for Men and Women[a]

Variable	r	b	Variable	r	b
Work-Family Strain—Men			**Work-Family Strain—Women**		
1. Hours per week worked	.33	.33	1. Hours per week worked	.17	.22
2. Age	−.21	−.25	2. Spouses' hours per week worked	.16	.14
3. Number of children in home	.09	.10	3. Number of children in home	.14	.14
			4. Age	−.17	−.10
R = .392 R² = .15			R = .310 R² = .10		
Depression—Men			**Depression—Women**		
1. Work-family role strain	.32	.32	1. Comparison of general financial situation	−.32	−.26
2. Comparison of wife's work status	−.23	−.12	2. Evaluation of spouse as provider	−.26	−.18
3. Comparison of own work situation	−.16	−.11			
4. Performance of "feminine" household tasks	−.14	−.10			
R = .393 R² = .17			R = .368 R² = .14		

[a]Coefficients are significant at the .05 level or above.

Earlier it was suggested that the division of labor in the household might be linked with work-family strain. But the extent of involvement in either masculine or feminine tasks was not related to the role strain of men or women. Comparisons of life situations with those of others and evaluations of competency in work and provider roles did not alter the role strain of either sex.

Depression

Corroborating other literature (Radloff, 1975; Pearlin & Johnson, 1977), women were significantly more depressed than men ($t = 4.11$; $p < .001$). To explore correlates of depression, work-family role strain was included with the variables described earlier. In contrast to the similarity of the factors that fostered work-family strain, conditions that produced depression in the two-job family varied for men and women (see Table 1). Work-family strain was the most important element in fostering depression among men ($b = .32$). Also men who felt they were comparatively worse off than men whose wives were full-time homemakers were more depressed ($r = -.23$), as were men who viewed their work situation as less desirable than that of other men their age ($r = -.16$). Finally, men who performed "feminine household tasks more often experienced greater depression ($r = -.14$). These four variables explained 17% of the variance in male depression.

A major source of depression among women was their perception of their financial situation relative to that of others. Women who evaluated their financial situation as poorer than that of other women their age were more depressed ($r = -.32$). Furthermore, when women devalued their husbands' performance as a provider, they exhibited more symptoms of depression ($r = -.26$). These two variables were the most important determinants of depression and accounted for 14% of the variance. When all variables were considered simultaneously, none of the other factors made a significant contribution to levels of female depression.

Work-Family Role Strain

Factors in the two-job family that fostered role strain were tied to time demands, both in the workplace and home and to stage in the life cycle. It is not surprising that hours per week spent at work were reflected in work-family strain. Because the wife's career is usually treated as secondary and an adjunct to that of the husband, it might be speculated that the wife's work time would place an extra burden on both spouses. But the wife's involvement in the labor force was not directly linked to the role strain expressed by the husband. Rather wives manifested greater strain if their husbands' involvement in work was more extensive. This may support Rowe's (1978) view that the husband's career comes first in the constellation of both spouses' use of time (p. 95).

Although younger couples reflected greater role strain, it was not all due to the presence of children. The data suggest that age also independently influenced the role strain of both sexes.

Individuals may experience less work-family strain as they grow older for several reasons. First of all, newly-acquired roles are especially stress-producing, and roles that require innovative behavior, such as those in the two-job family, generate greater role strain (Keith, 1979). Older persons will likely have had more work experience and are usually established in an occupation and/or a particular work setting. Furthermore, many older couples have probably been a part of a two-job family longer. Some young couples may be adjusting simultaneously to two new jobs and to recent parenthood. This suggests that we need to consider the work histories including the timing of entry into the labor force and job changes of both spouses in relation to stress and mental health.

Depression

Work-family role strain was a major determinant of depression among men. A deficit perspective described earlier speculates that the work as well as mental health of the husband may suffer when both spouses seek to juggle employment outside the home and family obligations. We did not have a direct measure of the impact of female employment on husband's success at work. But whatever the reasons motivating their wives' employment, men who felt comparatively deprived by their wives' absence from the home perceived their work more negatively and reported poorer mental health.

Another link between the two-career family and male mental health involved performance of "feminine" household tasks by men. Men whose wives spent more time in the labor force were more involved in "feminine" household tasks ($r = -.16$) which in turn were linked to greater depression. However, women's stress was not diminished by husbands' involvement in the household. The potential benefits of male assistance may have been offset by reluctance to share tasks, guilt, or the quality of the tasks that are done.

The major factors in depression among women were perceptions of their financial situation relative to that of others and their evaluation of husbands' performance as providers. Moreover, women tied evaluations of their financial status to perceptions of their husbands' adequacy in the provider role ($r = .28$), but both variables independently influenced women's depression. Most revealing was that women's evaluation of their own adequacy as earners did not correlate with perceptions of their general financial situation.

Work-family role strain did not directly affect the depression of women. Pearlin (1975) suggested that stress and depression among employed women and homemakers probably are due to the severe demands of their employment inside the home rather than work or a preference for work outside the home. It is also possible that women's dependence on males for financial security and their disappointment with male performance were indeed major factors in their depression.

Implications for Counseling

Both men and women may be disadvantaged by their somewhat traditional attitudes toward the provider role. Men and women in two-job families who held more traditional views of work and provider roles seemed to "pay" for their traditionalism with poorer mental health. One task of counselors, educators, and their clients will be changing and developing more accepting attitudes toward the role transitions that accompany the two-career family. But they also can create an awareness of the "costs" of maintaining expectations for traditional sex roles in a society in which two-job families will soon be

the modal pattern. Because factors that foster well-being in two-career families may be somewhat sex-linked, practitioners can alert clients that their spouses may be distressed by quite different situations. Practitioners also should consider stage in the life cycle and the work histories of their clients and examine new jobs and other changes as possible sources of strain and depression. This task will be especially difficult in families in which neither spouse has positive attitudes toward the employment of the wife.

REFERENCES

Berger, P., & Luckman, T. *The social construction of reality.* New York: Anchor, 1966.

Berkove, G. F. Perceptions of husband support by returning women students. *The Family Coordinator*, 1979, **28**, 451-457.

Booth, A. Does wives' employment cause stress for husbands? *The Family Coordinator*, 1979, **28**. 445-449.

Bryson, R., Bryson, J., & Johnson, M. Family size, satisfaction, and productivity in dual-career couples. *Psychology of Women*, 1978, **3**, 67-77.

Burke, R., Weir, T. Relationship of wives' employment status to husband, wife, and pair satisfaction and performance. *Journal of Marriage and the Family*, 1976, **38**, 279-287.

Campbell, A. The American way of mating marriage si, children only maybe. *Psychology Today*, 1975, **8**, 37-43.

Campbell, A., Converse, P., & Rodgers, W. *The quality of American life.* New York: Russell Sage, 1976.

Clark, R. A., Nye, F. I., & Gecas, V. Husbands' work involvement and marital role performance. *Journal of Marriage and the Family*, 1978, **40**, 9-21.

Gove, W. R. & Geerken, M. R. The effect of children and employment on the mental health of married men and women. *Social Forces*, 1977, **56**, 66-76.

Hopkins, J., & White P. The dual-career couple: Constraints and supports. *The Family Coordinator*, 1978, **27**, 253-259.

Keith, P. Correlates of role strain in the classroom. *Urban Education*, 1979, **14**, 19-30.

Keith, P., & Brubaker, T. Male household roles in later life: A look at masculinity and marital relationships. *The Family Coordinator*, 1979, **28**, 497-502.

Pearlin, L. I. Sex roles and depression. In N. Datan & L. Ginsberg (Eds.), *Proceedings of the fourth life-span developmental psychology conference: Normative life crises.* New York: Academic, 1975.

Pearlin, L. I., & Johnson, J. Marital status, life-strains, and depression. *American Sociological Review*, 1977, **42**, 704-715.

Radloff, L. Sex differences in depression: The effects of occupation and marital status. *Sex Roles*, 1975, **3**, 249-265.

Rowe, M. Choosing child care: Many options. In R. Rapoport & R. Rapoport (Eds.), *Working couples.* New York: Harper Colophon, 1978.

Seidenberg, R. *Corporate wives—corporate casualties.* New York: Doubleday, 1973.

Work Roles as Stressors in Corporate Families*

PATRICIA VOYDANOFF**

This paper discusses the impact of several work role stressors on corporate families: employment insecurity and career mobility, job content and satisfaction, amount and scheduling of work time, geographic mobility, and the corporate wife role. Coping strategies and supports used by corporate families are analyzed briefly.

There is a growing interest in examining the impacts of executive work roles on corporate families in spite of a general tendency on the part of corporations and executives to ignore or deny the relatedness of work and family roles. This position, referred to by Kanter (1977b) as the denial of connections, has been supported by a strong allegiance to the protestant ethic among corporate executives which includes high priority on work roles, strong dedication to achievement and advancement, and loyalty to the corporation. Executives have been expected to be "good family men" without having family obligations infringe upon work role responsibilities.[1]

Recent work indicates that there are several characteristics of executive employment that serve as family stressors which are related to low levels of marital satisfaction and family cohesion and to difficulties in performing family roles. Stressors are defined as problems requiring solutions or situations to which the family must adapt in order to maintain the functioning of the family system. Stressors can be of two types: (a) life events or acute changes affecting the family, and (b) relatively enduring situations requiring problem solving behavior or coping strategies (Moen, Note 1; Pearlin, Note 2). Several aspects of executive work roles function as chronic stressors in relation to the family, e.g., routine husband-father absence resulting from long hours and frequent travel, work-related stress associated with time pressure and mobility aspirations, and the tendency for a divergence of interests to develop between husband and wife. In addition to these relatively enduring stressors, more acute life-event stressors occur including geographic mobility and job transfers, nonroutine husband-father absence resulting from long-term travel assignments, and acute stress associated with status changes such as promotions.

Socioeconomic Status and Occupational Success

The literature on the relation between socioeconomic status and family life is extensive and the findings are quite consistent. Socioeconomic status is related to patterns of family behavior including division of labor,

*Paper presented at the Annual Meeting of the North Central Sociological Association, May, 1980. Preparation of this manuscript was supported by a grant from the American Council of Life Insurance.

**Patricia Voydanoff is Chairperson, Department of Family and Community Studies, Merrill-Palmer Institute, 71 East Ferry, Detroit, MI 48202.

(*Family Relations*, 1980, **29**, 489-494.)

[1] In this paper analysis is limited to male executives and their families. More research is needed to determine the extent to which the findings and conclusions apply to female executives and their families.

marital power and decision-making, and socialization practices and values. In addition, positive relations between socioeconomic status and marital happiness, cohesion and stability are reported from most research. Scanzoni (1970) has developed a model of family cohesion which places major explanatory power on the husband's success in the occupational sphere as measured by socioeconomic status. However, it has been reported recently that the relation between occupational success and marital happiness and cohesion is curvilinear with less satisfactory marital relationships being more prevalent among those who are most and least successful in the occupational world (Aldous, Osmond, & Hicks, 1979). This contrasts with Scanzoni's hypothesis of a direct relation between occupational success and marital happiness and cohesion. Aldous et al. (1979) supported their hypothesis by specifying some of the correlations reported by Scanzoni (1970) and Blood and Wolfe (1960) that indicated a leveling off or decrease in happiness and cohesion among those in higher occupational and income categories. They also cited Dizard (1968) who reported that, in his study of middle-class couples, those who were most successful in their occupations were most likely to have marital relationships deteriorate over time. He explained this finding by suggesting that a gulf develops between the husband and wife because of different life situation requirements.

It has been reported in other literature that a minimum level of income and employment stability are necessary for family stability and cohesion (Furstenberg, 1974). Beyond this minimum the family's subjective perception of adequacy becomes relatively more important in relation to happiness and cohesion (Oppenheimer, 1979; Scanzoni, 1970). Men with middle-level incomes and occupational status may be best able to combine work and family roles whereas those at the lower end have too few economic resources and those at the upper end have difficulty performing family roles (Aldous, 1969; Aldous et al., 1979; Kanter, 1977b). The evidence for this hypothesis is not conclusive; the hypothesis is quite provocative when viewed in the context of the analysis of executive work role stressors.

Executive Work Role Stressors

Job Security and Career Mobility

It has been noted in the recent business literature that executive employment is becoming increasingly insecure due to top-heavy managements, depressed industries, automation and computers, and managerial upheavals. It involves a greater likelihood of unemployment among all levels of management as well as decreasing opportunities for promotion into higher levels of management. Reactions to unemployment among the middle-class are relatively severe in terms of status loss and self-esteem; impacts on the family have not been studied (Braginsky & Braginsky, 1975; Briar, 1978; Elder, 1974; Goodchilds & Smith, 1963; Powell & Driscoll, 1973). Fineman (1979) reported that stress accompanies unemployment among managers in situations where managers are highly involved in their work, where unemployment coincides with family problems, and where repeated job-seeking attempts fail. Stress is lower among managers where job satisfaction and job involvement have been low, where managers interpret job loss as a challenge to meet or a problem to solve, and where they feel confident about their abilities to meet the challenge.

The highest rates of unemployment and economic uncertainty are still found within the lower and working classes. However, strong economic striving and desire for mobility among the middle class may have effects on the family comparable in some ways to the effects of job insecurity and fear of unemployment. In addition, those executives not meeting their achievement aspirations must adjust to the discrepancy between aspirations and accomplishments. Mizruchi (1964) saw the strain associated with this disparity as a major source of anomia in the middle class. Following Durkheim, he referred to this type of anomia as boundlessness. Part of the midlife crisis among executives centers on the need for middle-aged executives to come to terms with the discrepancy between current achievements and aspirations set earlier in their careers. Problems associated with mobility striving and gaps between achievement and aspirations have not been studied in relation to the family except perhaps for Blood and Wolfe (1960) who found that the wives of occupational strivers are less satisfied with their marriages than other wives with husbands in high status occupations.

Job Content and Satisfaction

It has been suggested that the content or requirements of the work roles of successful executives lead to or are accompanied by the development of personality traits or attributes that are inconsistent with successful family life. This incongruence is found on two levels. First, the personal traits needed for a happy family life are not necessarily compatible with those needed to become a successful executive (Bartolomé, 1972; Maccoby, 1976; Zaleznik, Note 3). Managerial careers stress the development of the "head" at the expense of the "heart" (Maccoby, 1976). Second, the husband and wife may grow apart psychologically and develop different interests as the husband grows in his career (Dizard, 1968; Foote, 1963; Levinson, 1964; Seidenberg, 1973). This is especially true if the wife is not employed outside the home.

Research on job satisfaction and the family complements the analysis of occupational success discussed above because job satisfaction may be positively related to family role participation and marital happiness except for those with the highest levels of job satisfaction, i.e., a curvilinear relation may exist (Aldous et al., 1979). Bailyn (1970) found a positive relation between job satisfaction and marital happiness for couples in which the husband was family oriented. However, she found a negative relation between husband's job satisfaction and couple happiness for those couples in which the husband was career oriented and the wife family oriented. Thus, the Aldous et al. (1979) hypothesis that high levels of job satisfaction can hinder marital satisfaction is supported among the couples fitting the general orientation of many corporate families, i.e., a career-oriented husband and a family-oriented wife.

Amount and Scheduling of Time

Executives tend to work long hours and to take work home frequently. Findings on the impact of number of hours spent working on family roles are not conclusive. Time spent working is related to family strain (Mortimer, Note 4); however, the number of hours worked does not significantly influence the performance of family roles except for recreation (Clark, Nye, & Gecas, 1978). Pleck (1977) has suggested that attitudes toward family role performance are more important than work time, i.e., executives can choose to spend their off-work time, limited though it may be, either in family activities or other leisure-oriented pursuits.

It may be that the timing of work role activities has a greater effect on the family than the number of hours worked. Those who travel extensively or work evenings and weekends may find it difficult to fulfill some aspects of family roles including companionship with spouse and children, attendance at family and school functions, and participation in household duties (Culbert & Renshaw, 1972; Kanter, 1977b; Renshaw, 1976; Young & Willmott, 1973).

Geographic Mobility

Frequent transfers have been considered an integral part of moving up the corporate ladder for executives. In recent years, however, some executives and some corporations have been reexamining the costs and benefits associated with corporate transfers. Increasing, though still small, numbers of executives are refusing transfers (Costello, 1976). Personal and family considerations top the reasons for refusal. Corporations are beginning to seek ways to ease the strain of transfers for their employees and their families.

A wide range of family responses to frequent moves has been reported in the literature. In some situations these moves have been found to be stressful for all family members (Tiger, 1974); in others, families have little difficulty adjusting (Jones, 1973; McAllister, Butler & Kaiser, 1973). It is necessary to consider the conditions under which moving is stressful. Factors making a difference in adjustment include the number and timing of moves, degree of family cohesion and integration, ages of children, and the extent to which the wife has difficulty making new friends and transferring her credentials and contacts (Margolis, 1979; Portner, 1978; Renshaw, 1976; Jones, Note 5). After many moves some corporate wives give up trying to become part of yet another community and become isolated and depressed (Seldenberg, 1973).

Role of the Corporate Wife

The executive role has been analyzed as one example of the two-person career, i.e., an occupation in which the wife has well defined duties that are an integral part of the husband's occupational role (Papanek, 1973). These include supporting the husband in his work, taking care of the home so that the husband can spend more time at work and be able to relax when at home, participating in volunteer work to develop business contacts, entertaining work associates, and attending work related social functions (Kanter, 1977a, 1977b). The role also is associated with several problematic characteristics—frequent moves, lack of personal identity development, difficulty in integrating the husband into family activities, lack of parallel growth between husband and wife, and myriad psychological disturbances such as depression and alcoholism (Kanter, 1977a, 1977b; Seidenberg, 1973; Vandervelde, 1979). Information on the prevalence of these problems is limited; most of the data come from corporate wives in clinical settings.

Corporate wives are less likely to be employed than other women partly because their husbands' work roles impose constraints on their employment (Mortimer, Hall, & Hill, 1978). In spite of these constraints, however, wife employment is increasing among women with high educational levels because of changes in sex role orientation and increased occupational opportunities. If the wife also has a career, she is likely to experience role overload because she may continue to fulfill traditional family responsibilities in addition to full-time employment (Holmstrom, 1972).

Coping Strategies and Supports

Within the limits of the current literature, several relations between executive work role stressors, family roles, and cohesion have been documented. Within the context of current employment practices it is important to examine coping strategies and supports used by corporate families to moderate the impact of work stressors.

Boss, McCubbin, and Lester (1979) have outlined three coping strategies used by corporate wives in dealing with husband-father absence: fitting into the corporate life style, developing self and inter-personal relationships, and establishing independence and self-sufficiency. A related study of the wives of Navy servicemen revealed five coping patterns—maintaining family integrity, developing interpersonal relationships and social support, managing psychological tension and strain, believing in the value of spouse's profession and maintaining an optimistic definition of the situation, and developing self reliance and self-esteem (McCubbin, Boss, Wilson, & Lester, Note 6). Mortimer (Note 7) has shown the importance of the wife's support of the husband's work in mediating the relation between job-induced strain and marital satisfaction. Burke and Weir (1975, 1977) also reported that satisfaction with the husband-wife helping relationship effectively mediated between job and life stress and several measures of well-being including job, marital, and life satisfaction and mental and physical well-being. This work suggests the importance of coping strategies and supports within the family itself for limiting the impacts of work role stressors.

Several organizations are attempting to deal with stress in corporate families by holding "executive seminars." In these seminars, the strains and pressure of corporate life are discussed. Executives and their wives are helped to develop personal and family resources to handle their problems. The Harvard Business School offers a course for married students and their spouses on how executives can meet the demands of both work and family responsibilities (Greiff, 1976). The Menninger Clinic seminars on midlife transitions among executives deal with psychological resource development and the integration of work and family roles (Rice, 1979). Others bring together husbands and wives to discuss issues relating to corporate life and marriage (Becerra, 1975). Seminars also have been held to deal with the stresses associated with business travel (Culbert & Renshaw, 1972).

The reduction of work and family stress is also dealt with in the literature for corporate executives and their wives. The American

Management Association recently published a "how to" book for executives who want to achieve success in both marriage and corporate careers (Ogden, 1979). Hall and Hall (1979) have developed many practical suggestions for dealing with stress and role overload among two-career couples. The literature written for corporate wives is also changing. Earlier writings stressed the importance of the corporate wife in smoothly handling family life so that her husband could devote himself to his work. A recent book tells corporate wives how they may become more independent without hurting their husbands' careers (Vandervelde, 1979).

Much more needs to be done to develop coping strategies and supports for corporate families. This work should progress on several levels—encouraging the development of internal coping strategies for family units and individual family members; providing group supports for families and individual members, e.g., seminars of various types; and developing community supports for corporate families, e.g., child care for two-career families. Based on McCubbin (1979) these strategies and supports need to be oriented toward both chronic and acute stressors.

REFERENCE NOTES

1. Moen, P. *Patterns of family stress across the life cycle.* Paper presented at the Annual Meeting of the National Council on Family Relations, Boston, 1979.
2. Pearlin, L. I. *The life cycle and life strain.* Paper presented at the Annual Meeting of the American Sociological Association, Boston, 1979.
3. Zaleznik, A. D.C.S. *Isolation and control in the family and work.* Paper presented at the Symposium on The Family: Setting Priorities, Washington, DC, 1978.
4. Jones, S. *Corporate policy on the transferring of employees: Sociological considerations.* Paper presented at the Annual Meeting of the North Central Sociological Association, Louisville, 1976.
5. McCubbin, H. I., Boss, P. G., Wilson, L. F., & Lester, G. R. *Developing family invulnerability to stress: Coping patterns and strategies wives employ in managing family separations.* Paper presented at the 9th World Congress of the International Sociological Association, Uppsala, Sweden, 1978.
6. Mortimer, J. T. *Work-family linkages as perceived by men in the early stages of professional and managerial careers.* Paper presented at the Annual Meeting of the Society for the Study of Social Problems, Boston, 1979.

REFERENCES

Aldous, J. Occupational characteristics and males' role performance in the family. *Journal of Marriage and the Family*, 1969, **31**, 707-712.

Aldous, J., Osmond, M., & Hicks, M. Men's work and men's families. In W. Burr, R. Hill, I. Reiss, & F. I. Nye (Eds.), *Contemporary theories about the family.* New York: Free Press, 1979.

Bailyn, L. Career and family orientations of husbands and wives in relation to marital happiness. *Human Relations*, 1970, **23**, 97-113.

Bartolomé, F. Executives as human beings. *Harvard Business Review*, 1972, **50**, 62-69.

Becerra, M. Marriage and the corporation. *Nation's Business*, 1975, **63**, March, 82-84.

Blood, R. O., & Wolfe, D. M. *Husbands and wives.* New York: Free Press, 1960.

Boss, P. G., McCubbin, H. I., & Lester, G. The corporate executive wife's coping patterns in response to routine husband-father absence. *Family Process*, 1979, **18**, 79-86.

Braginsky, D. D., & Braginsky, B. M. Surplus people. *Psychology Today*, 1975, **9**, 68-72.

Briar, K. H. *The effect of long-term unemployment on workers and their families.* Palo Alto: R & E Research Associates, 1978.

Burke, R. J., & Weir, T. The husband-wife relationship. *The Business Quarterly*, 1975, **40**, 62-67.

Burke, R. J., & Weir, T. Marital helping relationships. *The Journal of Psychology*, 1977, **95**, 121-130.

Clark, R. A., Nye, F. I., & Gecas, V. Husbands' work involvement and marital role performance. *Journal of Marriage and the Family*, 1978, **40**, 9-21.

Costello, J. Why more managers are refusing transfers. *Nation's Business*, 1976, **64**, October, 4-5.

Culbert, S. A., & Renshaw, J. R. Coping with the stresses of travel as an opportunity for improving the quality of work and family life. *Family Process*, 1972, **11**, 321-337.

Dizard, J. *Social change in the family.* Chicago: University of Chicago Press, 1968.

Elder, G. h. *Children of the great depression.* Chicago: University of Chicago Press, 1974.

Fineman, S. A psychosocial model of stress and its application to managerial unemployment. *Human Relations*, 1979, **32**, 323-345.

Foote, N. N. Matching of husband and wife in phases of development. In M. B. Sussman (Ed.), *Sourcebook in marriage and the family.* Boston: Houghton Mifflin, 1963.

Furstenberg, F. Work experience and family life. In J. O'Toole (Ed.), *Work and the quality of life.* Cambridge: MIT Press, 1974.

Goodchilds, J. D., & Smith, E. E. The effects of unemployment as mediated by social status. *Sociometry*, 1963, **26**, 287-293.

Greiff, B. S. The executive family seminar: A course for graduate married business students. *American College Health Association*, 1976, **24**, 227-231.

Hall, F. S., & Hall, D. T. *The two-career couple.* Reading, MA: Addison-Wesley, 1979.

Holmstrom, L. *The two-career family.* Cambridge: Schenkman, 1972.

Jones, S. B. Geographic mobility as seen by the wife and mother. *Journal of Marriage and the Family*, 1973, **35**, 210-218.

Kanter, R. M. *Men and women of the corporation*. New York: Basic, 1977. (a)

Kanter, R. M. *Work and family in the United States: A critical review and agenda for research and policy*. New York: Sage, 1977. (b)

Levinson, H. *Emotional problems in the world of work*. New York: Harper, 1964.

Maccoby, M. The corporate climber has to find his heart. *Fortune*, December, 1976, pp. 98-108.

Margolis, D. *The managers*. New York: Morrow, 1979.

McAllister, R., Butler, E., & Kaiser, E. The adjustment of women to residential mobility. *Journal of Marriage and the Family*, 1973, **35**, 197-204.

McCubbin, H. I. Integrating coping behavior in family stress theory. *Journal of Marriage and the Family*, 1979, **41**, 237-244.

Mizruchi, E. *Success and opportunity*. New York: Free Press, 1964.

Mortimer, J., Hall, R., & Hill, R. Husbands' occupational attributes as constraints on wives' employment. *Sociology of Work and Occupations*, 1978, **5**, 285-313.

Ogden, R. W. *How to succeed in business and marriage*. New York: AMACOM, 1978.

Oppenheimer, V. K. Structural sources of economic pressure for wives to work: An analytical framework. *Journal of Family History*, 1979, **4**, 177-197.

Papanek, H. Men, women, and work: Reflections on the two-person career. *The American Journal of Sociology*, 1973, **78**, 852-872.

Pleck, J. H. The work-family role system. *Social Problems*, 1977, **24**, 417-428.

Portner, J. *Impacts of work on the family*. Minneapolis: Minnesota Council on Family Relations, 1978.

Powell, D. H., & Driscoll, P. F. Middle-class professionals face unemployment. *Society*, 1973, **10**, 18-26.

Renshaw, J. R. An exploration of the dynamics of the overlapping worlds of work and family. *Family Process*, 1976, **15**, 143-165.

Rice, B. Midlife encounters: The Menninger seminars for businessmen. *Psychology Today*, 1979, **12**, 66-74, 95-99.

Scanzoni, J. H. *Opportunity and the family*. New York: Free Press, 1970.

Seidenberg, R. *Corporate wives-corporate casualties?* New York: AMACOM, 1973.

Tiger, L. Is this trip necessary? The heavy human costs of moving executives around. *Fortune,* September 1974, pp. 139-141.

Vandervelde, M. *The changing life of the corporate wife*. New York: Jecox, 1979.

Young, M., & Willmott, P. *The symmetrical family*. New York: Penguin, 1973.

Family Life and the Police Profession: Coping Patterns Wives Employ in Managing Job Stress and the Family Environment*

PETER MAYNARD AND NANCY MAYNARD,
HAMILTON I. MCCUBBIN, AND DAVID SHAO**

Family life in the police profession is stressful. This study examines the coping strategies wives employ in the management of the hardships associated with this style of life. The coping patterns of Developing Self Reliance, Accepting the Demands of the Profession, Building Social Support, and Maintaining Family Integration, reported by 42 wives, were associated with specific dimensions of family functioning—Interpersonal Relationships, Personal Growth and System Maintenance. The importance of coping as a meaningful target for family counselors and prevention oriented family life educators is underscored.

Stress is an integral part of the life of a professional police officer. Police often encounter stressful situations in their daily work, and these stressors have cumulative effects. Police officers reveal physical health problems at a significantly higher rate than the general public (Richard & Fell, 1975). Jacobi's study (1975) of stress-related disa-

bilities in the Los Angeles Police Department revealed high incidences of high blood pressure, peptic ulcers, and hyperacidity. Kroes (1976) reported abnormally high rates or coronary mortalities among law enforcement officers. Depression, suicide, alcoholism and other forms of chemical dependency have also been reported in association with job stress of police officers (Herman, 1975; Schwartz & Schwartz, 1975).

The stressors of life-threatening events, armed conflict, and other risks associated with the police profession also impact upon family life. Kroes (1976) offered extensive documentation of the hardships families face including the psychological fears of injury, social stigma, and trying to manage seemingly unpredictable work schedules. Kroes (1976) and Reiser (1975) reported marital conflicts associated with spouses being overwhelmed by the job. Hageman (Note 1) described police officers who learned to cope with job stress by psychologically detaching themselves from experiences on the job. Marital difficulties emerged in those situa-

*This project was conducted as part of the Family Impact Training Grant, National Institute of Mental Health awarded to the Family Study Center, University of Minnesota. Dr. McCubbin's involvement was supported by a grant from the Agriculture Experiment Station, University of Minnesota, St. Paul.

**Peter Maynard is Associate Professor, and Nancy Maynard a Special Instructor, Department of Human Development, Counseling and Families Studies, University of Rhode Island, Kingston, Rhode Island. Hamilton I. McCubbin is Professor and Chair, Department of Family Social Science, University of Minnesota, St. Paul, Minnesota. David Shao is Associate Professor, Department of Industrial Engineering, University of Rhode Island, Kingston, Rhode Island.

(*Family Relations*, 1980, **29**, 495-501.)

tions where spouses used detachment to manage stressors in family life. Hageman also reported that as the length of service increased, so too did the usage of this denial coping mechanism and, accordingly, for some, marital satisfaction and happiness decreased.

Prior studies of the police profession and its impact on family life have tended to emphasize the negative consequences of stress upon the marital relationship and upon family life. Studies to date have not examined what coping strategies wives find helpful in managing the hardships of this unique profession. If we had a clearer picture of the range of coping strategies spouses employ and which strategies appear to strengthen the family environment, we could respond to their needs more appropriately. Coping itself becomes a meaningful target for family counselors and prevention-oriented family life educators who often are called upon to assist these families directly or indirectly through family life education programs. The study of police officer families and the coping strategies spouses employ in managing occupational stress and the family environment is the focus of this exploratory investigation.

Subjects and Procedures

The subjects of this investigation were 42 wives of police officers in a large metropolitan police department in the Midwest. They were randomly selected from a roster of currently married officers. To maintain confidentiality the researchers were not given direct access to the master roster, but worked through a liaison officer who made the initial contacts with the officers and their families and sought their voluntary involvement in this study. Of the 50 randomly selected families contacted, 42 wives agreed to participate in the study and were interviewed by the authors for a period averaging 2½ hours. Wives also were asked to complete questionnaires regarding coping, stress, and family functioning.

The wives ranged in age from 22 to 50 with a median age of 31. They were married a median length of 8.7 years with a range of 2 to 28 years. For all but three of the wives, this was their first marriage. The majority (34) had 2 children with a range of 1 to 10 children. The wives had completed a median of 13 years of formal education. A small but notable percentage (27%) of these wives were full-time homemakers. Of those employed outside the home, the majority (64%) were employed full-time.

Instruments

Coping, defined as behavior strategies for managing strain in the family, was measured through the use of a self-report, 58-item questionnaire—*Inventory of Coping Strategies, Family and Police Career Form W* (McCubbin, Maynard, & Maynard, Note 2). This inventory was patterned after the *Coping with Separation Inventory* (CSI) (McCubbin, Dahl, Lester, & Boss, 1978). The revised coping questionnaire included coping items which focused on: (a) social support (Kaplan, 1977; Cobb, 1976)—the wives' relationship to the community in gaining support; (b) family resources (Burr, 1973, 1976; Hill, 1949)—the wives' management of intra-family resources, such as parent-child relationships; and (c) psychological techniques (Lazarus, 1966)—the wives' management of psychological tension through such strategies as eating, dieting, and sleeping. The coping items from the CSI were altered to fit the police profession but with every effort to maintain the original coping patterns of: (a) *Maintaining Family Integration*; (b) *Developing Self-Reliance and Self-Esteem*; (c) *Developing Social Supports*; (d) *Maintaining an Optimistic Definition of the Situation and Accepting the Demands of the Profession*; and (e) *Managing Psychological Tension*. The psychometric details of the CSI and these sub-scales are reported elsewhere (McCubbin, Boss, Wilson, & Lester, in press). Wives completing the inventory were asked to rate how helpful they found each coping behavior to be to them in managing the hardships of life in the police profession. The ratings ranged from 1 to 4, with the higher score indicating the greater helpfulness.

Family Environment Scale. To examine the relation between coping and family functioning, the *Family Environment Scale* (Moos, 1974) was included in this study. The Family Environment Scale (FES) is composed of 10 sub-scales that measure the interpersonal relationships among family members, the directions of personal growth that are emphasized in the family, and the basic organizational structure of the family. The psychometric details of the FES are discussed elsewhere (Moos, 1974). The five subscales (cohesion, expressiveness, conflict, independence, and control) that focus on "family functioning" and that have received emphasis in prior studies were included in this research effort:

A. *Family Interpersonal Relationship Dimensions*
    1. *Cohesion*—or the extent to which family members are concerned, helpful and supportive of each other.
    2. *Expressiveness*—or the extent to which family members are allowed and encouraged to act openly and to express their feelings directly.
    3. *Conflict*—or the extent to which the open expression of anger and aggression and generally conflictual interactions are characteristic of the family.

B. *Family Personal-Growth Dimensions*
    4. *Independence*—or the extent to which family members are encouraged to be assertive, self-sufficient to make their own decisions, and to think things out for themselves.

C. *System Maintenance Dimensions*
    5. *Control*—the extent to which the family is organized in a hierarchical manner, the rigidity of rules and procedures, and the extent to which family members order each other around.

The analysis of wives' responses to the coping inventory revealed that 37 of the 58 items were rated as not helpful. The resultant 21 helpful items were analyzed using the SPSS principal factoring with iterations method. The four factors were rotated to a varimax solution. These four factors, now called coping patterns, represented 78% of the variance of the original correlation matrix.

The first coping pattern, *Developing Self Reliance*, is composed of four coping behaviors. These items center around the wives' efforts to be independent and to develop them-

Table 1
Factors Structure: Wives' Coping Patterns Associated
with Life in the Police Profession

Coping Patterns	Coping Factors and Factor Loadings			
	I	II	III	IV
Factor I: Developing Self Reliance				
7. Trusting my husband	.68			
16. Becoming more independent	.79			
20. Telling myself I have many things to be thankful for	.56			
37. Developing myself as a person	.72			
Factor II: Adapting to Demands of the Profession				
13. Accepting this is a demanding and stressful job		.67		
15. Accepting my husband will be away a lot		.70		
52. Believing things will always work out for the best		.63		
53. Establishing a family routine not dependent on husband being around		.47		
56. Believing this is our style of life and I should enjoy it		.63		
Factor III: Building Social Support				
38. Involvement in social activity with friends			.76	
42. Talking to someone about how I am feeling personally			.87	
43. Going shopping by self with friends or with children			.57	
44. Engaging in satisfying relationships			.54	
Factor IV: Role Maintenance				
14. Being a supportive wife				.82
55. Planning special events for the whole family				.71
51. Eating together as a family				.37
Eigen Values:	4.04	2.44	2.15	1.85
Pct. of Variance:	30.1	18.1	16.0	13.8

selves as individuals. Coping Pattern II, *Accepting the Demands of the Profession*, includes five behaviors that are concerned with the wives accepting the police job as demanding of them, and adopting the belief that this is their chosen life style and so things will work out. *Building Social Support*, the third Coping Pattern (III), focuses upon the wives' interactions with friends and other special relationships. These behaviors involve developing meaningful and supportive relationships outside the family unit. Coping Pattern IV, *Maintaining Family Integration*, emphasizes the wives' efforts to perform the traditional role of "supportive" wife that includes organizing family activities and promoting family integration. Coping scale scores were computed for each of these four patterns by means of an unweighted summing of the wives' "helpfulness" ratings (1-4) across behavior items in each pattern.

Because the ratio (2:1) of subjects to number of coping items falls short of the desired ratio (5-10:1) for factor analytic procedures, caution is suggested in accepting the reliability of these factors. However, in comparing both the coping items and the four coping patterns with those identified in a prior study (McCubbin, Boss, Wilson, & Lester, in press), some confidence is gained in the applicability and reliability of the factors. The Cronbach alphas computed for each of the coping patterns derived in this investigation indicated respectable reliabilities (.75, .77, .75, .67).

Coping and Family Functioning

The analyses of these coping patterns with the five indices of family functioning indicated that not only are these coping efforts helpful to wives in managing the strains of life

with a policeman-husband, they also appear to contribute to family functioning. As indicated in Table 1, the effort of wives to be *Self-Reliant* is positively associated with family "cohesiveness" ($r = .43$, $p < .01$), family "expressiveness" ($r = .31$, $p < .02$) and "independence" ($r = .35$, $p < .01$). Additionally, effort to *Accept the Demands of the Profession* is positively related to "independence" in the family ($r = .13$, $p < .05$). Concomitantly, the effort to *Build Social Supports* for herself and members of the family is inversely related to "control" in the family ($r = -.28$, $p < .04$). The final coping pattern of *Role Maintenance* is inversely related to "independence" ($r = -.33$, $p < .01$), and "conflict" ($r = -.33$, $p < .01$).

Discussion

This investigation appears to complement recent investigations designed to identify measurable dimensions of wives' coping responses in managing the hardships in family life associated with occupational stress. The importance of the present investigation is seen in its identification of coping patterns that not only tend to facilitate the wives' adaptation to strains of life associated with the law enforcement profession, but also facilitate family system adaptation to stress. Building on both the classic studies of family stress (Burr, 1973, 1976; Hill, 1949), and the more recent investigations of wives' coping with family separations (McCubbin, Dahl, Lester, Benson, & Robertson, 1976; Boss, McCubbin, & Lester, 1979; McCubbin, Boss, Wilson, & Lester, in press), the line of inquiry pursued herein offers exploratory empirical evidence of four functionally valuable coping patterns. These patterns serve to characterize adaptive behavior of families under stress.

Table 2
Correlations between Family Environment and Police Wives' Coping Patterns

Indices of Family Functioning	Self Reliance	Accepting the Demands of the Profession	Social Support	Role Maintenance
Cohesion	.43***	.22	−.18	−.02
Expressiveness	.31**	.07	.17	−.10
Conflict	−.12	−.06	.06	−.33***
Independence	.35***	.13*	.06	−.33***
Control	.00	.13	−.28*	.09

*$p < .03$.
**$p < .02$.
***$p < .01$.

The findings of this investigation may be compared with previous clinical investigations that have emphasized family dysfunction and the deleterious effects of the police occupation on family life. According to these results, there are at least four types of coping responses that may be helpful for such families. Wives are called upon to attend to themselves, their strengths and self reliance. Additionally, they find value in *developing social supports* from the community for themselves and other members. Wives are called upon to make a concerted effort to *accept the demands of the profession* while, predictably, they provide leadership in keeping the family *functioning together as a unit*. When viewed in the context of the family processes, the four coping patterns emerge as conscious efforts to promote family organization, maintain emotional stability, and promote the independence of family members and their personal growth and development.

The family *interpersonal relationship dimensions* of cohesion, expressiveness, and conflict appeared to be directly related to the coping strategies wives employ in the management of stress. The extent to which family members are helpful and supportive of each other, and the degree to which family members are allowed and encouraged to act openly and express their feelings directly were positively associated with their efforts to be self sufficient and independent. The amount of conflict or the extent to which the family expresses anger and aggression and generally conflictual interaction appeared to be lessened by wives' efforts to do things as a family unit and to organize family social functions. One wife realized that she had become increasingly depressed by the demands of her husband's profession. In response, she decided to extend herself and build a family life in which she played a more prominent role. She made an effort to express her feelings about the job and what it was doing to her, her husband, and her family. To gain support she became involved in a voluntary organization and assumed a leadership role as a member of the board of directors.

The *personal growth dimension* of family life, represented by the FES measure of independence, was also related to wives' coping.

The extent to which family members are encouraged to be assertive, to make their own decisions, and to think things out for themselves, is positively associated with both wives' *Developing Self Reliance*, and *Accepting the Demands of the Profession. Independence,* on the other hand, was inversely related to *Role Maintenance*. Personal growth in the family appeared to involve a delicate balance of wives' coping strategies directed at self reliance, accepting a way of life, and promoting family togetherness. For many wives, accepting the demands of the profession was not merely acquiescing to the occupation. Wives took deliberate steps to minimize the impact of the occupation on their lives. Those who had their own careers or vocations continued to work part or full time. Other wives dealt with specific problems in creative ways. For example, many wives mentioned the problem of their spouses' "fraternity" and social drinking that followed the second shift in the evening. One wife hired a baby sitter for 10:30 p.m. on every Friday and Saturday night that her husband worked. She would pick him up at the precinct station and they would make it a night out.

The *system maintenance dimensions* of family "control," or the extent to which the family is organized in a hierarchical manner with rigidity of rules and procedures, was inversely related to *Building Social Support*. Wives' efforts to develop amd maintain family relationships, friends, and special relationships that are supportive for them and other family members appeared to contribute to reducing the amount of control in the family. Most wives reported how meaningful it was to have friends and associates with whom they could share the pleasurable experiences as well as the negative situations that police officers' wives experienced. One woman member stated that after hearing from another wife that "rookie fever" was a symptom of the new police academy graduate, she was better able to deal with the problem and its ramifications in their family life.

Coping with the strains of family life in the police profession appears to be an ongoing process of checks and balances, a system of adaptive compromises. This complex interplay among coping patterns is infrequently referred to in the literature; it is seldom apparent in the study of short-term, single-stressor events. Wives faced with the reality of chronic stress appear to pace themselves throughout life through the use of personal, social, and intra-family coping strategies. In asserting themselves through *Developing Self Reliance* and *Accepting the Demands of the Profession*, they are able to facilitate family cohesion, expressiveness, and independence. Through such coping efforts as *Developing Social Support* and *Maintaining Family Integration*, they appear to be able to minimize conflict and control in the family. However, in emphasizing *Role Maintenance*, wives also face the risk of reducing independence in the family. It appears that the family will constantly strive for an adaptive balance that not only preserves the stability and cohesiveness of the family unit, but also permits family members to develop themselves as individuals and increase their social and psychological autonomy. Achieving and maintaining this delicate balance between family functioning and individual development appears to be one of the major objectives of coping behaviors in families.

Although the sample consisted of intact families most of whom were relatively successful in their adjustment, there were families who had difficulties. A few wives were not able to achieve a balance in coping and were unsuccessful in managing the stress associated with the police occupation.

Two wives who expressed feelings of being isolated and under extreme pressure by the police department's inordinate demands on family life, stated that their marriage was deteriorating. Both said they felt very alone and at times very depressed. Although there was a predisposition among many of the wives interviewed to feeling pressured because of the public's questioning attitude toward law enforcement officers and the department's unpredictable work hours, these women expressed concern that they did not have friends with whom they could talk about the specific hardships they faced.

Because police families are at risk for divorces and family crises, the positive coping strategies identified in this study could serve as a point of departure for building long-range programs to assist police families in the management of some of the predictable stressors associated with their profession. Based on the present data, it is suggested that an emphasis on positive coping mechanisms could ultimately result in more meaningful payoffs in work with police families under stress.

The fact that the police department, the police union, and its women's auxiliary cooperated in this study indicates that there is a sincere interest in understanding the hardships families face. The information provided by this study should prove helpful for the development of prevention-oriented programs for families who must cope with this predictably demanding occupation.

REFERENCE NOTES

1. Hageman, M. J. Occupational stress of law enforcement officers and marital and familial relationships. Paper presented at the Annual Meeting of the American Sociological Association, Chicago, 1977.
2. McCubbin, H. I., Maynard, P. E., & Maynard, N. E. *Inventory of coping strategies*. St. Paul, MN: Department of Family Social Science, University of Minnesota, 1978.

REFERENCES

Boss, P. G., McCubbin, H. E., & Lester, G. The corporate executive wife's coping patterns in response to routine husband-father absence. *Family Process*, 1979, **18**, 79-86.

Burr, W. *Theory construction and the sociology of the family*. New York: Wiley, 1973.

Burr, W. *Successful marriage: A principles approach*. Homewood, Ill.: Dorsey, 1976.

Cobb, S. Social support as a moderator of life stress. *Psychosomatic Medicine*, 1976, **38**, 300-314.

Herman, M. F. Police suicides revisited. *Suicide*, 1975, **5**, 5-20.

Hill, R. *Families under stress: Adjustment to the crises of war and separation and reunion*. Westport, CT: Greenwood, 1949.

Jacobi, J. H. Reducing police stress: A psychiatrist's point of view. In W. H. Kroes & J. J. Hunnell (Eds.), *Job stress and the police officer*. Washington, DC: National Institute for Occupational Safety and Health, (HEW Publication No. 76-1187), pp. 85-106.

Kaplan, A. *Social support: The construct and its measurement*. Unpublished Bachelor's Thesis, Brown University, Providence, RI, 1977.

Kroes, W. H. *Society's victim—the policeman*. Springfield, IL: Charles C. Thomas, 1976.

Lazarus, R. S. *Psychological stress and the coping process*. New York: McGraw-Hill, 1966.

McCubbin, H. I., Boss, P. G., Wilson, L. R., & Lester, G. R. Developing family invulnerability to stress: Coping patterns and strategies wives employ. In J. Trost (Ed.),

The family and change. Sweden: International Library Publishing, in press.

McCubbin, H. I., Dahl, B. R., Lester, G. R., Benson, D., & Robertson, M. L. Coping repertoires of families adapting to prolonged war-induced separation. *Journal of Marriage and the Family*, 1976, **38**, 461-471.

McCubbin, H. I., Dahl, G., Lester, G. R., & Boss, P. Coping with Separation Inventory (CSI). San Diego, California: Naval Health Research Center, 1978.

Moos, R. *Family environment scale and preliminary manual*. Palo Alto, CA: Consulting Psychologists Press, 1974.

Reiser, M. "Stress, distress and adaptation in police work." In W. H. Kroes & J. J. Hunnell (Eds.), Job stress and the police officer. Washington, DC: National Institute for Occupational Safety and Health (HEW Publication No. 76-187), 1975, pp. 17-25.

Richard, W. C., & Fell, R. D. Health factors in police job stress. In W. H. Kroes & J. J. Hunnell (Eds.), *Job stress and the police officer*. Washington, DC: National Institute for Occupational Safety and Health (HEW Publication No. 76-187), 1975, pp. 73-84.

Schwartz, J. A., & Schwartz, C. B. The personal problems of the police officer: A plea for action. In W. H. Kroes & J. J. Hunnell (Eds.), *Job stress and the police officer*. Washington, DC: National Institute for Occupational Safety and Health (HEW Publication No. 76-187), 1975, pp. 130-141.

The Impact of the Environment on the Coping Efforts of Low-Income Mothers*

DIANA DILL, ELLEN FELD, JACQUELINE MARTIN,
STEPHANIE BEUKEMA, AND DEBORAH BELLE**

Interviews were conducted with 43 low-income mothers concerning the ways they found to maintain their well-being while living under highly-stressful conditions. This paper discusses the environmental impact at four points of the coping process. Frequent and severe threats to the individual's well-being, differing life contexts upon which threats impinge, limited options for addressing a problem, and lack of environmental response complicate the individual's coping efforts. Case material is presented and its theoretical relevance discussed.

Welfare mothers and other poor women are often depicted as, among other things, unable to manage their own affairs. Such stereotypes are frequently based on the assumption that the woman is ultimately in control of, and therefore responsible for, the forces that affect her life. If we look more closely, however, it becomes apparent that environment has a powerful impact on their efforts to cope with daily life.

Recent research has produced models of coping which systematically incorporate the effects of the environment. Lazarus, Averill, and Opton (1974) have developed a "sources of variance" model of coping which includes the effect of situational cues on the cognitive mediation of threat and response. Coping is defined as "problem-solving efforts made by an individual when the demands he faces are highly relevant to his welfare . . . and when

these demands tax his adaptive resources" (p. 250). The process of coping involves, first, the recognition and interpretation of threat and, second, the "perception of the range of coping alternatives through which harm can be mastered, or beneficial results achieved" (p. 260).

In this paper, we use this conceptual model to distinguish those aspects of the coping process which are influenced by the environment. Threats to an individual's well-being may arise out of the environment or from within the person. We will address only those threats which originate in the environment. The individual recognizes those threats in a unique way, assessing the threat in terms of current danger and its effect on ongoing life. Situational and life-contextual cues are used in this assessment. In response to the perceived threat, the person searches for means of overcoming it, whether by direct action or by intrapsychic processes which relieve unpleasant affect. In the effort to cope, the person can only deploy whatever environmental and personal resources are available or perceived to be available. Finally, the environment can oppose or facilitate the person's efforts to master the threatening situation. The response of the environment may in turn affect the individual's motivation and self-esteem. Each of these

*This work is supported by grant No. MH 28830 from the Mental Health Services Branch of the National Institute of Mental Health. Susan Salasin is Project Officer and Deborah Belle, Principal Investigator.

**Diana Hill, Ellen Feld, Jacqueline Martin, Stephanie Beukema, and Deborah Belle are with the Stress and Families Project, Harvard Graduate School of Education, Cambridge, MA 02140.

(*Family Relations*, 1980, 29, 503-509.)

points of environmental impact will be discussed in this paper.

Methods

The Stress and Families Project[1] (SFP) has investigated several hypothesized relationships among low-income mothers' life circumstances, their mental health, and their maternal behavior, in order to locate points at which interventions might be successful in protecting mental health and family functioning.

The Sample

Forty-three Boston-area women ranging in age from 21 to 44 and representing every legal marital status were recruited with their families for the study. Twenty of these women were single-parent heads of household and 23 lived with husbands or other male partners. Per capita income for the families ranged from $500 to $4,000, which meant that families living far below federal poverty lines, as well as some living just above the poverty line, were included in this study. Thirty-three of the families studied were currently receiving AFDC benefits, and an additional two families has received such benefits at some time in the past. The sample included 21 black women and 22 white women. Each research family included at least one child between the ages of 5 and 7. Respondents' attained educational level ranged from fourth grade to graduate school. Families were paid $150 for their participation in the study and were recruited through a variety of community channels.

Data Collection

Intensive interviews were conducted with each woman concerning many facets of her life. As part of this larger study, a coping interview was designed to explore the ways women found to maintain their well-being while living under very stressful conditions.

To this end, each woman was asked to list her most stressful experiences, either current, past, or future. She was then asked to choose any four of the situations for an in-depth discussion. Probing questions were designed to tap various aspects of the situations, including the types of personal strain associated with the problem, the strains on the woman's household, and her satisfaction with her management of the situation and its ensuing stress. Also investigated were the availability of social and psychological resources. Finally, the woman was asked to discuss what she had learned in each specific instance. A total of 128 situations was reported.

The Impact of the Environment on the Coping Process

In the following pages, the content of the situations reported during the coping interviews will be used to illustrate the impact of the environment at four points of the coping process. In addition to anecdotal data drawn from these interviews, other data collected as part of the Stress and Families investigation will be utilized. Case material will be presented and its theoretical relevance discussed.

1. *Environmental threat.* Low-income mothers tend to have very stressful lives. Life events which require change and readjustment are one potent source of threat. On a checklist of 91 life events,[2] the SFP respon-

---

[1]For a fuller exposition of the stresses experienced by low income mothers, and the effect of these on their mental health and maternal behavior, the reader is referred to the Stress and Families Project report: *Lives in stress: A context for depression*, available from the Stress and Families Project, Harvard School of Education, Cambridge, Massachusetts, 02140.

[2]The Life Events Measure was developed for the particular purposes of the Stress and Families Project by Vivian Parker Makosky (1980). Ninety-one life events were included in this checklist, some drawn from the Holmes and Rahe (1967) and Dohrenwend checklists (Dohrenwend, Krasnoff, Askenasy, & Dohrenwend, 1978) and others included in order to more fully represent the universe of events to which low-income mothers are particularly vulnerable (e.g., household violence, change in child-care arrangements, unwilling participation in a sexual act). For each event, the respondent was asked whether or not it had happened to her during the past two years, and if so how many times. Scores were also obtained for the Holmes and Rahe and Dohrenwend scales mentioned above. Respondents reported a mean of 14.1 events on the Holmes and Rahe scale and a mean of 13.2 events on the Dohrenwend scale; therefore, they also reported high scores on lists which are widely used and not tailored to this particular population. Test-retest reliability has not yet been established for this measure, therefore the data are used in a descriptive manner only.

dents reported a mean of 14.1 events during the previous two years in which they had been the central figure (Makosky, Note 1). In contrast, most community surveys report an average of one or two events a year (Coates, Mayer, Kendall, & Howat, 1976; Dohrenwend, 1973). Many of the reported events required major readjustment. Reporting on events which had occurred in the two years preceding the interview, 26 respondents (62%) reported deaths of family members or friends, 16 (38%) reported illnesses or accidents which required hospitalization or surgery, 24 (57%) respondents reported 41 instances in which they had been a victim of a crime, and 15 (36%) reported large drops in income. In 37 reported incidents, respondents were victims of violence.

Ongoing conditions which make continuing demands on the individual's resources are another powerful source of threat. Compared to national averages, all of the respondents lived in high-density, high-crime neighborhoods. Only half (58%) of the respondents knew a month ahead of time how much money they would have coming into their households. One-third of the respondents said that they did not have enough money to buy adequate food for their families. Twenty-three percent rated their health as poor or very poor. Forty-eight percent reported that at least one child had problems in school.

Life events and life conditions such as the above severely threatened the well-being of the women interviewed. One woman discussed a particularly stressful period of her life. Her husband supported the family, which included eight children, through a home-based business for which the family truck was essential. The truck broke down at Christmas time, when the children were expecting new boots, and one daughter needed expensive dental treatment. The respondent, who was diabetic, learned that she had also developed rheumatoid arthritis. The family was not supported by welfare and not eligible for Medicaid benefits, and their medical bills precluded fixing the truck. The family business came to an effective halt and financial crisis ensued.

Another woman discussed her mental health. She had lost her mother when she was a young child, and three of her own children had died young. In the three years preceding the interview, her father, the father of her children, and her sister all died, and her son was sent to jail. So many losses had precipitated a severe depression.

A widow who supported two young children on an annual income of $5,500 was slowly going blind. Her husband had recently died and the family income plummeted. Her blindness, not yet severe enough to make her eligible for benefits for the blind, and her children's regression into constant quarrelling, compounded this woman's troubles.

Another woman said: "My life has always been a manner of coping with one thing or another. I get through one thing to find another coming up. Sometimes it feels as if everything is coming in all at once."

The question that arises from this case material is whether severe and chronic threats require forms of coping that differ from those used to address everyday problems. Traditional psychoanalytic theories of stress management contain the assumption that, as situations pose greater threat to the self, coping mechanisms become more primitive, less reality-oriented, and increasingly costly to the individual psyche (Freud, 1946; Menninger, 1954). Although researchers differ in how they define coping and defense, coping is generally conceived as rational, reality-oriented strategies employed in response to a lesser degree of threat. In contrast, defensive strategies are less reality-oriented and flexible, distort one's perception of the threatening event, and are used in situations which pose greater threat to the individual (Haan, 1977; Lazarus et al., 1974). Bernard, Ottenberg, and Redl (1965) reviewed studies of individuals exposed to chronic stressful circumstances of a dehumanizing nature, that is, circumstances over which they have no control. They demonstrate the predominant use of defense mechanisms such as denial and distortion. Managing long-term stress may involve mechanisms different from those used to address a transient crisis, and with longer duration of stress the strategies become decreasingly action-oriented and more oriented toward defense. Defensive strategies would presumably be less successful in reducing the objective threat than are coping strategies.

2. *Contextual cues determine experiences of stress.* If threat is defined as the objective condition, stress may be defined as the person's perception of and emotional response to that condition. Perception of threat may be understood as arising out of what Lazarus et al. (1974) have termed "primary appraisal." Situations are appraised as more or less threatening depending on personality factors which predispose the individual to attend to certain cues in the situation. While individual personality factors do affect the way people view situations, we have found that one's environment is an important determinant of whether a situation will be appraised as stressful, and of how the stress will be construed.

Three SFP respondents who had recently returned to school discussed problematic pregnancies. These women differed in life circumstances and therefore differed in how they construed their pregnancies. One woman had been intimidated by her college experience and wanted to enjoy her life more. Her grandmother, however, was very ambitious for her and insisted that she finish her education. Pregnancy gave this woman an excuse for leaving school which her grandmother would accept. Another woman became pregnant unexpectedly. Education and family life were equally important to her. She wanted to bear the child, but worried that the newborn child would interfere with her schoolwork and the happiness of her other children. Her decision was further complicated by her partner's increasing job responsibilities which made him less available to share household duties and child care than he had been previously. The third respondent, a single woman, felt already overstressed by lack of income and by conflicting responsibilities at work, at school, and at home caring for a young daughter when she became pregnant. She did not want to make a commitment to the father of this child, and carrying the pregnancy to term would have meant interrupting her education, which was central to her self-esteem.

We present this simple illustration to show that responses to problematic situations have histories to them, and suggest contexts surrounding a problem as well as the problem itself. Many coping researchers have attempted to hold situations constant as a point of comparison among individuals and their choices of coping strategies, without, however, addressing this issue of differential impacts. We have seen that a woman's life context, as well as the unique way in which she views her world, play important roles in how threats are construed. Superficially similar situations can not be considered functionally similar across individuals unless the meaning of the situation is held constant as well. It is therefore important to understand how a threat is interpreted when comparing and assessing coping strategies.

3. *Limited options for managing stress.* Lazarus et al. (1974) distinguish "primary appraisal," or the recognition and interpretation of threat, from "secondary appraisal" in their conceptualization of the cognitive mediation of threat and response. "Secondary appraisal" is the search for a means of mastering threats to one's well-being. For each individual faced with problematic circumstances, the universe of potential strategies for mastering these problems is limited. It is limited, first, by how the threat was interpreted. Just as a newspaper selects and reports only a portion of the events which finally appear as a news story, so do each of us limit our perception of events to those features which are personally salient. Thus we respond to the event-as-perceived rather than to the total stimulus field. Potential strategies for addressing problems are further limited by the predicted cost of an imagined strategy to the person's self-esteem, and by the person's predictions about the effectiveness of the strategy of choice.

Personal predispositions in addition to those mentioned above can limit one's choice of coping strategy, but the environment may also effectively limit options for addressing a problem. One of the SFP respondents wanted to work. She hoped that working, by helping her feel useful, would make her feel more worthwhile as a person. She also wanted to increase her family's income. She found, however, that potential employers would not consider her. They gave as reasons her lack of references, her unsteady work history interrupted by childbirth, and her child care responsibilities which they assumed would conflict with her work. She would have to have already demonstrated her working ability in order to get a job. Another woman, separated from her husband and left with a very low income, articulated the dilemma she faced in attempting to "become (her) own woman":

I thought that working and having my daughter in school was the solution to my problems. But it is not because I don't make enough. The main reason I went back to work was to stimulate myself, to get on my own, and to feel independent. My job is comfortable, but not exciting in any way. If I were making enough money, I could sit back and stay there. So in a way I am glad I'm not. I have no choice but to look at alternatives. The reason I decided to make a decision is because I can't make ends meet on $80 a week. I can't even pay a babysitter. I was as well off not working full-time (while on welfare) but working part-time, if not better. I went to work in the first place because welfare is degrading.

Sometimes the most obvious coping strategy becomes incredibly complicated, full of costs to the respondent which may finally outweigh the benefits which she hopes to achieve. Washing machine repairs involve welfare vouchers for which payment may take many months. Attempts to address children's behavior problems quickly involve the school system, health and mental health services, and social workers, and women must weigh the costs of humiliating intrusions against the likelihood that their child will eventually be helped. Experience with such intrusion has led at least one woman to consider that option closed. Another woman mentioned that she would not seek counseling for her own emotional problems, because she was afraid that her children would be taken away from her.

Options for coping effectively with some problems may simply not be available to a women already hampered by inadequate financial resources and lacking the power, status, language, information, or appropriate advocates to move institutions in her favor. The strategy with which a woman eventually addresses a problem will often be a compromise between what the environment allows and what she wants and is capable of accomplishing, thus her performance may not accurately reflect her ability. When low-income mothers' coping strategies are assessed, the researcher should consider whether or not the optimum strategy would have been possible for the woman to accomplish, given her circumstances.

4. *The environmental response to efforts at mastery.* Low-income mothers constitute a special group in that they depend heavily on public institutions for support and basic services. The environment may affirm or deny a woman's efforts to master stressful circumstances. The SFP respondents provided us with numerous examples of how public institutions, primarily the public welfare system, were unresponsive to their efforts to cope with adverse situations. Attempts to alter situations directly were frequently met with resistance or resulted in little, if any, improvement, with the unfortunate result that women felt they had little control over the forces and policies which determined their lives and the lives of their children.

One respondent discussed the frustration of trying to get appropriate help for her young son who was dyslexic and emotionally disturbed. She tried and failed to get him an early learning abilities evaluation through his school. She also tried and failed to have her son placed in a Big Brother program, in after school day care, and in a special school for the learning-disabled. Because she was not able to obtain the help she needed from these institutions, through no failure of effort or imagination on her part, she felt guilty and inadequate as a mother, and worried that her son's problems, left untreated, would only get worse. When another woman sought psychiatric help for her child, the mental health worker was more concerned about her capacity to mother than about her worry over her son. She did not receive the help she had sought and finally enlisted legal aid to resist the invasion of her privacy which resulted from her efforts.

A third respondent waited six months to get welfare approval of the furniture voucher and assistance with her utilities bills which had been promised to her. During the six-month period, she repeatedly visited the welfare office without receiving any information on her case. Her lawyer finally determined that her caseworker had been laid off several months before. A black woman's three sons were bussed to school in a white community which had recently been the scene of inter-racial violence. Her sons were afraid to go to school and complained that they weren't being taught anything. She tried many times, without success, to transfer them to another school district. Finally, she considered sending them to live, apart from her, in another city where she felt they could go to school without fear. Another woman has had her apartment ruined by leaking water. Public health officials declared the apartment unsafe, but the public housing authority never came to make repairs. She appealed to everyone she could find to listen to her case, even calling in the local media for an exposé. Her suit is now pending in court, while water continues, years later, to leak into her apartment.

In these examples, persistent, energetic, imaginative, and versatile strategies were used in efforts to alter threatening situations. These strategies were ineffective, not because they were deficient, but because the institutions simply would not respond. A study of coping would not be complete without reference to the outcomes of efforts made to master threatening situations. Outcomes must be addressed in terms of the environmental factors which have influenced them, and also in terms of their ultimate effects on the individual. These issues have received little attention since naturalistic observation of these processes has been neglected. The environmental response, however, is an influential factor in the coping process. We have seen that respondents' environments have often sabotaged their efforts to cope. If coping efforts are continually ineffective, regardless of the essential adequacy of the strategies chosen, a woman will perceive herself as ineffectual and incompetent in those spheres. We must wonder to what extent these experiences will generalize to her overall self-esteem. In his conceptualization of the inferiority complex, White (1959) locates its origins in the individual's repeated failure to achieve mastery. Seligman (1975) has shown that persistant ineffectiveness under stressful circumstances results in decreased motivation, or "learned helplessness." One SFD respondent poignantly addressed this issue. Of her repeated unsuccessful efforts to find work she said: "I constantly worry about my own worth. I begin to question my role here on earth."

Conclusion

We have tried to demonstrate the impact of the environment on four points of the coping process, as it is experienced by low-income mothers, and to draw implications from this case material for coping theory. These implications may be summarized as follows: First, environments may differ in the nature and frequency of threats posed to the individual, with deleterious effects on coping ability the result of severe and chronic threat. Second, the context in which threats arise plays an important role in determining how that threat is perceived and experienced; thus, situations of similar content cannot be considered functionally similar for individuals. Third, environments may differ generally in the breadth of options for addressing threatening situations which they allow. What may seem like poor coping strategies are often the result of severely limited options. Finally, the environment responds to a person's strategy, often in ways which negate the coping effort. The environmental response is in turn evaluated by the person in terms of its reflection on her competency. In most cases, the women we have interviewed have very little objective control over the institutional forces in their lives and those affecting the lives of their children. Many low-income mothers would profit from recognition, by those who work closely with them, that much in their circumstances is outside their control. Family workers could be instrumental in helping their clients distinguish situations where control may be effectively exercised from those over which they have little control, so that responsibility would not be assumed without control. Their self-esteem could be supported if their failures to achieve results were not always taken—by themselves and others—as evidence of incompetence and unworthiness.

REFERENCE NOTE

1. Makosky, V. *The correlates of stress.* In Stress and Families Project, *Lives in stress: A context for depression.* Unpublished report, 1980. (Available from Department of Psychology, St. Lawrence University, Canton, NY 13617).

REFERENCES

Bernard, V., Ottenberg, P., & Redl, F. Dehumanization: A composite psychological defense in relation to modern war. In M. Schwebel (Ed.), *Behavioral science and human survival.* Palo Alto: Science and Behavior Books, 1965.

Coates, D., Mayer, S., Kendall, L., & Howat, M. Life-event changes and mental health. In I. G. Sarason & C. D. Spielberger (Eds.), *Stress and anxiety* (Vol. II). Washington, DC: Hemisphere, 1976.

Dohrenwend, B. Social status and stressful life events. *Journal of Personality and Social Psychology,* 1973, **28,** 225-235.

Dohrenwend, B., Krasnoff, L., Askenasy, A., & Dohrenwend, B. Exemplification of a method for scaling life events: The PERI life events scale. *Journal of Health and Social Behavior,* 1978, **19,** 205-229.

Freud, A. *The ego and the mechanisms of defense.* New York: International Universities Press, 1946.

Haan, N. *Coping and defending.* New York: Academic Press, 1977.

Holmes, T., & Rahe, R. The social readjustment rating scale. *Journal of Psychosomatic Research,* 1967, **11,** 213-218.

Lazarus, R., Averill, J., & Opton, E. The psychology of coping: Issues of research and assessment. In G. Coelho, D. Hamburg, & J. Adams (Eds.), *Coping and adaptation.* New York: Basic Books, 1974.

Menninger, K. Regulatory devices of the ego under major stress. *International Journal of Psychoanalysis,* 1954, **35,** 412-420.

Seligman, M. *Helplessness.* San Francisco: W. H. Freeman, 1975.

White, R. Motivation reconsidered: The concept of competence. *Psychological Review,* 1959, **66,** 297-333.

Rural Plant Closures: The Coping Behavior of Filipinos in Hawaii*

The coping behavior of families facing plantation closures is evidenced in their jobseeking, in their dependence on social alliance systems, and in the role changes they experienced within their families. Their behavior was constrained by expectations derived from earlier actions by the plantation companies and by government, as well as sometimes being limited by low levels of education and English-speaking ability.

The loss of a job is obviously stress inducing, particularly when the perceived prospects of finding another source of income are somewhat remote. This can be particularly severe for people living and working in a "company town" when its primary source of employment closes. Not only do people lose their jobs, they must often consider moving elsewhere to find another job. In the process, the entire town may find its continued existence threatened. The "ghost towns" of former mining areas are vivid reminders of the possibilities facing any small community that is economically dependent on one company or on a specialized economic activity.

Coping behavior in these situations involves attempts to foresee opportunities as well as to adjust to new uses of the families' financial, labor, property, and social resources. New jobs, including self-employment, are the obvious solution. Government programs often are built around solving the dilemma in that way, but related programs to assist with any coping efforts beyond the search for new jobs are weak or non-existent.

If the new jobs are not found (or created), then other forms of coping become more prominent. Property and savings may be converted to income to provide economic support in the absence of employment. Other members of the family may take jobs, for even if the worker who was laid off is fortunate enough to find a new job, it is likely to pay less than the previous employment. Such changes in labor force participation bring about pressures for changes in family roles and responsibilities for household tasks. Ultimately, and often only as a last resort, the family may elect to uproot itself from its network of family and friends in order to pursue employment opportunities in another community.

Numerous studies of job displacement (Haber, Ferman, & Hudson, 1963; Owen & Belzung, 1967; Dorsey, 1967) have examined the employment seeking experiences of people following the massive localized unemployment caused by shutdowns of large plants. Findings of such studies generally indicate that: (a) government is usually somewhat inept and ineffective in its efforts to improve localized economic conditions; (b) new industries rarely take up the slack; (c) older workers are likely to take early retirement or part-time employment; (d) the less-educated

*Funds for this study were provided in part through Title V of the Rural Development Act of 1972.

**Robert N. Anderson is Associate Professor of Agricultural and Resource Economics, and Coordinator of the Center for Nonmetropolitan Planning and Development, University of Hawaii, Honolulu, Hawaii, 96822.

(*Family Relations*, 1980, **29**, 511-516.)

and the older workers are less successful in seeking new employment; (e) jobs are typically found through informal social networks rather than through employment services and formal hiring campaigns; (f) the percentage of employed women increases substantially; (g) most families move elsewhere only as a last resort.

The cases of plantation closings observed in Hawaii exhibited characteristics that were virtually identical to the findings just noted, but with some additional aspects that arose from the nature of the nonmetropolitan company towns and the histories of the people involved. This article draws on data of varying types derived from three somewhat separate studies of five rural areas in Hawaii, two of which had lost their sources of primary employment (a sugar plantation, including a processing mill, and a pineapple plantation). Data came from three surveys of families (N = 221, 212, and 48), and particularly from lengthy periods of participant observations. Families of Filipino ethnicity were the focus of study, since, as a group, they were thought to be less equipped to deal with economic setbacks. Their lack of formal education levels, their low levels in understanding English, and their immigrant status were perceived as disadvantages in the labor markets outside the plantation structures.

As a general observation, Filipino families in rural Hawaii were observed to exhibit considerable thought and activitiy in pursuit of the best social and economic options available to them. Even in the face of discouraging news about plantation shutdowns, considerable anticipatory discussion occurred concerning the possibilities of self-employment, job-training, moving to another community, or even preventing the plantation from closing. Even our researchers working in the communities were frequently consulted for new information or assessments of tentative plans. The ultimate behavior and decision processes were complex and interwoven.

Hawaii's Filipinos have traded lives of extreme rural poverty in the Philippines for somewhat better conditions in Hawaii, even though they are often still in poverty in terms of U.S. standards. In the Philippines, work had been without supervision in a wide range of agricultural tasks which could occupy all of a person's waking hours, and which required complex skills inherited from generations of farmers in that region. However, only a low level of subsistence was possible under existing conditions. In contrast, plantation work in Hawaii consisted of closely-supervised, simple, repetitive tasks on a rigidly-designed schedule. Plantation workers who were driven to control their work lives without being supervised, who were innovative, or who were socially abrasive lasted only a short time in the plantation work system.

As a result of this work history, when the workers were displaced from their plantation jobs they seldom were skilled in tasks that other employers found appealing, and they seldom possess the personal initiative and self-assertiveness necessary to become self-employed or even to pursue new employment aggressively. Our interviews with plantation employees indicated they believed that diligence, subservience, and amiability were the important qualities for work success. Conspicuously not mentioned were knowledge, experience, intelligence, and innovativeness.

Job Seeking

Prior to the plantation closings, about three-fourths of the families said they would depend on the government to help them if the plantation shut down. This expectation proved to be somewhat unrealistic, for in cases where layoffs had occurred five years ago or earlier, very few families (12%) had received government assistance beyond small amounts of unemployment compensation, and only very few jobs in the long run were gained from companies receiving special consideration by government in order to take up the economic slack created by the plantations going out of business. As a stopgap measure, programs such as CETA did provide employment for less than one-fifth of the former plantation workers (excluding retirees). Less than 10% of the families expected their union or relatives and friends to be of help. Nevertheless, most new jobs were secured through these sources, and the union proved very instrumental in persuading government to undertake helpful actions.

Some of the workers feared they would have problems in seeking certain types of employment because of arrest and conviction records for gambling or cockfighting. Both activities are not necessarily considered socially undesirable within the plantation community, for a number of well-respected leaders in these towns frequently pursue such activities. However, the mainstream culture outside the plantation communities, whose members control most non-plantation jobs, does not share the same attitudes. A number of our informants (17%) simply lied about their police records when they applied for new employment. None reported that this false information had been discovered, presumably because little or no verification was done by the new employer.

Very few (3%) of the respondents perceived any racial discrimination in their search for employment. If anything, a type of reverse discrimination may still occur, for just as plantation management had preferred Filipinos for employment in the fields, a few employers reportedly are fairly blatant in their preference for hiring Filipinos for certain types of poorly-paid jobs, such as hotel maids or housekeepers.

One of the basic problems faced by the displaced worker is to learn how to behave "appropriately" in an employment interview or in a new work setting. For example, some of the Filipino men recounted that they found themselves somewhat immobilized in the presence of a perceived social superior. Coaching on how to sell one's self to a prospective employer was considered crucial by a number of the former plantation workers who received such assistance through their former union.

Among the major obstacles facing most of the older former plantation workers were a lack of English language ability and low levels of literacy. Past government programs in basic education had usually failed dismally due to the lack of culturally, emotionally, and linguistically compatible instructors. Consequently, the former plantation employees generally had unreceptive attitudes toward any formal training courses that might prepare them for new employment. The respondents in our informal discussions expressed a desire for courses to be taught on a far more personal and informal basis than they had

been led to expect. They also feared that they might be grouped in classes with people who had more advanced skills, thus subjecting them to potential ridicule by their classmates. One such experience was enough reason for many of them to not return to that or subsequent courses. In other words, it seems that many problems could be avoided by a more effective classification and grouping of students for the classes, as well as simply attempting to establish more informal, friendly and personal means of instruction.

Considerable anxiety was experienced by former plantation employees who were "tested" in some way as part of a job application process or who were hired on a probationary status. Although their behavior in the context of testing clearly reflects their perception that success is dependent upon the skills they display, almost all discussion with family and friends about the experience is couched in terms of luck or chance. In this way failure is not shamefully acknowledged as being the result of inferior skills or other personal deficiencies. Equally important, if successful they are also thus able to mitigate the tension and envy that would develop among their less fortunate friends.

In other words, by verbally attributing success or failure to luck rather than personal behavior, stress is somewhat lessened. Such conversations should be recognized as social devices only, for only in a few instances was actual behavior observed to accord with such beliefs. The intensity of effort displayed in job tests and during probationary periods belied any conviction that luck or fate determined personal failure or success. Based on these observations most efforts to persuade a jobseeker to not adopt a fatalistic approach to employment success would be ill-founded, for the jobseeker may have valid reasons for describing his perceptions about employment processes in ways that are substantially different than his actual perceptions.

One of the reasons the families did not feel compelled to move elsewhere in order to find jobs was the expectation that government would prevent their living conditions from dropping below untenable levels.

In the face of being unable to prevent the plantation from closing and lacking confidence in being able to succeed in other employment, they resigned themselves to the possibility of government assistance:

> "This is where Hawaii is very much ahead of the Philippines. Here, the government won't let you down. When you are poor, there is the welfare program to turn to."

> "When you no get job, you can get unemployment compensation. When you retire, you get Social Security. Good life over here."

> "Why should we have compunctions about going on welfare? The hippies do it, the Hawaiians do it, so we do it too."

Social Alliance Systems

Various studies (Stout, Morrow, Brandt, & Wolf, 1964; Gore, 1973) have shown that small town closeness and ethnic homogeneity are important conditions that mitigate the stressful effects of various crises. In particular, social networks have been demonstrated to be important resources in coping with stress-inducing dilemmas (Tolsdorf, 1976; Liem & Liem, 1978; Gore, 1978).

The older male immigrants observed were not highly assimilated into U.S. mainstream culture. Their exposure to mass media has been negligible, for their English language ability is very limited. For example, almost all of the men over age 60 were unaware of Nixon's resignation. They seldom have maintained viable personal relationships with people in the Philippines. Consequently, their social networks and continued interactions with the outside world (via intermediaries) were heavily dependent upon the maintenance of the rural communities where they have lived for decades.

Following the Immigration Act of 1965, the rapid influx of women from the Philippines led to a resurgence of a number of community celebrations similar to those held in the rural Philippines. The facilities and much of the operational expenses were provided by the plantation companies. The closing of the plantations and the consequent general gloom that settled over the communities were sufficient obstacles to prevent the continuation of such celebrations. These celebrations were not only enjoyable recreation, but they were important devices to build community identity and social support systems.

The Filipinos observed in this study who were experiencing economic stress have been able to rely upon an intricate network of powerful alliances and mutual assistance that is far too complex to describe in detail here. Basically, there is a recognized commitment to a concept of mutual obligations, often being formalized through ceremonies, although not specified in detail (Lebra, 1975). The system has worked fairly well, but its success depends upon the continued economic health and integrity of the community. If the families move elsewhere, they lose most of the benefits of the system, and if economic distress is widespread throughout the community, the system is not of much help.

As the families have dealt with plantation shutdowns, the usefulness of the alliance system has differed markedly in the various communities. In communities in which the plantation company "persuaded" people to move elsewhere, the system essentially collapsed. In communities in which the residents were able to retain control of the homes and community facilities, the alliance system continued to be an effective vehicle for rallying the community around strong negotiating positions that have led to greater concessions by the government and plantation management.

The alliance system can thus be a source of support in the face of plantation shutdowns, although it does curb somewhat a family's mobility to move elsewhere. As an example of the latter, the union was sent back to the negotiating table after it had won concessions of re-employment in plantations elsewhere in the state. The workers were interested in higher severance pay rather than equivalent jobs in other communities. Quite simply, they were reluctant to abandon, among other things, their carefully nurtured social capital that was coexistent with the community's viability.

Role Changes

In one community that experienced a plantation shutdown, survey results seven years later showed that about one-third of the wives of the former plantation workers stated they had entered the labor force after the shutdown to counter the income losses resulting from the unemployment or lower wages received by their husbands after their job loss. About 40% of the wives in the community had already taken non-plantation employment before the news of the plantation's impending closing, so the phenomena of "working wives" was not new to the community. However, it was new to some families, and it was particularly viewed as a mixed blessing in the cases in which the husband was unsuccessful in finding employment.

As male workers were laid off, the dynamics of marital role definition, when added to other pressures, often led to considerable stress within the families. This was particularly the case in the families in which the husband was considerably older than the wife. (Comparable data from communities not experiencing employment problems unfortunately were not gathered.)

"May-December" marriages (i.e., at least 15 years age difference between the spouses) were fairly common in the households studied. These age discrepancies resulted directly from U.S. immigration restrictions, which from 1946 until 1965 effectively prevented women from coming to Hawaii from the Philippines. By then, the men who had immigrated were often past age 50. The women they found most appealing and who were most willing to come to Hawaii were often under age 30. Age is usually not the only discrepancy in such marriages, for these younger women are usually far better educated and more capable of dealing with the mainstream culture of Hawaii. Thus, they come into the marriage with considerable strength and capacity to dominate many of the household decisions. Accustomed to household chores from long years of bachelorhood, the men are usually amenable to performing tasks that would be resisted by other men in the same culture.

Despite this situation of mild role-reversal already occurring prior to the plantation shutdown, the loss of breadwinner status by the husband was seen as a significant disturbance to their recognized family roles. Many (43%) of the husbands in the "May-December" marriages adamantly resisted the idea of their wives seeking employment, even though they may not earlier have opposed the idea when

their roles as breadwinners were considered secure. Such opposition was not nearly as apparent (6%) in families in which the husbands were younger and better educated.

In other words, the resistance of the older men was not simply a matter of having more traditional cultural beliefs or somehow being more resistant to women's "liberation"; they felt more threatened because the basis of strength for their family role typically was far more eroded already than was the case in marriages in which the spouses were more nearly equal in age and education.

The women in the "May-December" marriages also expressed concern about this erosion of their husbands' family role, although they often felt economically compelled to seek employment. They were particularly concerned that their children would become disrespectful to their unemployed fathers, and were often times observed to require their children to seek their father's permission for various activities, which generally was not the case prior to the layoffs. The wives also were observed reminding the children, as a means of preserving the husband's breadwinner status, of the long years of toil by the husband for the family's welfare.

In a very few cases, the role denigration experienced by the husbands was so acute that they virtually abandoned all status and power in the household. They would refuse to discipline their children or to participate in any family-oriented events in the community. Their social activities became limited to gambling and drinking with male friends. The wives had no choice but to take completely dominating roles in the household. However, such cases were less than 10% of the "May-December" marriages.

Conclusion

The limited observations of the studies reported in this paper suggest that families may have unrealistic expectations concerning the experiences they face when the community's major source of employment threatens to close. New jobs may indeed become available, and the plant may not close after all. Job-seeking behavior can be enhanced by formal counseling, but the most frequent useful sources of information concerning job availability appear to be an informal network of friends and relatives. While this social network system can be an important resource in dealing with the problems of unemployment, the families were somewhat constrained in their search for employment by their reluctance to move elsewhere, which would mean abandoning much of their social alliance system.

The economic stresses experienced by families in which the male parental role was already somewhat eroded led to an even greater deterioration of their culturally-prescribed status. This occurred in spite of deliberate efforts by the families to prevent such an undesired change.

Government programs in job-training were weak because of cultural insensitivity, but government efforts to provide interim employment directly were useful. Unemployment compensation and other transfer payments were also helpful, but only on an interim basis.

Family counseling in the situations described in this paper must not only be based upon a realistic anticipation of future employment possibilities in the area, but an understanding of the socio-cultural aspects of family behavior is also vital. Perceptions derived solely from mainstream cultures or, even worse, from naive ideas such as fatalism can only lead to inappropriate strategies and responses.

REFERENCES

Booth, A. Does wives' employment cause stress for husbands? *The Family Coordinator*, 1979, **28**, 445-449.

Brinkerhoff, D., & White, L. Marital satisfaction in an economically marginal population. *Journal of Marriage and the Family*, 1978, **40**, 259-267.

Dorsey, J. The Mack case: A study in unemployment. In O. Eckstein (Ed.), *Studies in the economics of income maintenance*. Washington, DC: The Brookings Institution, 1967.

Gore, S. The effect of social support in moderating the health consequences of unemployment. *Journal of Health and Social Behavior*, 1978, **19**, 157-165.

Gore, S. *The influence of social support and related variables in ameliorating the consequences of job loss*. Unpublished doctoral dissertation, University of Pennsylvania, 1973.

Haber, W., Ferman, L., & Hudson, J. *The impact of technological change*. Kalamazoo, MI: W. E. Upjohn Institute for Employment Research, 1963.

Lebra, T. An alternative to reciprocity. *American Anthropologist*, 1975, **77**, 550-565.

Liem, R., & Liem, J. Social class and mental illness reconsidered: The role of economic stress and social support. *Journal of Health and Social Behavior*, 1978, **19**, 139-156.

Owen, J., & Belzung, L. An epilogue to job displacement: A case study of structural unemployment. *The Southern Economic Journal*, 1967, **33**, 395-408.

Stout, C., Morrow, J., Brandt, N., & Wolf, S. Unusually low incidence of death from myocardial infarction. *Journal of the American Medical Association*, 1964, **188**, 845-855.

Tolsdorf, C. Social networks, support, and coping: An exploratory study. *Family Process*, 1976, **15**, 407-417.

Unemployment and Family Stress: A Reassessment*

L. EUGENE THOMAS, ESTHER MCCABE, AND
JANE E. BERRY**

Past research, particularly that dating from the Depression of the 1930s, suggests that unemployment tends to precipitate crises for many families. Two small-scale studies are reported in which it was found that unemployed managers and professionals did not report strain on family relationships. A review of other studies conducted in the present decade indicate that for a majority of families, including white- and blue-collar workers, crisis does not accompany husbands' unemployment. Three causes for the apparent changes the impact of unemployment has upon families are discussed: improved financial support for the unemployed; erosion of the psychological importance of work; and changing sex roles.

It has come to be held more or less axiomatic among social scientists that unemployment tends to have a severe negative impact upon individuals, resulting in family stress and disorganization (e.g., Moen, 1979). Studies dating from the Depression of the 1930s indicate that unemployment can have a devastating effect upon men, leading to lowered morale, depression, anxiety, and other negative emotional states (cf. Eisenberg & Lazarsfeld, 1938, for a summary of the literature from that period). Subsequent research (Braginsky & Braginsky, 1975; Leventman, 1976; Powell & Driscoll, 1973) has tended to replicate these earlier findings, and further,

significant psychosomatic disabilities have been found to be connected with unemployment (Karl & Cobb, 1970). In an intensive study of the closing of one plant, for example, Slote (1977) found that over half of the displaced workers suffered from psychosomatic symptoms, including ulcers, arthritis, serious hypertension, and alcoholism.

Given these individual effects of unemployment, it is not surprising to find that unemployment often has a negative impact upon families. Cavan (1959), in a review of the family literature from the Depression and later, noted that unemployment often led to disorganization and rearrangement of roles within the family. Studies from that period indicated that fathers tended to lose authority over wives and children, especially if the wife took a job (Stouffer & Lazarsfeld, 1937). Ginzberg (1971) noted that the failure of men to bring home a paycheck led to disturbed sexual relationships as well. He quoted one woman who asserted, "F.D.R. wears the pants in this family—he gives us our money" (p. 231). Concerning the long-term effect of unemployment, Ginzberg observed, "We found . . . disorganization in the lives of adults and children which resulted when work was no longer

*Research reported in this study was supported by a grant from the University of Connecticut Research Foundation. The authors wish to acknowledge the assistance of Moira Birmingham in collecting and analysing the data.

**L. Eugene Thomas is Associate Professor, Human Development and Family, the University of Connecticut, Storrs, CT 06268. Esther McCabe is Associate Professor, Design and Resource Management, the University of Connecticut. Jane Berry is Assistant Professor in Residence, Design and Resource Management, the University of Connecticut.

(*Family Relations*, 1980, **29**, 517-524.)

the fulcrum around which his life and the members of his family was organized." He further noted, "There were early developmental disturbances in children growing up in households where the father did not work" (pp. 230-231).

With this research in mind, it was expected that a similar degree of disruption and stress would be found when a study of managers and professionals who had changed careers in mid-life was undertaken. Little evidence of family disruption was found, however, and most of the respondents (72%) indicated that the change had been good for their families (Thomas, 1980). This was especially interesting in view of the fact that many of the men in changing careers had moved to lower status jobs with less pay.

One major difference between current mid-life career changers and unemployed workers studied during the Depression is that contemporary mid-career changers typically chose to make the change in jobs (Thomas, 1977), whereas unemployment during the Depression was involuntary. In order to replicate the earlier research more closely we decided to conduct another study in which men who were involuntarily unemployed would be examined. The findings from this study will be reported first, and then other research on the impact of unemployment upon families in the decade of the 1970s will be examined.

Divergent Evidence

As with the study of mid-life career changers, men were sampled who were middle-aged (35-54) and had, before their period of unemployment, held professional or managerial positions (*Dictionary of Occupational Titles* categories 0 and 1). Questionnaires were distributed by employment counselors at eight state employment offices in an industrialized New England state. A total of 90 questionnaires were returned, representing 31% of those distributed.

Respondents reported a high level of educational preparation: all had completed high school, 65% had completed college, and 27% had earned graduate degrees. The high SES level of the sample was further indicated by the fact that prior to their unemployment two-thirds reported having had family income

over $25,000, and a third were in excess of $30,000. This level of education and income is not surprising, however, when it is remembered that these men had held either middle- or upper-middle level management positions (52%), had been engineers (20%), or were in teaching or the helping professions.

Respondents, who had been unemployed from a month to over a year, reported dramatic drops in income following their job loss. Almost half (46%) reported current family income of less than $7,000 a year, and an additional 29% had incomes between $7,000 and $16,000. Despite the dramatic drop in income, only 3% reported having to rely on food stamps; only 4% had been forced to sell property for current income; and only 7% reported receiving significant financial help from family or friends. In sum, these families had suffered significant drops in income as a result of unemployment, but most were able to live on their reduced family income without financial sacrifice or severe loss of status.

We were especially interested in learning how these events had affected family relationships. In particular, we wanted to know if the loss of earning power had led to a loss of status for the husband. If there had been a loss of status, we would expect respondents to report a deterioration of relationships with wives and children, since this was often the observed pattern reported for the unemployed and their families in earlier studies.

Only in about a third of the cases (37%) did respondents report a negative effect in their relationships with their wives (Respondents were asked, "How has your being unemployed affected your relationship with your spouse?"). Almost half (48%) reported no change at all, and 15% reported that their relations with their wives had actually improved since their job loss. Even less negative impact was reported for relationships with children (using an open-ended question similar to that used for spouse, "How has your being unemployed affected your relationship with your children?"). While 17% reported some negative effect, over half (53%) indicated that there had been no change in relations with their children, and 11% stated that there had been an actual improvement since they became unemployed. Moreover,

78% of the respondents indicated that they had received adequate emotional support since losing their job. Interestingly, when families experiencing the greatest loss of income were compared with those having least loss (using a median split), no significant differences were found on any of the measures of family relationships.

When we completed analyzing the data we were faced with a dilemma in interpreting our findings. Our first inclination was to conclude that respondents simply were lying about their relationships with their families; or, that our respondents represented a self-selected minority of those for whom unemployment had not been stressful, while the majority of non-responders may have experienced greater family stress. Alternately, if some credence is given to the findings from this small-scale study, it could be that unemployment does not affect middle-class professionals as severely as it does blue-collar workers (on whom most previous research has been conducted). Or finally, it might be that the impact of unemployment upon families is not as severe today as it was during the Depression of the 1930s.

Somewhat perplexed by our data, and unable to decide among the alternative interpretations, we presented a preliminary report of our findings at the National Council on Family Relations annual meeting in New York (McCabe, Thomas, Birmingham, & Berry, Note 1). Since that time other researchers have begun to report data similar to what we found. We will briefly present the findings from several of these studies, and then consider factors which may account for a different level of family impact which unemployment may have today.

Further Divergent Research

Although recent research on the impact of unemployment upon families has been sporadic and isolated, several studies have emerged which agree in essence with the findings from our research. Powell and Driscoll (1973), in a study of unemployed professionals quite similar to our sample, found that at one stage in adjusting to unemployment (the third stage, a time of vascillation and doubt) family relationships were strained, but during the other stages relationships with family members did not suffer. In their sample only 20% of the men were in the stage of vascillation and doubt, with the majority (52%) having moved beyond to a stage of personal malaise and cynicism. Although this final stage involved personal discomfort for the respondents, relations between husbands and wives were found to have improved markedly from that of the third period. Interestingly, it was found that in families where sex roles were strictly defined, the most severe marital difficulties developed. During the final stage of adjustment, roles began to shift to less sex role distinction, and it was at this time that husband-wife relations showed marked improvement.

Other research suggests that unemployment in the 1970s has not proved to be as disruptive for blue-collar workers either. Root and Mayland (Note 2) conducted a series of longitudinal interviews with workers and their wives following the closing of a packing plant, in order to determine the impact upon individuals and families. Most of the workers lost a significant proportion of their family income as a result of the closing, with the period of their unemployment varying from less than a month to over a year. When asked what effect the closing had had on their families, most (40%) indicated that it had been generally good, and an additional 27% reported that its effect had been neutral or both good and bad. Less than a third of their respondents (30%) reported that there had been only a negative effect on their family. Length of unemployment was not found to be significantly associated with whether respondents viewed the closing as generally good or bad for their families. In fact, those who had been unemployed over a year had a higher percentage (50%) who rated the effect as generally good, than did those unemployed for a shorter time (27% unemployed less than one month, and 36% of those unemployed one month to a year, reported a positive effect).

At the time of the final interview, couples were asked the following questions, in seeking to relate their experience to research from the 1930s:

Many years ago—during the Depression— studies of long-term unemployed men sug-

gested that the husband lost respect because he was unemployed. This was reflected in increasing marital conflicts, blaming the husband for unemployment, constant nagging, sharp criticism in front of the children, and so on. How is it with you folks, do either of you believe the husband has lost respect since the plant closing? (Root & Mayland, Note 2, p. 13)

Root and Mayland found that in only four instances was there a positive response to this question, while 62 workers and their spouses, representing 94% of the respondents, said no.

These studies, plus data presented in this paper, suggest that unemployment may not be as disruptive of family relationships at the present time as it proved to be in earlier decades. We will, therefore, turn to a discussion of the factors which might best account for this difference, and then examine the implications this might have for anticipating the impact of unemployment and underemployment upon families in the future.

Discussion

There have been countless changes in the social and economic conditions since the 1930s, many of which could affect the impact of unemployment upon families. The following three factors appear most important for understanding changes in the effect of unemployment on family relationships:

Changed Economic Conditions

Of the factors which could mitigate the impact of unemployment on family functioning, the most obvious is change in the financial status of the unemployed. During the Depression there was very little financial support available to persons who lost their jobs, short of going on relief, and even this wasn't available until families had exhausted all their financial resources. Most families did everything in their power to avoid the loss of status accompanying reduction to the poverty level, since the receipt of relief was looked upon as incurring a dread social stigma (Ginzberg, 1942). The absence of unemployment compensation and other financial cushions meant that loss of a job often brought economic deprivation (Komarovsky, 1940), with the attendant disruption of family relationships.

In contrast, the unemployed in recent years have had a number of financial support systems to fall back upon, including severance pay, unemployment compensation, food stamps, medicare, and ADC, as well as employment opportunities for spouses. As a result, few unemployed families today suffer the level of financial deprivation which was common even a few decades ago. Estes and Wilensky (1978) found that over half of their sample of unemployed professionals in the early 1970s reported experiencing no heavy financial stress, a percentage similar to that reported by Little (1976) with another sample of unemployed professionals. Not surprisingly, the longer the men were unemployed, the higher percentage had working wives (Little, 1976), with 69% of those unemployed eight months or longer reporting that their wives were employed. In a time of general economic dislocation, as in the Depression of the 1930s, that would not have been possible, of course.

Unemployed professionals would be expected to have greater resources to survive the loss of the major wage earner's salary than would blue-collar or even skilled workers. But in their study of blue-collar workers who lost their jobs when their plant closed, Root and Mayland (Note 2) found that although families experienced appreciable drop in annual family income (the modal group lost $4,000), few families were reduced to the poverty level, and the average income for families after the plant closing was still over $10,000. Here, too, wives provided considerable help to families, with two-thirds of the families reporting that wives were working after the plant closed (compared to only one-third prior to husband's unemployment).

This is not to suggest that unemployment no longer can cause financial distress for families. But for the majority of the population today, society has provided a financial floor beneath which they are not allowed to sink, thereby removing the threat of severe financial deprivation which was the common lot of families of the unemployed in earlier days.

Change in the Psychological Importance of Work

In addition to changed economic conditions which tend to lessen the impact of unemployment, there are indications that the place which work holds in the lives of individuals has also begun to change. Traditional psychological theory has considered work as providing a central stabilizing force in life, "binding the individual more closely to reality" (Freud, 1930, p. 36). Erikson (1963) suggested that work plays a central place in helping develop one's sense of personal identity, and Henry (1971) has argued that work serves as the major socializing force in adult life, playing a crucial role in the psychological space of the individual. Thus, it was not surprising that men suffered psychological pain and often deterioration when they lost their jobs (Sofer, 1970). As one writer, reflecting on interviews with the unemployed during the Depression, observed, "Emotionally, the nearest counterpart to this experience is the loss of love the child suffers from a rejecting mother, especially a child who 'has not done anything' to deserve it" (Ginzberg, 1942, p. 442).

There are indications that the psychological centrality of work, what has been termed the Protestant Ethic, has eroded significantly in recent years (Ginzberg, 1971). As a result, personal identity appears to be less centrally focused on one's work life. It is hard to provide firm evidence for this, but a number of indicators point in this direction. The increasing popularity of the notion of mid-life career change suggests this, along with the increasing importance of leisure in life style. For instance, a journalist quoted a Washington woman visiting Los Angeles as observing, "When I meet someone at a Washington party, within 10 minutes I know whether he's on the Hill or at State. Here, I know whether he's a skier or a sailor" (Morgan, 1976, p. 64). The journalist notes in passing that California tends to be a "preview state": things tend to happen there first.

Among professionals and managers, for whom it has been suggested that personal identity and work are most closely entwined, there is evidence that loss of job in recent years has not proven as psychologically devastating as traditional psychological theory would lead one to expect. Little (1976) found that half of his respondents had positive feelings about their job loss, saying that it gave them time for other interests, a stimulus for change, or (comprising the largest number) an opportunity to make a change they had thought about making anyway.

Similar responses were given by laid-off, blue-collar workers studied by Root and Mayland (Note 2). Of those who felt the plant closing was good for their families (some two-fifths of the sample), the most common observation was that it offered an opportunity. As one man put it, "I had always wanted to get out of Armour, to try something else— the closing allowed me to do that" (p. 7). It is significant that Estes and Wilensky (1978) found that for over half of their respondents (58%), morale of unemployed professionals was not significantly different from that of their counterparts who were continuously employed. Only those unemployed who experienced severe financial hardship were found to be lower in morale.

Part of this psychological invulnerability to unemployment may be due to the fact that unlike the Depression era, individuals do not blame themselves for their job loss. Research on unemployed professionals (Little, 1976; Estes & Wilensky, 1978), as well as blue-collar workers (Root & Mayland, Note 2), bears this out. Little (1976) suggests that the unemployed role has become a socially accepted one today, whereby the individual is not held responsible for his inability to perform. "Like the sick role," Little observes, "the unemployed role may be a welcome haven from everyday obligations, with the added bonus that, when unemployed, one does not have to stay in bed" (p. 265).

This is not to argue that unemployment is psychologically painless for everyone. Powell and Driscoll (1973) and others (Braginsky & Braginsky, 1975; Leventman, 1976) have found that continued unemployment can still lead to depression and cynicism. But even in those cases where the individual suffers psychological distress, there are indications that this does not necessarily result in disturbed family relations. In our sample of unemployed professionals and managers we found that although the majority said that their job loss had had either no effect, or had actually improved their family relationships, a majority (59%) indicated that being unemployed had had a negative effect on them personally, and most of the remainder (37%) said that the experience had had at least some negative impact.

In reconciling these findings, it is possible that we have been too ready to expect that personal dissatisfaction leads inevitably to family dissatisfaction. The decreasing centrality of the work role appears to have allowed men to separate the professional and personal lives such that dissatisfaction in one does not necessarily spill over into the other. Powell and Driscoll (1973) found that during the final stage of adaptation to unemployment, although individuals became cynical and resigned, relations with their wives actually improved. Further support for the independence of family satisfaction from the career realm came from a study by Oliver (1978) of career changers, satisfied non-changers, and dissatisfied non-changers. For all three groups little connection between career satisfaction and life satisfaction was evident: 92 of the 94 men in his sample (98%) saw career and life satisfaction as two distinctly separate entities. In view of the fact that these men closely associated life satisfaction with the status of their family relationships, it would follow that dissatisfaction with career does not necessarily lead to family discord.

Change in Sex Roles

One final factor which may tend to lessen the impact of unemployment upon families is the movement toward equality of the sexes and a diminishing of sex role stereotyping. Evidence from the Depression (Cavan, 1959), as well as the present decade (Powell & Driscoll, 1973) indicates that those families in which sex roles are more rigidly defined experience the greatest difficulty when the husband is unemployed. Powell and Driscoll further found that in the final stage of adjustment to unemployment, when roles began to be shared more equally, relations between husbands and wives became markedly better.

The cause for the relationship between sex-role stereotyping and family discord is not hard to guess. A husband who is able to help with housework without feeling a loss of masculinity would be able to feel that he was still useful to the family, despite his unemployment. Conversely, Powell and Driscoll (1973) found that families in which the husband refused to help with housework, although he was around the house all day, were most likely to experience strained husband-wife relationships. Further, a husband whose masculinity is not threatened by deviations from strict sex-role stereotypes would be more likely to encourage his wife to seek employment, and thereby reduce the financial stress to which his family was subjected.

There are indications that men are increasingly accepting of their wives' occupational achievement. Richardson (1979) found that, contrary to much social science theory and popular speculation, wives holding superior occupational positions to those of their husbands did not have less satisfactory marriages. In an analysis of cumulative NORC data from 1972-1977 he found that those families in which wives held higher status jobs (20% of the families in which both spouses worked) marital satisfaction was no lower than those families in which occupational status was equal (52%) or husbands' status higher (28%). There was a tendency for older couples to report lower marital satisfaction when the wife held a higher prestige job than for younger couples, suggesting a secular change is taking place.

Conclusion and Implications

Findings from a small-scale study of unemployed managers and professionals indicated that although these men experienced some personal distress from their unemployment, the majority reported that their family relationships had not been adversely affected. The limitations of this study, both a small response rate, and the problem of less than candid response to sensitive self-report questions, made us hesitant to make any generalization claims for our study. Subsequent research, utilizing differing populations and research methods, has begun to accumulate which replicates the findings from our sample. Although hardly definitive, these findings suggest that unemployment may now be less disruptive to family functioning than it was in earlier decades.

Three trends were identified which may be responsible for this change: (a) improved financial provision for the unemployed, such that families are not brought to financial ruin when the major wage earner becomes unemployed; (b) changes in the psychological importance of work, whereby individuals appear to be less threatened by loss of job, viewing it as less their own responsibility, and not the source of their total identity; and (c) changes in sex role stereotyping, such that unemployment and a working wife is not so great a threat to the husband's self-esteem, and families are consequently able to adapt to changes brought on by unemployment.

Of these trends, it would appear that all three have sufficient momentum that they are not likely to be reversed in the near future. It seems that our society has, indeed, moved into a new era in which the place of work is being radically re-defined (Ginzberg, 1971). Changes in financial support and re-defined sex roles may be two consequences of this emerging post-industrial society, making it possible for individuals and families to adjust to the dislocations and radical changes inherent in modern social structure.

It is well to remember, however, that severe economic conditions might reverse these trends. The financial stress of the Depression led to increased sex-role differentiation, which persisted beyond the period of economic stress (Elder, 1974). If the country should enter another period of severe economic depression like that of the 1930s, and political and economic pressure should lead to removal of the programs which provide an economic safety net for unemployed families, there is no guarantee that the observed trends will continue. It is possible that families of the unemployed will again suffer the stress and disruption which was experienced in the Depression of the 1930s.

In sum, the relationship between unemployment and family functioning is the result of dynamic social and economic forces which are subject to further change. Those whose professional concern is for the health and well being of families should be aware of the potential for such change, and should be ready to point out the consequence of policies which threaten to lead to a repetition of the trauma that unemployed families experienced during the Depression of the 1930s.

REFERENCE NOTES

1. McCabe, E., Thomas, L. E., Birmingham, M. T., & Berry, J. E. *Mid-career unemployment and the family.* Paper presented at the annual meeting of the National Council on Family Relations, New York, 1976.
2. Root, K. A., & Mayland, R. L. *The plant's closing, what are we going to do?: Worker and family response to job displacement.* Paper presented at the annual meeting of the National Council on Family Relations, Philadelphia, 1978.

REFERENCES

Braginsky, D. D., & Braginsky, B. M. Surplus people: Their lost faith in self and system. *Psychology Today*, 1975, **9**, 69-72.
Cavan, R. S. Unemployment—Crisis of the common man! *Marriage and Family Living*, 1959, **21**, 139-146.
Elder, G. H., Jr. *Children of the great depression.* Chicago: University of Chicago Press, 1974.
Eisenberg, P., & Lazarsfeld, P. F. The psychological effects of unemployment. *Psychological Bulletin*, 1938, **35**, 358-391.
Erikson, E. H. *Childhood and society*, 2nd Ed., 1963, New York: W. W. Norton, 1963.
Estes, R. J., & Wilensky, H. L. Life cycle squeeze and the morale curve. *Social Problems*, 1978, **25**, 277-292.
Freud, S. *Civilization and its discontents.* London: Hogarth Press, 1930.
Ginzberg, E. Work: The eye of the hurricane. *Humanities*, 1971, **7**, 227-242.
Ginzberg, S. W. What unemployment does to people. *American Journal of Psychiatry*, 1942, **99**, 429-446.
Henry, W. E. The role of work in structuring the life cycle. *Human Development*, 1971, **7**, 125-131.
Karl, S. V., & Cobb, S. Blood pressure changes in men undergoing job loss: A preliminary report. *Psychosomatic Medicine*, 1970, **32**, 19-38.

Komarovsky, M. *The unemployed man and his family*. New York: Dryden Press, 1940.

Leventman, P. G. Nonrational foundations of professional rationality: Employment instability among scientists and technologists. *Sociological Symposium*, 1976, **16**, 83-112.

Little, C. B. Technical-professional unemployment: Middle-class adaptability to personal crisis. *The Sociological Quarterly*, 1976, **17**, 262-275.

Moen, P. Family impacts of the 1975 recession: Duration of unemployment. *Journal of Marriage and the Family*, 1979, **41**, 561-572.

Morgan, T. The good life: Along the San Andreas Fault. *New York Times Magazine*, July 4, 1976, 17-21, 59-76.

Oliver, R. *Midlife unrest, midcareer unrest, and second careers among executive and professional males*. Unpublished doctoral dissertation, California School of Professional Psychology, Los Angeles, 1978.

Powell, D. H., & Driscoll, P. F. Middleclass professionals face unemployment. *Society*, 1973, **10**, 18-26.

Richardson, J. G. Wife occupational superiority and marital troubles: An examination of the hypothesis. *Journal of Marriage and the Family*, 1979, **41**, 63-72.

Slote, A. *Termination: The closing at Baker plant*. Ann Arbor: Survey Research Center, 1977.

Sofer, C. *Men in mid-career: A study of British managers and technical specialists*. Cambridge: University Press, 1970.

Stouffer, S. A. & Lazarsfeld, P. F. *Research memorandum on the family in the Depression*. New York: Social Science Research Council, 1937.

Thomas, L. E. A typology of mid-life career changers. *Journal of Vocational Behavior*, 1980, **16**, 173-182.

Thomas, L. E. Mid-career change: Self-selected or externally mandated? *The Vocational Guidance Quarterly*, 1977, **25**, 320-328.

Managerial Behavior and Stress in Families Headed by Divorced Women: A Proposed Framework*

CHERYL A. BUEHLER AND M. JANICE HOGAN**

Female-headed families are vulnerable to high levels of stress following divorce. A framework is proposed which conceptually links economic stressors and family management patterns. Ecosystem and management perspectives are offered as an integrated framework. Implications given for public policy and educational programming aimed at stress reduction and improved management in families headed by divorced women are based on this framework.

Although managerial behavior is not specifically addressed in the divorce literature, several scholars recognize the need for adjustments to the change in resources that result from a change in family structure (Spanier & Lachman, Note 1; Ross & Sawhill, 1975; Brandwein, Brown, & Fox, 1974). Family management, defined as goal-directed behavior using decision-making, valuing, planning, and organizing processes to guide resource use, is offered as one approach for guiding families toward successful adjustment following divorce.

An ecosystem approach is proposed to study the relationship between stress and single-parent family management behavior. From this perspective, factors within the family system—members' roles, their resource base, values, standards and goals—are linked interdependently. A change in one part of the system, such as the wife-mother taking primary responsibility for family economic support, will produce a change in all other parts of the system, given enough time for the process to transmit signals, and enough magnitude for the change to transmit itself through the linkage network. How does the family reorganize routine and nonroutine task performance such as day-to-day child care and income tax preparation? What input does the ex-spouse, extended family, friends or others in the environment provide to the system? How do female-headed families adjust their expenditure patterns to accommodate diminished financial resources? If they increase their market work time, how do they adjust their family system time? Which standards and goals are adjusted as system resources are changed?

The ecosystem approach emphasizes the linkage between the environment and the family system (Paolucci, Hall & Axinn, 1977). Social environmental systems, such as the labor market, the courts, the non-custodial parent, and the kin network, interface with the single-parent family system. Stress is created when environmental demands and supplies place constraining influences on the family. Using an ecosystem-managerial framework emphasizes the dynamic *process* of family functioning and underscores the interdependence among numerous stress factors.

*Support for this project is from the Minnesota Agricultural Experiment Station.

**Cheryl Buehler is a teaching and research assistant and Janice Hogan is an Associate Professor in the Department of Family Social Science, University of Minnesota, St. Paul, MN 55108.

(*Family Relations*, 1980, **29**, 525-532.)

Family Economic Stressors and Divorce

While female-headed families comprise 15% of the population, they account for 49% of all of the families in poverty (Epenshade, 1979). Stressors that help account for their economic status are downward economic mobility, changes in the source of income, and adjustments in the standard of living. These economic changes may increase the family's vulnerability to the initial stressor event, and over time, reduce the family's regenerative power.[1] According to Schlesinger (1973), the financial need of one-parent families is their greatest problem. The 1976 median income of female-headed families was about one-half of husband-wife families: $8,554 for female-headed families compared with $17,022 for husband-wife families (U.S. Bureau of Census, 1977). When parents divorce, the family loses an adult wage earner (most likely the primary earner), and also experiences the loss of economies of scale. This means that two households are now being maintained, which is more costly per family member than maintaining one household.

A large number of previously nonpoor wives and children suffer downward economic mobility following divorce (Brandwein, et al., 1974; Duncan, 1975). Explanations given for this change include economic discrimination against women, conflicts between labor market and home responsibilities, and a reluctance of both ex-husbands and outside agencies to help the female head. Lowered income may mean a drop in the consumption level, often including a change to poorer housing accommodations in a lower socio-economic neighborhood.

For many families, changes in net worth contribute to downward economic mobility. Net worth, a measure of assets and liabilities, is a function of the property settlement and the family financial status prior to the divorce. Assets may include cash, home ownership,

and insurance policies; liabilities include the home mortgage, insurance premiums, and consumer credit obligations. Hampton (1975) found that the assets of savings and home ownership are good indicators of family economic well-being. He reported that more ex-wives (39.7%) than ex-husbands (30.7%) owned their own homes. This is because more wives receive custody of the children and are consequently awarded the family home in the property settlement.

Caution may be necessary when either net worth or money income are used as sole indicators of economic well-being. Net worth provides little information about the flow of income. Because of generally low incomes of single-parent families, a small cash flow imposes a serious economic constraint on the management ability of the divorced mother, regardless of actual net worth. On the other hand, with a higher asset level, she may have more time and flexibility when seeking employment. Therefore, net worth and average monthly cash flow are both important management variables.

Families headed by younger mothers are more likely to be living in poverty. Mothers under 25 with children under six had a poverty rate of 82.7% (U.S. Bureau of Census, 1977). Each additional child diminishes the woman's prospects for economic security through employment because of the changed ratio of expenses to income. Thus, the more young children in a family, the greater the demands and complexity of family management. Potentially, additional members add human resources but this benefit is offset by the increased dollar cost of child rearing and the need to meet multiple standards and goals. According to Melson (1980), the organizational demands and tensions of family life are likely to increase with the size of the family group.

On the other hand, children may contribute their human resources to assist in reaching family goals. As they get older they are better able to help with household tasks and care of younger siblings. Glasser and Navarre (1965) found that one way mothers handled role overload was to have children help with household tasks and chores. This served as a continuous resource for the family, motivating change in the role descriptions. Also children

---

[1]Burr (1973) defines *vulnerability* to stress as variation in a family's ability to prevent a stressor event or change in the family system from creating some crisis or disruptiveness in the system. *Regenerative power* is the variation in the ability of the family to recover from a crisis. We refer to this variable as the family's *reorganizational ability*.

may assist in improved management by serving as a motivating force for setting new goals.

From an ecosystem perspective, falling and rising levels of resources (monetary and human), affect the family's ability to transact with the environment and impact on the patterns of family interaction. Distress from interpersonal relationships, strain from role overload, and concern over financial matters, are likely to reduce the mother's energy and her sense of control over the family's situation. All these hardships interact to reduce her level of management ability, at least for a period following the divorce.

Source of Income Changes

Female family heads receive their income from both earned and unearned sources. Wages and business investments are classified as earned income, whereas child support, alimony, public assistance and relatives' grants are classified as unearned income. Because of the uncertainties of the unearned income to their economic well-being, the earning potential of the female family head is crucial.

Earned income. Most female headed families receive their main source of income from wages. Bane (1976) found that 58% of the female family heads worked during 1972; 31.4% of them worked full-time, year-round. She reported that average earnings for full-time, year-round employed female heads were 58% of her male counterpart. Reasons for this differential in wages include lack of job skills and experience, irregular work histories, sex discrimination in hiring practices, and lack of satisfactory child care options (Glasser & Navarre, 1965; Stein, 1970).

Fulfilling the provider role and other parenting responsibilities are very demanding of the female head's human resources. A mother of three children who reluctantly gave up full-time employment stated, "I found the job rewarding but also very draining—I was attempting to take care of the kids and see friends sometimes—this plus being exhausted from the emotional upheaval—it was just too much." In the short term, employment may not relieve stress but create it. And in the long run, such nonemployment periods create unstable employment histories, a major factor in low earning power.

Women who are more flexible in their perception of appropriate sex role behaviors appear better able to handle new role expectations, such as that of primary provider. According to Brown and Manela (1978), nontraditional sex role attitudes are associated with lower distress, greater well-being, increased self-esteem, more personal growth, and an enhanced sense of personal effectiveness, regardless of the divorced head's age, race, education, and employment status. Thus, in order for female-headed families to reorganize successfully, each woman will need to examine her own synthesis of sex role attitudes and potential changes in roles. Children may also need to adjust their role perceptions.

Unearned income. Child support and alimony payments are low and irregular. According to the 1978 census, 42% of divorced women with children were awarded child support; the mean amount of this support was $2,450 per year. Only 5% of divorced women were awarded alimony (U.S. Bureau of Census, 1978). Concurrent with the issue of low awards is the high default rate of payments. A Wisconsin study[2] revealed that 38% of the fathers paid alimony and child support in the first year subsequent to divorce; 42% made no payments at all. After four years, 67% of the fathers ceased paying child support and alimony. The number of female-headed families receiving welfare income is less than common folklore would indicate. Hampton (1975), using the Michigan panel data, found that only 13% of the divorced women with families were receiving public assistance.

The reliability of the sources of income is closely related to the ability to plan expenditures, the woman's sense of personal control, and her self-esteem. According to Bould (1977), dollars which were obtained from unreliable and unstable sources have controlling and stigmatizing characteristics; such sources result in a condition of economic dependency which has potentially negative ef-

---

[2]Citizens Advisory Council on the Status of Women, *Memorandum: The Equal Rights Amendment and Alimony and Child Support Laws.* Washington, DC: U.S. Government Printing Office, January, 1972.

fects in terms of self-respect. She also found that sources of income which are unstable, such as child support and welfare, contribute to low personal control; whereas, sources of income that adequately fulfill the provider role in stable, normatively acceptable ways contribute to a high sense of personal control. A sense of identity and self-esteem are closely related to the concept of how much control a person feels over their life situation (Gray, 1978; Melson, 1980; and Ryan, 1976).

Standard of Living Changes

Level of living, the family's present state of well-being, is often quite different from their standard of living, their aspired state of well-being. This discrepancy, defined as subjective well-being, can be analyzed by looking at economic, social, and psychological factors (Strumpel, 1976; Yuchtman, 1976). Since many families headed by divorced women suffer from downward economic mobility, the question of *who* single-parent families compare themselves with—other families headed by divorced women, husband-wife families, or their own family before the divorce—is proposed as an important adjustment factor. *Until the female-headed family shifts its reference point from the family economic state before the divorce to a new reference point, the discrepancy between standard of living and level of living will continue to be a major source of stress.*

Management Variables

It is proposed that female-headed families can reduce some of the stress that follows divorce by implementing new management behavior. Stress-reducing managerial behavior includes: (a) setting new goals, (b) adjusting the level and standard of living, (c) exploring new resources and reorganizing routines to maximize resource effectiveness, and (d) redefining role expectations and negotiating task performance responsibilities. Specific behavior may include using community resources such as Displaced Homemaker Center, Parents without Partners, and child care cooperatives, to assist in formulating and reaching new goals. Children's responsibilities for household care may be increased to include a wider variety of required tasks. For example, teenagers may assume some of the shopping and chauffeuring responsibilities for the family. Each of these managerial changes requires decision-making.

Decision-making is particularly crucial for the single-parent family because of the need to establish roles, rules, and routines that are based on a different family composition and resource base. Potentially, the single-parent family can reduce stress by creating new courses of action and modes of functioning. For example, adjusting the standards for food preparations, laundry, and cleaning to allow children to successfully participate in task performance may improve family functioning. Paolucci, Hall and Axinn (1977) state that decision-making functions to bring about nondisruptive change and to maintain the family's most important values.

A high level of stress produces an avoidance of decisions. According to Janis and Mann (1977), a moderate degree of stress induces vigilant seeking and weighing of alternatives and motivates work toward a good solution; high levels of stress produce defensive avoidance and hypervigilance (a state of immobilization and sometimes panic). Thus, the levels of stress and the managerial pattern of behavior are linked. The literature suggests several basic patterns of family decision-making behavior in response to the stress of divorce.

Survival Pattern

The families with high stress levels may only be able to make decisions about survival —making it through today and trying to block out decisions about tomorrow. Such decision behavior has a *present* time orientation and an avoidance of using a future orientation which involves greater risk and uncertainty. While daily decisions and routines are crucial elements in successful family management, it is hypothesized that the absence of decisions about new goals, standards, resources, and roles will lock divorced families into a low level of functioning.

Survival patterns of management may persist because of the commitment by the single parent to provide the same level of living experienced in a two-parent household. In these families, stress is a product of the family's commitment to the old standards and goals which were established with a higher level of human and monetary resources. Predictably, family stress is generated by the family's inability to alter these standards and goals and to bring them in line with a realistic assessment of available family resources.

A decision dilemma for some families is estimating the future level of available resources. The more uncertain the female head is of child support payments, success in the labor market, and receipt of other income, the greater the stress. Planning ahead assumes a predictable source and amount of resources and control over resource use.

Incremental Pattern

As single-parent families attempt to reduce stress, they may use an incremental pattern. This pattern involves family efforts to implement small changes that are perceived as low risk alternatives. In contrast to goal setting and resource projection that are based on long-range perceptions of optimal family functioning, incrementalism is moving in small steps toward improved management. The evolution of change may not be readily evident in families using the incremental pattern. However, in retrospect, family records and personal reflections would reveal gradual but definite adjustments in standards, goals, and task performance. Gray (1978) reported significant changes between six month interviewing sessions; individuals had developed more fully functioning time patterns, and were making decisions from a more autonomous position.

Types of incremental decisions will vary. Some female heads may pursue a goal of enlarging their social contacts. Some families may adjust their level of living by eating fewer meat-centered meals and changing their thermostat setting. Children may assume more responsibility for helping each other. Resources may be expanded by families participating in a neighborhood car pool for children's extra-curricular activities or by substituting bicycling and walking for chauffeuring activities. However, since most female-headed families are faced with relatively major changes in financial resources and parenting tasks following divorce, incremental

decision-making may not be a very effective strategy for reducing stress.

Comprehensive Pattern

Comprehensive management focuses on making and implementing a network of key, significant decisions. These central decisions include establishing a revised set of short and long range goals, determining which tasks need to be performed by whom, and implementing instrumental and expressive tasks so each person can grow and develop. Comprehensive management also includes day-to-day decisions involving the allocation of scarce resources.

Setting new goals may be motivated by the change in family composition. Some goals may be deferred or deleted due to changes in the family's resource base. The family's goal setting decisions may include entry into upward mobile careers and jobs, keeping a smooth running household, and maintaining and establishing meaningful interpersonal relations—with their children and with persons outside the family.

A divorced mother stated, "The hard part is having to make important decisions alone—not having anyone to share these with—having the feelings of sole responsibility" (Brown, Feldberg, Fox & Kohen, 1976, p. 123). Chiriboga, Coho, Stein and Roberts (1979) reported divorced mothers reduced stress through the use of support systems. Brassard (Note 2) found that the divorced mothers who had more healthy interaction with their children obtained support from several people within and outside the family unit. These family systems can be described as more open than those that did not use support networks as a resource input. Stress-producing demands resulting from many role obligations may be met through supplementing personal resources with support networks.

While in general the existence of a social network appears to be a beneficial resource in the divorced mother's pattern of managing the home, specific network input may be negative. According to Jauch (1977), some single parents considered in-laws supportive, whereas an equal number felt their in-laws were nonsupportive. On the other hand, the effect of establishing a new intimate relationship on both the divorced mother's level of stress and the family's reorganization is proposed as a helpful support (Hetherington, Cox & Cox, 1976; Roman & Haddad, 1978; Spanier & Lachman, Note 1). However, the children's perception of the new intimate relationship will affect its contribution as a supporting resource.

The relationship with the ex-spouse also contributes to the level of stress and management potential. Westman, Cline, Swift and Kramer (1971) and Brandwein et al., (1974) found that children were distressed with hostile parental relations. Stress was created when the children were forbidden to see the non-custodial parent and when there were financial and child care issues between the parents. Hetherington, Cox and Cox (1976) found that when there was agreement on child-rearing between divorced couples, the disruption in family functioning was less extreme and family stabilization occurred earlier. In sum, families with more optimal patterns of functioning were found to have resources of social and material supports as well as interpersonal relationships which promoted individual development, autonomy, and family unity.

Comprehensive patterns of management will include decisions about changing the level of consumption as the family adjusts to the pace of inflation and income reduction. For example, stress may be brought about by rising gasoline prices and the relatively insatiable preference of some family members to use the car. The stability or continuance of a family, in part, rests upon mediation of this type of conflict.

From a managerial perspective, values, goals, standards, and resources are interdependent. If a change in resources is of sufficient magnitude, family values, goals, and standards will be reorganized when enough time has lapsed for the family system to process the effect. Conversely, if the hierarchy of values, goals and standards is changed, then the use of resources will change. Comprehensive management is the process by which families can best adjust their values, goals, and standards to meet the needs of its members.

Conclusions and Implications

From an ecosystem perspective, changes in family composition motivate the female-headed family to employ stress-reducing behavior aimed at improved family management. A reduction in monetary resources and a shift in the primary nurturant and earner roles bring about system disequilibrium that should lead to attempts at making appropriate changes. Based on family management theory, the appropriate changes include setting new goals, adjusting level and standards of living, assessing family and environmental resources, and making new decisions about the allocation of resources to fit a revised style of life.

The level of stress that female-headed families report is related to their environment. Environmental systems that impact most on their stress level and management options include the courts, labor market, welfare services, and support networks. For example, the court system finalizes the child support awards, property settlements, and child custody-visitation rights. The equity and equality of legal decisions over time is reported to be a major managerial constraint and contributes to downward economic mobility, lower levels of living, and changes in net worth.

In summary, stress can be created or reduced by systems external to the family and by the family's internal managerial behavior. In their mediation role, counselors frequently assist family members in resolving problems that emerge from role conflict. And in their education role, family specialists develop programs to teach new skills in resource management and parenting (Nickols, 1979). These approaches focus on the need for single parents to modify and/or adjust to the stressor events.

Since single parent families are also linked to and supported by systems external to the family, practitioners need to be aware of the equity of rules and regulations used by these systems. This approach will necessitate the involvement of professionals in the arena of public policy as well as research, teaching and counseling.

Some questions emerge from this framework which family professionals may want to give increased attention to:

FAMILY RELATIONS

1. Which single-parent families lack the management skills to organize to reduce stress levels successfully? Would they attend classes and/or join support groups with members who have improved their family management? How can families who have a survival style change to a more optimal pattern of management? Under what conditions do families achieve comprehensive management patterns?

2. How can support systems be strengthened for single parent families? How can family educators assist relatives to develop supportive behavior for their divorced relatives?

3. Are the established guidelines for the determination of child support awards equitable for the children, the custodial parent, and the non-custodial parent/co-parent? Should child support payments include an acceleration clause that would link payments to the age of the child and the rate of inflation? How can the collection process be restructured to reduce the payment default rate? Should child support payments be collected through the courts?

4. Should more government grants be given for job counseling and training, subsidizing child care and housing, and short-term income grants during the transition into the labor market? Should alimony payments be based on the worth of homemaking as an economic contribution in addition to other criteria presently used? What is the economic worth of parenting and homemaking?

The issues raised in the proposed framework suggest that family researchers, educators, and counselors are needed to assist in reducing stress and improving management abilities of the single-parent families.

REFERENCE NOTES

1. Spanier, B., & Lachman, M. B. *Indicators of adjustment to marital separation and social policy issues.* Paper presented at the annual meeting of Eastern Sociological Society, New York, March, 1979.

2. Brassard, J. *Ecology of divorce: Case study analysis of personal and social networks and mother-child interaction in divorced and married families.* Paper presented at National Council on Family Relations Conference in Boston, 1979.

REFERENCES

Bane, M. N. Marital disruption and the lives of children. *Journal of Social Issues,* 1976, **32**, (1), 103-117.

Bould, S. Female-headed families: Personal fate control and the provider role. *Journal of Marriage and the Family,* 1977, **39**, 339-349.

Brandwein, R., Brown, C., & Fox, E. Women and children last: Social situation of divorced mothers and their families. *Journal of Marriage and the Family,* 1974, **36**, 498-514.

Brown, C., Feldberg, R., Fox, E., & Kohen, J. Divorce: Chance for a new lifetime. *Journal of Social Issues,* 1976, **32** (1), 119-133.

Brown, P., & Manela, R. Changing family roles: Women and divorce. *Journal of Divorce,* 1978, **1**, 315-328.

Chiriboga, D. A., Coho, A., Stein, J. A., & Roberts, J. Divorce, stress and social supports: A study in helpseeking behavior. *Journal of Divorce,* 1979, **2**, 121-135.

Duncan, G. J. Unmarried heads of households and marriage. In G. J. Duncan and J. N. Morgan (Eds.), *Five thousand American families: Patterns of economic progress* (Vol. 4). Ann Arbor, MI: Institute for Social Research, 1975.

Epenshade, T. J. The economic consequences of divorce. *Journal of Marriage and the Family,* 1979, **41**, 615-625.

Glasser, P., & Navarre, E. Structural problems of the one-parent family. *Journal of Social Issues,* 1965, **21**, 98-109.

Gray, G. The nature of psychological impact of divorce upon the individual. *Journal of Divorce,* 1978, **3**, 289-301.

Hampton, R. Marital disruption: Some social and economic consequences. In G. J. Duncan & J. N. Morgan (Eds.), *Five thousand American families: Patterns of economic progress* (Vol. 3). Ann Arbor, MI: Institute for Social Research, 1975.

Hetherington, E., Cox, M., & Cox, R. Divorced fathers. *The Family Coordinator,* 1976, **25**, 417-428.

Janis, L. I., & Mann, L. *Decision making: A psychological analysis of conflict, choice, and commitment.* New York: Free Press, 1977.

Jauch, C. The one-parent family. *Journal of Clinical Child Psychology,* 1977, **6**, 30-32.

Melson, G. F. *Family and environment: An ecosystem perspective.* Minneapolis: Burgess, 1980.

Nickols, Y. Resource management for single parents. *Journal of Home Economics,* 1979, **71** (2), 40-41.

Paolucci, B., Hall, O., & Axinn, N. *Family decision making: An ecosystem approach.* New York: Wiley, 1977.

Ross, L., & Sawhill, V. *Time of transition: The growth of families headed by women.* Washington, DC: Urban Institute, 1975.

Ryan, W. *Blaming the victim.* New York: Random House, 1976.

Schlesinger, B. The one-parent family in Canada: Some recent findings and recommendations. *The Family Coordinator*, 1966, **15**, 133.

Stein, R. L. The economic statistics of families headed by women. *Monthly Labor Review*, 1970, **93**, 3-8.

Strumpel, B. Economic lifestyles, values and subjective welfare. In B. Strumpel (Ed.), *Economic means for human needs*. Ann Arbor, MI: University of Michigan, 1976.

United States Bureau of the Census. *Household money income in 1975 and selected social and economic characteristics of households*. (Current Population Reports, Series P-60, No. 104). Washington, DC: U.S. Government Printing Office, 1977.

United States Bureau of the Census. *Divorce, child custody, and child support*. (Current Population Reports, Series P-23, No. 84). Washington, DC: U.S. Government Printing Office, 1978.

Westman, J., Cline, D., Swift, W., & Kramer, D. The role of child psychiatry in divorce. *Archives of General Psychiatry*, 1971, **70** (23), 405.

Yuchtman, E. Effects of social-psychological factors on subjective economic welfare. In B. Strumpel (Ed.), *Economic means for human needs*. Ann Arbor: University of Michigan, 1976.

Divorce: A Crisis of Family Transition and Change*

CONSTANCE R. AHRONS**

This paper presents a conceptualization of a normative process of divorce as a crisis of family transition. With the integration of family stress and systems theories, a series of five transitions are identified as normative. Within each of these transitions, stresses associated with major role transitions and common family coping strategies are identified. Rather than dissolving the family, divorce culminates in its redefinition from a nuclear to a binuclear system. The continuation of meaningful attachment bonds between parents and children can reduce major stresses associated with this complex process of family change.

Traditional views of divorce as an indicator of deviance are outdated since the divorced family is a variant life style selected by many American families (Glick & Norton, 1978). A recent increase in divorce research has yielded a greater focus on outcomes, yet the adjustment of individual family members, primarily women and children, still receives the greatest attention (Luepnitz, 1978; Magrab, 1978). Although some stages of the divorce process have been identified for adults (Brown, 1976; Wiseman, 1975) and for children (Gardner, 1976; Tessman, 1978; Wallerstein & Kelly, 1980), no literature exists which integrates the interaction between parents and children throughout the divorce process (Levitin, 1979). The practice literature has fol-

lowed a similar pattern and developed therapeutic approaches oriented toward individuals, primarily women and children. Published articles that include the divorced family in their treatment programs are rare (Goldman & Coane, 1977; Weisfeld & Laser, 1979).

The scarcity of research on the family processes of the divorced family results in part from the fact that the postdivorce family has no historical precedent in western society (Bohannan, 1971; Mead, 1971). Two recent studies, however, have included both parents and children in their designs and have contributed new knowledge about the effects of divorce of family members (Hetherington, Cox & Cox, 1976; 1978; Wallerstein & Kelly, 1980). These studies strongly suggest a process-orientation: the findings indicate a positive correlation between the divorced parents' relationship and their children's psychological adjustment.

Based on these and other results (Ahrons, 1979, 1980; Note 1) this paper focuses on relationships between former spouses in postdivorce families and is an initial step in conceptualizing divorce as a process of family change. The central assumption is that divorce is a crisis of family transition which causes structural changes in the family system. These transitions and the accompanying stresses

*Work on this paper was supported by a Biomedical Research Support Grant (Project #110824), University of Wisconsin Graduate School, and HEW-AoA Grant #90-A-1230 for Multidisciplinary Research on Aging Women, awarded to the Faye McBeath Institute on Aging and Adult Life, University of Wisconsin, Madison. The author wishes to thank Morton S. Perlmutter for his critical review and valuable comments.

**Constance R. Ahrons is Assistant Professor, School of Social Work, University of Wisconsin, Madison 53706.

(Family Relations, 1980, **29,** 533-540.)

can be understood through a synthesis of general systems and family stress theories. The process of divorce results in changes in the family system's characteristics (i.e., the rules by which family members relate), but it does not necessarily obliterate the parent-child unit. Systems theory helps describe this process of family change. Family stress theory (Burr, 1973) provides constructs for identifying and explaining the relationships between major stressors in the divorce process and their impact on the family and allows the further construction of a model for clarifying normative family transitions that result from the divorce process.

Transition and Family Stress

The divorce process can be viewed as a series of transitions that mark the family's change from married to divorced status, from nuclearity to binuclearity (Ahrons, 1979). Erickson's (1968, p. 96) concept of transition as "a turning point, a crucial period of increased vulnerability and heightened potential within the life cycle" has been expanded to include periods which may encompass entire series of events. Characterized by affective and cognitive distress, they often result in disequilibrium reaching crisis proportions (Golan, 1978). Watzlawick, Weakland and Fisch's (1974) concept of second-order change (i.e., radical or ruleless) sought to explain this process. Although we usually define transitions within developmental frameworks (e.g., birth of first child, retirement), some life transitions are unrelated to developmental or social time clocks (Neugarten, 1979). Divorce is an unscheduled life transition, and one-third to one-half of the married population will experience these stresses of transition in the life cycle of their family.

Unlike family crises of sudden onset, the divorce process begins long before the actual decision to obtain a legal divorce. It need not be a crisis of dismemberment (Hansen & Hill, 1964), nor does it necessarily follow the stages of other family crises (e.g., dying or alcoholism). Unlike a crisis precipitated by war or death, in which external causes separate marriage partners, divorce is an internal crisis of relationship. It is a deliberate disso-lution of the primary subsystem of the family and because of the sociotheologic sanctity of marriage, the family's identity appears shattered.

The degree of crisis, however, that the family experiences depends on a complex interaction of individual and family variables which act to mediate the individual and cumulative impact of the transitions. The dramatic role changes which accompany divorce are identified as major sources of divorce-related stress: the ambiguity that surrounds roles in the postdivorce family further complicates these role changes.

Based on Burr's (1973) propositions, it can be argued that the lack of clear role models for the divorcing relates inversely to the amount of crisis experienced: the less role clarity, the greater the crisis. In addition, McCubbin (1979) has postulated that the family's vulnerability to stress is influenced by the clarity of community expectations and norms. Given the role ambiguity for the divorced in our culture, the divorcing family is in a highly vulnerable state.

Our culture presently provides largely negative role models for the divorcing family. The focus of divorce literature on clinical samples of maladaptive responses to divorce has given rise to a distorted perception. Language for divorced families lacks the capacity to describe a present relational system except in terms of a past relationship, e.g., broken home, ex or former spouse. In his recent appraisal of divorce's effect on the institution of marriage, Weiss (1979) suggests we recognize the marriage of uncertain duration as a new marital form. If we follow Weiss's suggestion, we would then be normalizing divorce, enabling and allowing the eventual definition of a wide range of roles for postdivorce family relationships. The basis emerges for a model of the divorce process as normative, allowing for development of appropriate role models for divorcing families, thereby alleviating some of the major stresses currently necessitated by family change. While the divorce process includes the dissolution of many aspects of the nuclear family system, it also requires redefinition of the postdivorce family such that basic family needs, specifically the needs of the children, continue to be met.

Transitions and Family Change

In this framework five transitions are identified in the divorce process: (a) individual cognition, (b) family metacognition, (c) systemic separation, (d) systemic reorganization, and (e) family redefinition. Although they are presented sequentially in their ideal developmental order, *they usually overlap*. Each transition includes social role transitions encompassing a complex interaction of overlapping experiences. Bohannan (1971) has identified these experiences as: (a) the emotional divorce, (b) the legal divorce, (c) the economic divorce, (d) the coparental divorce, (e) the community divorce, and (f) the psychic divorce. These "stations of divorce" form some of the basic tasks to be accomplished in the transitions leading to family change.

Individual Cognition

Most spouses are slow to cognize the marital relationships as causing distress in the family. Spouses may acknowledge personal distress, but they then search frantically for less threatening causes, e.g., the need for more extrafamilial interests, a new house, or even another baby. Family conflicts may intensify during this period.

Characteristic of the coping mechanisms in this transition is the denial of marital problems (Wiseman, 1975; Weiss, 1976). Childhood depression or acting-out and clinical depression in one of the spouses are common responses to marital distress.

Spouses also resort to blaming to obtain respite from a situation perceived as intolerable. The marital conflict escalates and the search for the fault in the other spouse often results in his or her being labeled the culprit. This time can be a highly stressful one, especially for the children who often become pawns in the marital strife. Conflict-habituated marriages are less threatening to some families than the uncertainty and change that accompanies separation and divorce. When compared with divorced families, these highly conflictual "intact" marriages appear more damaging to children than the disorganization associated with divorce (Lamb, 1977; Magrab, 1978).

After one of the spouses (or sometimes both) has identified the source of stress as

the marital relationship itself, they seek a solution. The type of resolution chosen during this transition may vary with the couple's history of coping patterns (Hansen & Hill, 1964). They frequently decide the best resolution is to delay divorce until a less disruptive time. For example, they will have made a pseudodecision to stay in the marriage until, for example, the kids are grown. Other coping strategies include the decision to alter lifestyles and invest energy in extrafamilial interests while attempting to maintain the facade of an intact family. This process of emotional divorce, the withdrawing of emotional investment in the marital relationship, is self-protective and may have some positive individual benefits. Although withdrawal by one member will reverberate throughout the system, it is usually only one member who benefits. Emotional withdrawal may occur early in the cognition transition or only after many other coping behaviors have failed.

The duration of this transition depends on the coping behaviors employed and other factors related to the family's vulnerability to stress. Equilibrium in the family is usually maintained, albeit precariously, during this transition. Role patterns may remain undisrupted. Families frequently manifest internal stress by assigning one member the role of family scapegoat (Vogel & Bell, 1968).

Family Metacognition

The metacognitive process is family stocktaking. Information is exchanged, more or less openly in the family, of the realization that the problem is essential to the system (Flavell, 1979). This exchange of information sums up each family member's anticipatory anxieties. The metacognition is that the marriage is the source of the problems and may itself perish because of them. If the family can cope well enough to survive this transition, the physical separation will occur after assimilation of the problem, its potential solutions and anticipated family changes. This time can be used to prepare for the changes caused by physical separation without decisions based on anger. If the family has not employed this method of problem solving in past crises, however, it is not apt to do so at this time. Due to the persistent emotional bonds between spouses, regardless of quality, this period is marked by ambivalent feelings of love and hate, euphoria and sadness (Weiss, 1976).

The amount of crisis experienced may depend on whether the crisis is voluntary or inflicted (Hansen & Hill, 1964). Although Weiss (1976) noted no long-range differences between those who did and those who did not choose divorce, this factor appears critical in determining coping behaviors and the degree of crisis experienced in the early stages of the marital disruption. Based on the mutuality of the decision to separate or divorce, the leavers are more likely to feel guilt about disrupting the family; those left, more likely to experience anger and/or depression (Brown, 1976).

For some families this is the time of greatest disequilibrium: old roles have disappeared and new ones have not yet developed. The future appears ambiguous, and the family searches for role models. In striving for homeostasis the family may try to preserve old rules and rituals, but old patterns fail to provide comfort or unity. Children often begin to research divorce by seeking friends whose parents are divorced.

Systemic Separation

The actual physical separation may be met with great variations in family coping patterns. The degree of crisis depends on whether the family has completed the work of the other transitions prior to the physical separation. When spouses separate reactively, prior to metacognizing separation or divorce as a solution to the problem, crisis in the family system is more likely to arise. This frequently results in premature contact with the legal system: the adversarial nature of the system is readily available to punish the spouse. When the first two transitions have not been completed, the crisis at the physical separation transition is more likely to be disruptive to the family.

Couples commonly engage in a long transition of separation and reconciliation. In many families, parents separate and reconcile briefly, perhaps several times, because of feelings of ambivalence or guilt over the children's distress. The stress in families during these intermittent periods of separation and reconciliation may resemble the stress experienced by the MIA wives (Boss, 1977) and corporate wives (Boss, McCubbin, & Lester, 1979). In the most common divorced family form, mother and children remain as one unit while father moves out and functions as a separate unit. The mother-headed household faces a dilemma: should it reorganize and fill roles enacted by the physically absent father, or should it maintain his psychological presence in the system by not reorganizing. If the mother/children unit tries to reassign roles, the father's return will be met with resistance. If, on the other hand, they deal with father as psychologically present, they perpetuate family disequilibrium and stress. This cycle is typical of the stress endured during this period. The children face a difficult and very stressful transition with the family in a constant state of disequilibrium characterized by the boundary ambiguity (Boss, 1977) created by the father's intermittent exit and return. This "on-again-off-again" marital relationship often continues for years as the spouses resolve their ambivalences and make the transition to reorganization. This length of time is particularly required if a crisis of the first transition precipitated the physical separation without allowing for a reorganization.

Even families that have successfully completed the earlier transitions suffer stress during this period, although they may not face severe disruption. At this time they share their marital separation with extended family, friends, and the community as they begin the tasks of the economic and legal divorce. These mediating factors can help and/or hinder the transitional process. The family usually encounters the legal system at this time and faces additional stress as they confront hard economic and child-focused realities. This may also escalate the crisis, since spouses now need to divide what they had shared.

Although no-fault divorce legislation reflects changing social attitudes, the legal system still operates on an adversarial model. Based on a win-lose game, the legal divorce frequently escalates the spousal power struggle, adding additional stress to the already disorganized system.

Systemic Reorganization

The concept of family boundaries, rules which determine the parameters of the family system (Minuchin, 1974), helps to understand a major stress of this transition. In the earlier transition, the absence of clear boundaries creates much of the confusion and stress; in this transition, the clarification of boundaries generates the distress.

Rules defining when and how each of the parents continues to relate to the children are critical to the child's understanding of the divorce and to the consequent stabilization of the parent-child relationship. Each parent must establish an independent relationship with the child to pass this transition successfully, but the continuation of each parent-child relationship unit requires the continued interdependence of the former spouses. This paradoxical and complex process requires the clarification of roles and boundaries between parental and spousal subsystems (Ahrons, Note 2). The lack of role models and the absence of societal norms for a continuing relationship between divorced parents complicate this transition.

The final stage of adjustment has been traditionally the exclusion of the "problem member" from the family system. This process of "freezing out" (Farber, 1964), "closing ranks" (Hill, 1949), or "closing out" (Boss, 1977) is functional only when the father remains absent in the system. While the literature has not directly identified this final stage as part of the divorce process, ample evidence suggests that this coping strategy has been common both to divorced families and to our thinking about them. Clinical literature often cites a healthy adjustment to divorce as associated with termination of relationships between former spouses (Kressel & Deutsch, 1977). The label "single parent family" as a descriptor of divorced families indicates the assumption that divorce results in one parent leaving the system.

Recent research, however, revealed that this pattern of coping with postdivorce family reorganization results in increased individual stress and family dysfunction: the more the noncustodial father is "closed out" of the system, the more dysfunctional stress the system experiences. Noncustodial fathers with infrequent postdivorce contact with their children were reported to be more depressed (Greif, 1979), more dissatisfied with their relationships with their children (Ahrons, 1979), and more stressed regarding role loss (Keshet & Rosenthal, 1978; Mendes, 1976). Sole custody mothers were more depressed and overburdened by the responsibilities resulting from role overload (Brandwein, Brown & Fox, 1974; Hetherington et al., 1976; Weiss, 1980). Children with very limited or no father contact suffered the most severe developmental and emotional distress (Hetherington, 1979; Wallerstein & Kelly, 1980).

The nuclear family's reorganization through divorce creates new households with single parents *only* when one parent has no further contact with the family and no longer performs parental functions. The frequent creation of interrelated maternal and paternal households creates two nuclei which form one family system—*a binuclear family system* (Ahrons, 1979, 1980, Note 1).

Family Redefinition

This transition is a metacognition and conclusion to the reorganizational transition. How the divorced family defines itself, both to itself and to community and friends, is critical to the family's struggles with identity, boundaries, and individuation. Society's labeling of postdivorce families as deviant only increases the stress of this final transition. Postdivorce households "have one thing in common; they show an individual adaptation to an overall social situation that is poorly defined and morally unresolved" (Bohannan, 1971, p. 290).

The redefinition of relationships in the divorced family depends on the relationship between the parents. Although a continued, cooperative, and mutually supportive relationship between divorced parents reduces the crisis potential associated with divorce, its dynamics remain largely unexplored. The growing debate about custody rights reveals our lack of knowledge about the time-honored concept, "best interests of the child," and brings the custom of sole custody into serious question. A trend toward shared custody and coparenting seems to be emerging ("One child . . . ," 1979) which should have profound implications for the postdivorce family. Given current societal changes such as increased role sharing and equality in marriage, increase of women in the labor force, and increased parental involvement of fathers, the issue is clearly no longer *whether*, but *how* divorced parents can continue to share parenting effectively.

Although current research on joint custody is necessarily limited to small samples, an increasing pool of data suggests a range of coparental relationship patterns which permits both parents an active role in their children's lives (Sell, Note 3). One major component of the redefinitional process appears to be the parents' ability to maintain a child-centered relationship. For some this includes a personal continuing friendship, but for most it is less intimate and more instrumental (Ahrons, 1979, 1980, Note 1). Parents who share custody, however, experience great distress as they interact with social institutions, family, and friends. Institutions based on the nuclear family strongly resist the changes introduced by the binuclear family. For example, the desire of *both* parents to receive copies of their children's report cards and school announcements commonly meets with resistance. Extended family and friends view such relationships as embarrassing, deviant, or in some way pathological. However, observations reveal normative changes which may assist in postdivorce family redefinition. Greeting cards are not available to announce a divorce and to send to the newly divorced. Language norms also reflect change: phrases like "my son's mother" and "my coparent" are no longer so rare.

A family redefinitional process frequently includes remarriage and the introduction of stepparents into the postdivorce family. Remarriage creates a series of transitions beyond the scope of this paper, but which are part of the ongoing transition of family redefinition. For some families, a potential remarriage partner or spouse-equivalent may become part of the family system prior to the legal divorce and at the early phases of the reorganization transition. Some unnamed and thus unsanctioned relationships within the binuclear family structure take on an importance in the redefinitional transition (see Fig. 1). They are kin or quasi-kin relationships in the context of the postdivorce family.

Relationships between stepparents and parents in the binuclear family system provide an important emotional continuity for both parents and children. It facilitates this transition by redefining the divorced family so that the amount of relationship loss experienced by children and parents is minimized.

Conclusions and Speculations

The dramatic role transitions and systemic reorganization necessitated by divorce puts stress on the whole family. This can bring on critical family dysfunctioning in all the major transitions. Rather than dissolving the family, divorce creates the need to develop a new equilibrium over time, with specific structural and behavioral rules for a binuclear family system.

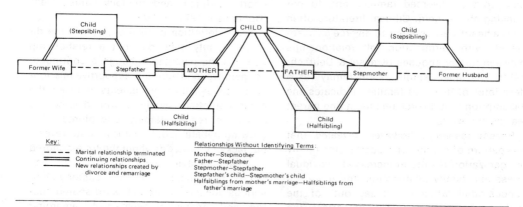

Key:
- – – – – Marital relationship terminated
- ═══════ Continuing relationships
- ─────── New relationships created by divorce and remarriage

Relationships Without Identifying Terms:
Mother—Stepmother
Father—Stepfather
Stepmother—Stepfather
Stepfather's child—Stepmother's child
Halfsiblings from mother's marriage—Halfsiblings from father's marriage

Figure 1. THE CHILD'S BINUCLEAR FAMILY SYSTEM

While this paper does not aim to present an intervention model, some clinical guidelines emerge. The maintenance of a good parenting relationship requires the redefinition of the divorced family to include both parents. The divorced spouses must be helped to disengage from spousal roles, at both the individual and interactive levels, while developing new rules and metarules for their continued relationship. Any attempt to redefine the boundaries of the coparental relationship must clarify boundaries within and between all the subsystems so that spousal roles do not contaminate parental roles. Therapists must especially work to clarify their personal perceptions and values about divorce, and to recognize the divorced family as a continuing family system. The transition from married to divorced can be less threatening if divorced parents know they can continue a coparental relationship. The binuclear family provides a family style which does not force the child to sever the bond with either parent, but which allows both parents to continue their parental roles postdivorce.

REFERENCE NOTES

1. Ahrons, C. R. *The continuing coparental relationship between divorced spouses*. Paper presented at the American Orthopsychiatric Association, Annual Meeting, April, 1980, Toronto, Canada.
2. Ahrons, C. *Redefining the divorced family: A conceptual framework for postdivorce family system reorganization. Social Work*, in press.
3. Sell, K. *Joint custody and coparenting*. Unpublished paper, Catawba College, North Carolina, 1979.

REFERENCES

Ahrons, C. The binuclear family: Two households, one family. *Alternative Lifestyles*, November, 1979, **2**, 499-515. 515.

Ahrons, C. Joint custody arrangements in the postdivorce family. *Journal of Divorce*, Spring, 1980, **3**, 189-205.

Bohannan, P. (Ed.) *Divorce and after*. New York: Anchor Books, 1971.

Boss, P. A clarification of the concept of psychological father presence in families experiencing ambiguity of boundary. *Journal of Marriage and the Family*, 1977, **39**, 141-151.

Boss, P., McCubbin, H. I., & Lester, G. The corporate executive's wife's coping patterns in response to routine husband-father absence. *Family Process*, 1979, **18**, 79-86.

Brandwein, R. A., Brown, C. A., & Fox, E. M. Women and children last: The social situation of divorced mothers and their families. *Journal of Marriage and the Family*, 1974, **36**, 498-514.

Brown, E. M. A model of the divorce process. *Conciliation Courts Review*, 1976, **14**, 1-11.

Burr, W. *Theory construction and the sociology of the family*. New York: Wiley, 1973.

Erikson, E. *Identity, youth and crisis*. New York: Norton, 1968.

Farber, B. *Family organization and interaction*. San Francisco: Chandler, 1964.

Flavell, J. Metacognition and cognitive monitoring: A new area of cognitive-developmental inquiry. *American Psychologist*, 1979, **34**, 906-911.

Gardner, R. A. *Psychotherapy with children of divorce*. New York: Jason Aronson, 1976.

Glick, P. G., & Norton, A. J. Marrying, divorcing and living together in the U.S. today. *Population Bulletin*, 1978, **32**, 3-38.

Golan, N. *Treatment in crisis situations*. New York: Free Press, 1978.

Goldman, J. & Coane, J. Family therapy after the divorce: Developing a strategy. *Family Process*, 1977, **16**, 357-362.

Greif, J. B. Fathers, children and joint custody. *American Journal of Orthopsychiatry*, 1979, **49**, 311-319.

Hansen, D. & Hill, R. Families under stress. In H. T. Christensen (Ed.), *Handbook of marriage and the family*. Chicago: Rand McNally, 1964, 782-819.

Hetherington, E. M. Divorce: A child's perspective. *American Psychologist*, October, 1979, **34**, 851-858.

Hetherington, E. M., Cox, M., & Cox, R. Divorced fathers. *The Family Coordinator*, 1976, **25**, 417-428.

Hetherington, E. M., Cox, M., & Cox, R. Stress and coping in divorce: A focus on women. In J. E. Gullahorn (Ed.), *Psychology and women in transition*. New York: John Wiley, 1979.

Hill, R. *Families under stress*. New York: Harper, 1949.

Keshet, H. F., & Rosenthal, K. M. Fathering after marital separation. *Social Work*, 1978, **23**, 11-18.

Kressel, K., & Deutsch, M. Divorce therapy: An in-depth survey of therapists' views. *Family Process*, 1977, **16**, 413-443.

Lamb, M. E. The effects of divorce on children's personality development. *Journal of Divorce*, 1977, **1**, 163-174.

Luepnitz, D. A. Children of divorce: A review of the psychological literature. *Law and Human Behavior*, 1978, **2**, 167-179.

Magrab, P. R. For the sake of the children: A review of the psychological effects of divorce. *Journal of Divorce*, 1978, **1**, 233-245.

McCubbin, H. I. Integrating coping behavior in family stress theory. *Journal of Marriage and the Family*, 1979, **41**, 237-244.

Mead, M. Anomalies in American postdivorce relationships. In P. Bohannan (Ed.), *Divorce and after*. New York: Anchor Books, 1971, 97-112.

Mendes, H. Single fatherhood. *Social Work*, 1976, **21**, 308-312.

Mendes, H. A. Single fathers. *The Family Coordinator*, 1976, **25**, 439-449.

Minuchin, S. *Families and family therapy*. Cambridge, MS: Harvard University Press, 1974.

Neugarten, B. L. Time, age, and the life cycle. *The American Journal of Psychiatry*. 1979, **136**, 887-894.

One child, two homes. *Time*, Jan. 29, 1979, p. 61.

Tessman, L. H. *Children of parting parents*. New York: Aronson, 1978.

Vogel, F. & Bell, N. W. The emotionally disturbed child as the family scapegoat. In N. Bell and E. Vogel (Eds.), *A modern introduction to the family*. New York: Free Press, 1968, 412-427.

Wallerstein, J. S., & Kelly, J. B. *Surviving the breakup: How children and parents cope with divorce*. New York: Basic Books, 1980.

Watzlawick, P., Weakland, J., & Fisch, R. *Change: Principles of problem formation and problem resolution*. New York: Norton, 1974.

Weisfeld, D., & Laser, M. Divorced parents in family therapy in a residential treatment setting. *Family Process*, 1977, **16**, 229-236.

Weiss, R. S. The emotional impact of marital separation. *Journal of Social Issues*, 1976, **32**, 135-146.

Weiss, R. A new marital form: The marriage of uncertain duration. In H. Gans, N. Glazer, J. R. Gusfield, & C. Jencks (Eds.), *On the making of Americans: Essays in honor of David Reisman*. Philadelphia: University of Pennsylvania Press, 1979.

Wiseman, R. S. Crisis theory and the process of divorce. *Social Casework*, 1975, **56**, 205-212.

The "Home Treatment": The First Steps in Trying to Cope With an Alcoholic Husband*

JACQUELINE P. WISEMAN**

Seventy-six wives of alcoholics were interviewed in depth concerning how they acted once they were certain their husbands had a drinking problem. Findings indicate that long before the husband seeks professional help, his wife is attempting to treat his alcoholism at home through a sequence of strategies which reflect her changing beliefs about the nature of alcoholism, her assessment of her current relationship with her husband, and her reaction to the failure of her most recent attempt to cope with this problem. Some of these wives' unsuccessful attempts at home treatment may be the behavior which professionals often view as pathological. Additionally, the home treatment represents strategies of amelioration under stress which probably contribute to such stress as well.

It is now recognized that alcohol addiction generates problems that extend beyond the heavy drinker to the family and particularly the spouse. Yet for several decades, when the spouse (and especially the wife) was the focus of research, primary emphasis was on her as an unwitting causal agent in her husband's problem drinking, due to the presumed presence of "pathological" personality traits such as dominance, dependency, or sadomasochism.[1] More recently, Steinglass and others (i.e., Steinglass [1976]; Steinglass, Weiner, and Mendelson [1971], Steinglass and Meyer [1977] and Paredes [1973])have taken a functionalist, systems approach and attempted to show that the wife is a part of a family "system" that may help maintain the husband's problem drinking. Where the focus has been on the coping behavior of wives of alcoholics, investigators have been concerned with her management of the problem over a considerable time span of his drinking career and do not detail early attempts to get him to stop or cut down (Jackson, 1954, 1956, 1959, 1962; Oxford & Guthrie, 1968). This effort to fit studies which compared the personality traits of wives of alcoholics with control groups (Corder, Hendricks, & Corder, 1964; Kogan, Fordyce, & Jackson, 1963; Kogan & Jackson, 1963; Mitchell, 1959; Rae & Forbes, 1966). Edwards, Harvey, and Whitehad (1973) examined this literature and concluded that wives of alcoholics exhibit stress that women with any marital problem might have. Paolino and McCrady (1977) report that evidence is lacking on both the existence of pathological traits of wives of alcoholics, as well as their apparent unconscious desire to keep their husbands drinking.

*This research was supported by NIAAA Grant No. 2 ROIAA 01456-03. I am indebted to members of the Social Research Group, University of California-Berkeley, who offered suggestions and criticisms when I presented an earlier version of this paper.

**Jacqueline P. Wiseman is Professor of Sociology, University of California—San Diego.

[1]See, for instance, de Saugy (1962), Futterman (1953), Kalashian (1959), Lewis (1937), Price (1945), and Whalen (1953). This research has been refuted to a great extent by

(*Family Relations*, 1980, **29**, 541-549.)

the wife into the etiology of alcoholism, or condense her attempts to cope with a husband's long drinking career into major stages, has resulted in ignoring what might be the first line of defense in the battle with a man's compulsive drinking behavior—the wife's early intervention efforts.

This paper contains a delineation of the many aspects of what will be referred to as the "home treatment" attempted by wives of alcoholic men as they try to handle their husbands' problem drinking in the privacy of their homes when they first become aware that he may be an alcoholic. Like the proverbial iceberg below the surface, there exists a career of amateur therapy by the wife of an alcoholic which is enacted long before her drinking husband comes to the attention of professionals in the field.

Shibutani (1961) has pointed out that all acts, even coping ones, depend on how the individual actor defines the situation and how he or she defines and symbolizes the meaning of any attempt at amelioration and the counterreactions these inspire. In the course of such definitions, the social actor takes into account how others feel about the action, and then moves tentatively toward it, "building it up" piece-by-piece, checking and re-checking the usefulness of the decision. Reports on the hidden drama of the home treatment indicate that maneuvers by the wife reflect her understanding of the nature of alcoholism, her adjustments to the reactions of her husband to reform attempts, and her changing perception of their relationship and her subordinate status vis-à-vis her spouse. Furthermore, there appears to be an *approximate* time order to the methods that are tried.

Wives of alcoholics who attempt to cope alone with the heavy drinking of their spouses find themselves in dual and somewhat contradictory roles: both therapist and close kin. Like the professional therapist, the wife searches for ways to help her husband with what she perceives to be a serious problem affecting both him and the entire family. Like many cases that therapists handle, the husband-client seldom admits he drinks too much. Again, like the professional, the wife gropes for ways of helping her "patient" in the face of his denial and even hostility to her efforts.

However, unlike the professional, the wife usually has an established and close relationship with the patient that existed *prior* to her attempts to help him stop his drinking. This has both advantages and disadvantages. Although this relationship may give the wife an edge over the professional in empathetic understanding, she is often, unlike the professional, the person with the *least power* in the dyad. This is quite the opposite from the professional relationship, where the therapist is seen to be of higher (or dominant) status in the role relationship with his client due to his acknowledged expertise.

Without this advantage, the wife of the alcoholic is forced to use approaches to her husband's problem drinking that do not depend on role power based on authority of knowledge and training. Thus, the stage is set for strategic interaction, since it is lack of power that is usually the genesis of inferior role position strategies. Yet, as will be seen, the approaches wives develop through trial and error bear a striking resemblance to some professional therapeutic stances.

Methodology

Seventy-six wives of alcoholics were interviewed in depth and also answered a five-page structured questionnaire concerned with pertinent background data. Wives were asked to discuss how they decided their husbands were alcoholics, what they did after they decided this, what persuaded them to try to get their husbands into professional treatment, how they handled this matter, their experiences (and their husbands') with professional treatment, and what effects the alcoholism of the husband had on their marital relationship and their lives in general.

Wives were recruited through an advertisement placed in newspapers in the city selected for the study. This approach is preferred over recruiting through Al-Anon because the latter offers a distinct philosophy of life to wives of problem drinkers, a fact which could confound the findings. Thus, Al-Anon members were interviewed only as they surfaced through advertisements.

Although the actual universe of wives of alcoholics is unknown, and thus cannot be compared with the sample, important demographic characteristics of the sample indicate that a desirably broad range of women participated in the study. The distribution by age, yearly income, education, and length of time drinking of wives (and the husbands they are reporting on) can be seen in Tables 1 through 4.

The wife's word that her husband is an alcoholic was accepted, because there was no way to check back with the husband inasmuch as many women came in secret to be inter-

Table 1
Age Distribution of Sample of Wives
of Alcoholics and Their Husbands

Age	Wives (n = 76) %	Husbands[a] (n = 76) %
20 or under	1	1
21-30	20	8
31-40	22	26
41-50	30	32
51-60	22	27
Over 60	5	6

[a]Age of husband was supplied by wife.

Table 2
Distribution of Yearly Family Income
of Sample of Wives of Alcoholics[a]

Total Yearly Income before Taxes	Wives (n = 72)[b] %
Under $5,000	7
$5,000-$7,499	8
$7,500-$9,999	5
$10,000-$14,999	35
$15,000-$19,999	15
$20,000 and over	15
Don't know	15

[a]Data were gathered in 1976 and 1977. Relatively low yearly income levels may reflect the marginal employment status of some men or a family dependent on a wife's income only.
[b]Refusals were excluded from the base.

Table 3
Educational Attainment of Sample of
Alcoholic Men and Their Wives[a]

Year in School Completed	Husbands (n = 72)[b] %	Wives (n = 72)[b] %
Elementary school only	7	—
Some high school	16	22
Vocational school	3	12
High school graduate	36	32
Some college	24	22
College graduate	6	8
Post graduate	8	4

[a]Educational attainment was thought to be a more stable social class indicator for the purposes of this study than occupation, since many men had lost their jobs or been demoted because of their drinking.
[b]No answers were excluded from the base.

Table 4
Length of Time Husband Has Had Drinking
Problem as Perceived by Wives of Alcoholics

Husband Has Had Drinking Problem	Wives (n = 76) %
Less than a year	1
1 to 5 years	9
6 to 10 years	21
11 to 15 years	13
16 to 20 years	26
21 to 30 years	11
31 years or more	15
Not certain, drank before marriage, etc.	4

viewed. However, there were reassuring indicators that the husbands who were discussed by their wives were indeed alcoholics: first, all had undergone some sort of treatment for their alcohol problem at least twice; additionally, the consistencies in the behavior of the husbands, as described by the wives, lend credence to the belief that a uniform population (in terms of the existence of problem drinking) was being tapped.

The Home Treatment

Wives of alcoholics were asked, "When you first decided that your husband was an alcoholic, what did you do? What did you do next? What did you do after that? Then, what did you do?" The aggregate behaviors reported had a time order—that is, almost all wives tried the same first approach to the problem of their husbands' alcoholism, and almost all adjusted their approaches to a series of failures in the same ways. However, many of these wives were offering retrospective data that spans 10 to 25 years of marriage. Some have said that they tried one thing and then another and then they would go back and try the entire repertoire again. Thus, the exact order of home treatment attempts cannot be known, although it would appear that the time order presented here is at least indicative of the general progression of events.[2]

The Direct Approach

At the outset, the wife saw her task as providing logical reasons to her husband for quitting his heavy drinking—arguments so persuasive that they outweigh any motives her

[2]It would be erroneous to perceive the ordered aspects of the wives' strategies as "stages" in the way that Jackson (1954, 1956) describes wives of alcoholics as they cope with their husbands' drinking over the years. They are, rather a logical (to the wives) trial-and-error progression.

husband may have for continuing. Although the wife probably had been told that alcoholism is a "disease," at this point she still believed her husband's drinking was voluntary. Thus, she initially proceeded on the theory that the use of alcohol can be halted or reduced if the drinker is persuaded of the necessity to do so.

Logical persuasion and its fate. When wives tried to "talk things over" with their husbands, most started out rather low key, affecting a casual attitude while still making their concern clear.

Usually, when we are alone, I tell him, "You gonna start to drink again, you better be careful." But I would not nag him. I'd say, "You're drinking again; you better be careful or you'll end up in trouble." Usually he says, "No, I won't, Babe."

(I'd say) "John, do you have to drink that much? Now is it really necessary?"

As can be seen, the early approach centers on suggestions for more moderate drinking, rather than stopping altogether. The responses by the men were, however, primarily defensive.

I'm taking care of myself. I'm not drinking so much now. Don't worry.

I'm not drinking too much. It's your imagination.

When convinced that a gentle nudge toward cutting down on alcohol intake is not going to work, wives escalated to "presenting a case." Their arguments usually had three major foci:

1. The husband had better start realizing that he has a real drinking problem, and his drinking has gotten out-of-hand.
2. His drinking is adversely affecting other areas of his life and relationships with others.
3. His drinking, if continued, will ruin his health.

Sample comments from wife-respondents were:

I told him that if he kept drinking, he'd be out of a job.

I tried to show him what was bothering me. The fact that we didn't have any money; the car; he has ulcers also . . . the fact that he was always complaining about a headache, his stomach and everything.

Wives reported that the reaction of some husbands to these stronger arguments remain mild, and even become conciliatory as they offer agreement and promises to cut down their drinking. However, these promises rarely were kept for long.

He was very intelligent, and he would always agree. Then he would really get drunk and get a big hangover and say, "That is it. You are right, honey, no more." I live in hope until the next time (he starts drinking again).

Nagging—Wives Escalate Their Campaign. If social bonds, especially those in the marriage relationship, are based on shared meanings, reciprocity, and trust, then it is not surprising that a great deal of strain was felt by the wife as she experienced the disappointment of a succession of such broken promises and that she moved from logical discussion to nagging.

I felt let down, you know. Somebody didn't keep their end of the bargain. Now I just don't believe him, and tell him so.

I'd be a screaming, nagging bitch, that's what I've become.

Husbands did not react to a wife's nagging and quarreling with the same equanimity they showed when she attempted logical persuasion. A frequent reaction was to suggest to the wife that she was driving him to drink by her continual complaining.[3]

Well, he said I was nasty when he drank, so this is why he drank. Who wants to come home to a nasty woman? I admit I did start to get nasty.

It is at this juncture that men used counter criticism to end the nagging *and* to explain their drinking.

Once he said, "You're too fat. Stop eating and I'll stop drinking."

The above strategy placed the wife in a no-win position. Logical discussion and sweet reasonableness do not result in any long-term reform. When she became more forceful, he began to blame her for his excessive drinking.

---

[3]Some social workers believe that complaining wives do drive their husbands to drink, and take as one therapeutic mandate teaching the wife not to be hostile to her husband. See, for instance, Cheek, Franks, Laucius, & Burtle (1971).

In despair and desperation, these women turned to a persuasive strategy used by many women in other situations—emotional pleading and threatening (Safilios-Rothschild, 1969).

Emotional pleading and threats to leave. Wives' descriptions of how they acted when they became too emotional to continue to discuss their husbands' drinking dispassionately indicated they still believed that their spouses could stop drinking if they wished. Wives also hoped their husbands' love would cause these men to cease their excessive alcohol intake in order to end her unhappiness.

> *I begged him. I pleaded, I cried. I was very emotional and I cried and said that if loved me, he wouldn't do this to me and the children.*

Husbands who were constrained when their wives raised the subject of their heavy drinking calmly and who limited themselves to counADDRcharges when wives made accusations produced some defensive escalation (Schelling, 1963) and exhibited anger when approached by an emotion-wrought wife.

> *He said, "Well, you go your way and I'll go mine. I am not an alcoholic."*

With talk on all levels failing, but still holding to the belief that their husbands could voluntarily stop their drinking, wives of alcoholics often turned next to threats of separation or divorce. The purpose, however, was to hasten reform and ultimately to salvage the marriage. These women hoped *not* to have to carry through on their threat.

> *At that time, I threatened: "You either stop or I will leave." I guess that when I said I would leave him, I hoped that it would sort of, you know, make him realize.*

Husbands responded to these threats primarily with cavalier disinterest, although remorseful promises (such as they made in response to tearful pleas) were sometimes forthcoming. These drinking husbands appeared to be guessing that there was a lack of real seriousness in the threat. They may have known that it is economically very difficult for the average wife to manage such a move on her own—especially if small children are involved. They also may have counted on their wives lacking the courage for such a drastic

action. Women, themselves, admitted these problems. They said:

> *The threats I used to use on him would roll off his back and he would say, "Well, maybe you're right, maybe we should give up and quit and get a divorce."*

James and Goldman (1971) and Estes (1974) have noted that wives of alcoholics often develop an entire repertoire of coping styles for living with an alcoholic. As one fails to produce the desired results, another is tried. The findings of this study—more narrowly focused on the early period of trying to get alcoholic husbands to stop drinking excessively—substantiate these two reports. Starting with the direct approach, wives passed through logical discussion, emotional pleading, nagging, and threats, and then often go back to some one of these methods in the hope that they would yet be effective. It is at this juncture of failing several times at various direct approaches that wives began to develop indirect moves—strategies they hoped would help the husband cut down on his drinking *without his being aware of the fact the wife was trying to change his behavior.*

The Indirect Approach

The development of hidden anti-drinking strategies signals a turning point in the wife's view of alcoholism and her power to do anything about it. She no longer sees excessive drinking as so completely voluntary and is beginning to consider the possibility that his drinking is a compulsion.

Her assessment of their relationship changes as well. She has learned that he will not stop drinking just for her sake, nor does he show concern at the ritual threat of separation. Because of this, she often feels a loss of closeness with her husband. At the same time, she may also experience feelings of being more aware than her husband of the danger he is in. Using a type of reasoning that is startlingly like that of professional therapists, wives try out a range of behind-the-scenes manipulative approaches to managing the husband's environment in such a way that he either has less desire or less opportunity to drink.

Acting "normal" or "natural". One indirect approach is not unlike the so-called therapeutic milieu that enjoyed popularity in treating mental illness in the 1960's (Rapoport, 1959). The essence of the method is that professional therapists construct the environment of the alcoholic in such a way that he will experience less stress and have a reduced desire to drink. The wife, lacking the resources of an institution, must therefore create the nonstressful environment within her limited sphere of power and competence.

The wifely version of the therapeutic milieu is what wives referred to as acting "normal" or "natural."[4] The wife stopped trying to persuade her husband to stop his heavy drinking. Instead, she pretended the drinking or the drunken behavior was not occurring. Often the wife will try this method after deciding that the daily hassle of the direct confrontation was useless, as well as being hard on her emotions. It should be stressed, however, that "acting normal or natural" was more than just resignation. It was a mode of "reasonable" behavior that wives assumed in reaction to their husband's drinking; it was intended to elicit the same type of "reasonable" behavior in return.

I acted a lot of ways when he was drunk. Inside, I acted like, "Let's pretend it is not happening." Now, I try to act like a normal person (like he thought I was abnormal) *because I thought if I acted normal in some way, that he would act normal . . .[emphasis added]*

A major setting for these attempts to act natural was the home at the end of the day when the husband returned quite obviously drunk. The wife then tried to act like she thought she would act if her spouse were sober.

(When he came home) I just talked to him like I'm talking to you. I just pretend like nothing is wrong. Sometimes it would work and other times he would keep at me 'til I got mad.

In an effort to reduce such strain, wives of alcoholics used props and activities to aid in acting natural. Often they went on a self-conscious and feverish round of cleaning and cooking activities when their husbands came home drunk, for it is easier to play-act at "naturalness" if one has some concrete routine involving behavior that will take up excess nervous energy.

(I act normal by) being in the garage washing, in the den, or finding something to do—nervous energy. I am so busy with things that I don't even pass the kitchen to see what he is doing.

Goffman (1968) discussed the strains that develop in the family of a deviant (in this case, a mentally ill member) when loved ones try to help him, and keep him from harming himself, while at the same time working hard at appearing "normal" so that such surveillance is not noticed. The problematic person also notices the forced normalcy but pretends to be unaware of being watched. Thus, the interaction becomes stilted and the home becomes "an insane place."

Taking over. A touching extension to acting natural is added by the wives who actively attempted to make all facets of the home and marriage better for their husbands by taking over anything that might put demands on their mates or upset them. In addition to trying to be better wives and housekeepers, such women took care of more details of running the house and other areas of life. Their hope was that an extremely pleasant, burden-free atmosphere would reduce their husband's need for liquor.[5] It is quite possible that this coping approach is the foundation for the traits of "dominance" and "desiring a dependent marriage partner" that were earlier ascribed to the wife of an alcoholic by psychiatrists and social workers.[6]

_____

[5] Obviously, as the drinking continues, the wife must take over for practical as well as altruistic reasons.

[6] Like all research topics, interest in the coping patterns of wives of alcoholics, the psychological sources of her reactions to her husband's drinking, as well as the effect of her behavior on his imbibing have been in and out of fashion. In the 1940s, 1950s and early 1960s, emphasis was on her "pathological" personality traits. It was also suggested that she somehow manipulated her husband into being an alcoholic and/or remaining one. Thus, the wife was seen as an important link in the etiology of alcoholism. In the late 1960s, studies failed to find personality differences between these wives and women in marriages

_____

[4] The strategy of "acting natural" appears to transcend cultural boundaries. Finnish wives of alcoholics also described this ploy (Wiseman, 1976).

I do all the shopping. I take him to work and bring him home, pick him up from work, and I pay the bills and, you know, things like that. Well, I thought it would help him, that I could, you know, help with some of the responsibilities. I thought maybe he could have been tired—they need a drink to relax. I thought that might be the problem.

Another indirect strategy involved selecting "safe," non-drinking companions or visitors for social occasions.

I tried getting us involved with people that didn't drink as much as we did, but he found them very dull.

If he would say, "I am going to go out for a little while," I'd say, "Take Mike with you." He is five years old. I figure if he (the husband) has the child with him, he would not go to the pub.

Wives also tried to manipulate the money available to their husbands for alcohol. Those wives who had direct access to the family money and got the paycheck first, hid the checkbook or hid extra money. Wives who found it difficult to physically withhold or hide money, however, took a more indirect course and often attempted to spend so much that there was little or no money left for alcohol.

Neither approach was successful in preventing most husbands from getting money to buy alcohol. Desperation finally drove the wife of an alcoholic at one time or another to try and curtail the supply of liquor available in the home. They poured out liquor, smashed bottles wherever they found them, or hid the liquor supply from their husbands. This direct

and time-worn strategy is more histrionic than really helpful to finding a solution for the problem.

Industrial therapy. Quite often part of the therapeutic milieu in the mental hospital or institutional setting is what has been termed "industrial therapy" (Belknap, 1956; Wiseman, 1970). This "I.T." refers to routine work around the ward, which is assigned to patients in an attempt to keep them out of trouble, taking up free time with a "useful pursuit." A variation of this approach has been invented by wives of alcoholics, who exhibit great versatility in the creation of tasks and a subtlety of task management. Because their rather special form of industrial therapy grew out of their subordinate position in the marriage dyad, however, wives attempted to increase the number of activities where their husbands usually and voluntarily drink less. By this strategy, women reduced their spouses' intake without creating an awareness of manipulation.

I try to keep him busy. I bought paintings for him . . . You know, those paint-by-the-numbers things.

I tried to interest him in reading, but that didn't work. (I tried) gardening . . . We did a lot of gardening together. We planned out our landscaping and, of course, the house which I thought was the final, ultimate . . . Eventually, I had to subcontract practically everything, because he just could not grasp hold of it . . . it didn't work.

Drinking along with him. With some vague intent of forcing him to "share the supply," or "showing him," or "letting him see what it is like to be living with an alcoholic," or forcing him to "cut down in order to be a better example to her," some wives turned to a dangerous and dramatic strategy—they tried to drink as much as the men did. Most wives found this an impossible task; they usually were unable to match their alcoholic spouses drink for drink. Either they became ill and passed out, or they retreated from the approach upon becoming frightened that they themselves might be developing a serious drinking problem.

Other wives reasoned that if a husband's drinking could be restricted to the home, he

---

where alcoholism was not a problem, and it was thought that any emotional problems a wife might have were the result of the stress caused by living with him. At this time, there was more focus on how this stress, however understandable, might result in her acting in ways to undermine his treatment—however sincerely she might want to help her husband stop drinking. Thus, emphasis was on how to counsel her to help him. In the 1970s, these two concerns were, to some extent combined in the systems approach to alcoholism. Here, the wife was seen as part of a family system which when adjusted to his drinking unknowingly perpetuated it. Practical focus here is on family therapy to make wives of alcoholics aware of the system which has been created and to enable them to handle their behavior in such a way as not to perpetuate it.

would drink less. To get him to drink at home, they start drinking with him, trying to create a party atmosphere that would be competitive with the inviting social milieu of the bars he frequented. But, as with "use the supply" and "fighting fire with fire" approaches, most wives found the "home party" strategy failed because they couldn't match their husband's intake stamina.

> It was great (drinking with him at home), but then after two or three drinks, I had enough and I was ready to go to bed. By then he was so happy . . . he'd want me to sit with him 'till three o'clock, and if I refused, and say, "I have to go to work, I don't want to drink more," then, well, he'd go out. So you see, there was no way of stopping him.

Miscellaneous indirect strategies. In their desperation to turn back the tide of their husbands' increasingly heavy drinking, wives also tried a variety of other strategies—all covert in nature and some reflecting what stress can do to a person's powers of reasoning.

> I tried behavior modification. The biggest behavior mod I've done is definitely withhold sex.

> I remembered he loved his boots, and I thought somehow, if I do something to these boots so he can't wear them to go out drinking, then he won't go; (so) I hid them.

The "Hands-off" Approach

After extensive efforts at various aspects of home treatment, wives began to feel (sometimes through counseling or at Al-Anon) that they personally could do little about their husband's drinking. McNamara (1960) has pointed out that for many wives, this is a relief.

> I figure after trying everything out, I figure let me leave him alone. It will either kill him or cure him, or something, but let him do it on his own. I cannot fight him. I fight, I get less results, so I figure let me let it be.

After allowing the problem to lie fallow for a time, however, the wife finally turned to professional help for her husband. She realized at last her inability to do anything to help him. This awareness signals a greater acceptance of the illness theory of problem drinking, as well as a definite end to any hope of handling the problem within the family. The home treatment was terminated. Coping began to focus on how to adjust to an alcoholic in the family. Parenthetically, contact with alcoholism treatment professionals, initially on behalf of her husband, may eventually result in the wife arranging for counseling for herself.

Summary and Conclusions

Well before a man's drinking problem emerges to engage the attention of professionals in the field, his wife is usually attempting to cope through what might be termed "the home treatment." Wives start out certain their special marital relationship, plus the objective facts of their husband's increased alcohol intake and its obvious results, will mean that the spouse will yield to a logical argument. They soon discover that they are trying to dissuade a man from a behavior that at present defies logic.

Wives turn next to emotional pleading and threats followed by a series of indirect strategies that signal a change from perceiving the husband's heavy drinking as a voluntary act to viewing it as a compulsion or illness. Among the indirect strategies are some intended to create a stress-free environment for the husband and thus eliminate his need to drink. These strategies are what wives refer to as "acting natural" (pretending he is not drunk and making no fuss about it), and "taking over" (handling all tasks and chores connected with the household). Wives also will drop drinking friends of their husbands and take up non-drinking companions; they will attempt to keep their husbands from having money to spend on alcohol; and sometimes they will destroy the home supply of liquor. They also may attempt to drink with him as a means of getting him to reduce his own intake. None of these efforts work.

These home treatment approaches remind us that the first type of coping behavior people select when a stressful problem strikes seldom includes adjustment to the many facets of their changed circumstances created by the problem. More often it is a valiant attempt to return to some less painful status quo. Furthermore, as with the case of alcoholism, many coping efforts take place in a knowledge vacuum, without counseling or professional help. These coping strategies by wives of alcoholics are the individualistic (and somewhat naïve) attempts to handle things alone with methods that have the potential of doing more harm than good.

Additionally, a most important aspect in understanding each spouse's effect on the other is that the wife must live, in a very literal sense, with her therapeutic failures. She gets no surcease on nights or weekends. That is the hardest part of all for her and an important factor for the study of interaction with an alcoholic over time. One wife[7] who had been both in the role of a professional (a social worker) and the wife of an alcoholic was quite aware of this:

> I tried to think of him as sick, but it was hard to do. I knew he was sick, but I had to stand him. I had worked with alcoholics as a social worker, but it's different living with one.

If these wives could be reached by educators and counselors in this early stage of their husbands' problem drinking, they might be saved the disappointment of futile attempts to "cure" their husband's alcoholism single-handedly. Furthermore, the emotional stress and ultimate alienation these efforts cause in both spouses (which may actually exacerbate the drinking) could be avoided. Most important, wives might be given instructions on more fruitful approaches to handling an alcoholic husband in the beginning stages of his drinking career.

---

[7]This quote comes from a Finnish wife, indicating, again, how the effects of an alcoholic in the family are strikingly similar, despite cultural differences (Wiseman, 1976).

REFERENCES

Belknap, L. Human problems in a state mental hospital. New York: McGraw-Hill, 1956.

Cheek, F. E., Franks, C. M., Laucius, J., & Burtle, V. Behavior-modification training for wives of alcoholics. Quarterly Journal of Studies on Alcoholism, 1971, 32, 456-461.

Corder, B. F., Hendricks, A., & Corder, R. F. An MMPI study of a group of wives of alcoholics. Quarterly Journal of Studies on Alcohol, 1964, 25, 551-554.

deSaugy, D. L'alcoolique et sa femme: Etude psychosociale et statistique sur les conditions de leur developpement individuel et de leur vie en commun. Hygiene Mental, 1962, 51, 81-128, 145-201.

Edwards, P., Harvey, C., & Whitehead, P. C. Wives of alcoholics: A critical review and analysis. Quarterly Journal of Studies on Alcohol, 1974, 34, 112-132.

Estes, N. J. Counseling the wife of an alcoholic spouse. American Journal of Nursing, 1974, 74, 1251-1255.

Futterman, S. Personality trends in wives of alcoholics. Journal of Psychiatric Social Work, 1953, 23, 37-41.

Goffman, E. Insanity of place. Psychiatry, 1968, 32, 357-388.

Jackson, J. K. The adjustment of the family to the crisis of alcoholism. Quarterly Journal of Studies on Alcohol, 1954, 4, 562-586.

Jackson, J. K. The adjustment of the family to alcoholism. Journal of Marriage and the Family, 1956, 18, 361-369.

Jackson, J. K. Family structure and alcoholism. Mental Hygiene, 1959, 43, 403-406.

Jackson, J. K. Alcoholism and the family. In D. J. Pittman & C. R. Snyder (Eds.), Society, culture, and drinking patterns. New York: Wiley, 1962.

James, J. E., & Goldman, M. Behavior trends of wives of alcoholics. Quarterly Journal of Studies on Alcohol, 1971, 32, 373-381.

Kalashian, M. M. Working with the wives of alcoholics in an out-patient clinic setting. Journal of Marriage and the Family, 1959, 21, 130-133.

Kogan, K. L., Fordyce, W. E., & Jackson, J. K. Personality disturbances in wives of alcoholics. Quarterly Journal of Studies on Alcohol, 1963, 24, 227-238.

Kogan, K. L., & Jackson, J. K. Role perceptions in wives of alcoholics and of non-alcoholics. Quarterly Journal of Studies on Alcohol, 1963, 24, 627-639.

McNamara, J. H. The disease conception of alcoholism: Its therapeutic value for the alcoholic and his wife. Social Casework, 1960, 41, 460-465.

Mitchell, H. E. The interrelatedness of alcoholism and marital conflict. American Journal of Orthopsychiatry, 1959, 29, 547-559.

Orford, J. F., & Guthrie, S. Coping behavior used by wives of alcoholics: A preliminary investigation. International Congress of Alcohol and Alcoholism, Proceedings, 1968, 1, 97.

Paolino, T. J., & McCrady, B. S. The alcoholic marriage: Alternative perspectives. New York: Grune & Stratton, 1977.

Paredes, A. Marital-sexual factors in alcoholism. Medical Aspects of Human Sexuality, 1973, 7, 98-115.

Price, G. M. A study of the wives of twenty alcoholics. Quarterly Journal of Studies on Alcohol, 1945, 5, 620-627.

Rae, J. B., & Forbes, A. R. Clinical and psychometric characteristics of the wives of alcoholics. British Journal of Psychiatry, 1966, 112, 197-200.

Rapoport, R. N. Community as doctor: New perspectives on a therapeutic community. London: Tavistock, 1959.

Safilios-Rothschild, C. Patterns of familial power and influence. Sociological Focus, 1969, 2, 7-19.

Schelling, Thomas C. The strategy of conflict. New York: Oxford University Press, 1963.

Shibutani, T. Society and personality. Englewood Cliffs: Prentice-Hall, 1961.

Steinglass, P. Experimenting with family treatment approaches to alcoholism, 1950-1975: A review. Family Process, 1976, 15, 97-123.

Steinglass, P., & Moyer, J. K. Assessing alcohol use in family life: A necessary but neglected area for clinical research. The Family Coordinator, 1977, 26, 53-60.

Steinglass, P., Weiner, S., & Mendelson, J. H. A systems approach to alcoholism: A model and its clinical application. Archives of General Psychiatry, 1971, 24, 401-408.

Wiseman, J. P. Stations of the lost: The treatment of skid row alcoholics. Englewood Cliffs, NJ: Prentice-Hall, 1970.

Wiseman, J. P. Early diagnosis and therapeutic strategies on the home front. (Part I of The other half: Wife of an alcoholic in Finland.) Alkoholipolitikka, 1976, 41, 62-72.

The Hyperactive Child as a Source of Stress in the Family: Consequences and Suggestions for Intervention*

CAROLYN BALKWELL AND CHARLES F. HALVERSON, JR.**

Selected literature on childhood hyperactivity and suggestions for management of this behavior syndrome are reviewed in this article. It is argued that little consideration has been given to the consequences for parents and siblings of having a hyperactive child present in the family setting. Furthermore, it is suggested that little attention has been focused on the implementation of management techniques.

Hyperactivity, or the hyperkinetic syndrome, has been widely discussed in the literature of such varied fields as child development, psychology, medicine, and education. Such interest is readily understood when one realizes that the estimates of the number of afflicted children vary from 3% to 10% of the *entire* school-age population (Sleator, von Neumann, & Sprague, 1974). Etiology of the disorder, typologies of children exhibiting this behavior, descriptions of the identifying symptoms, methods of measuring the phenomenon, and suggestions for managing the hyperactive child have all received wide-spread attention. Little has been written, however, about the consequences for the parents and siblings of living with a hyperactive child. Depending on the severity of the hyperactivity, the management program utilized, and the availability of helping networks, this impact may be relatively mild or severely stressful.

*The authors are grateful to Richard C. Endsley and James Walters for valuable comments on an earlier draft of this paper. Any errors which remain are solely the responsibility of the authors.

**Carolyn Balkwell is a doctoral student, and Charles F. Halverson, Jr. is Associate Professor, Department of Child and Family Development, University of Georgia, Athens, Georgia 30602.

(*Family Relations*, 1980, 29, 550-557.)

Etiology and Identifying Symptoms of Hyperactivity

Disagreements exist concerning the likely causes of the hyperactivity syndrome in children, but most authors have suggested that there is probably some biological mechanism involved. Also, in the vast majority of cases, the behavior is believed to be neither willful wrongdoing on the part of the child nor solely the result of sociopathic family situations.

Ross and Ross (1976) have maintained that unique etiological subgroups exist in the hyperactive population even though the tendency has been to treat the phenomenon as having a single cause. Children with quite disparate medical and psychological problems may be diagnosed as hyperactive. In some children, suggested causal agents appear to be inherited familial or genetic factors (Morrison & Stewart, 1971, 1974) that may take the form of imbalances in the neurotransmitters of the central nervous system, possibly involving the reticular activating system which functions to filter out irrelevant environmental stimuli (Silver, 1971). It has been proposed that any relevant genetic factor is probably sex-linked because approximately eight times as many males as females are afflicted with the syndrome (Woodard & Brodie, 1974).

Others have found that the frequency of minor physical anomalies, which may be caused by either genetic factors or teratogenic agents (i.e., agents which cause abnormal growth of the fetus) operating in early pregnancy to affect both the central nervous system and the surface of the body, are related to hyperactive behaviors in males (Halverson & Victor, 1976; Quinn & Rapoport, 1974; Rapoport, Quinn, & Lamprecht, 1974). The nature of the relation between hyperactivity and minor physical anomalies is less clear for females: although intractible, females with high anomaly scores were more frequently described as shy and withdrawn rather than as overactive or aggressive (Waldrop & Halverson, 1971).

Organic brain damage and brain dysfunction also have been suggested as antecedents of hyperactivity in some children. Abnormal EEG's have been noted in many of the children who had been referred for behavior disturbances of a hyperactive nature (Prechtl & Stemmer, 1962). Histories of complicated pregnancies, difficult deliveries, and/or postnatal illnesses have been related to the abnormal brain activity in these children. Mothers of hyperactive boys often report bleeding during pregnancy (Quinn & Rapoport, 1974), and an association has been observed between abnormally short or long labors and hyperactivity; however, aside from the use of forceps, other commonly damaging prenatal and postnatal factors do not appear to be related to hyperactivity (Minde, Webb, & Sykes, 1968). A series of minor injuries, no one of which appears serious, may affect the diencephalon (including the hypothalamus) and, thereby, distort the patterning of the stimuli that are received from the sensory receptors (Laufer, Denhoff, & Solomons, 1957). It has been noted, however, that the neurological signs and EEG abnormalities that sometimes are associated with hyperactivity are consistent with either an interpretation of brain damage or of delayed maturation of the central nervous system (Satterfield, Cantwell, Saul, Lesser, & Podosin, 1973).

Allergies to food additives and dyes may be at the root of hyperactive disorders in some children (Feingold, 1975). However, it should be noted that carefully controlled studies indicate that the proportion of the hyperactive population which is so afflicted may be relatively small and may consist entirely of preschool-age children (Harley, Matthews, &

Eichman, 1978; Harley, Ray, Tomasi, Eichman, Matthews, Chun, Cleeland, & Traisman, 1978; Williams, Cram, Tausig, & Webster, 1978). Other environmental factors, such as low-level radiation or exposure to lead, have been the suspected causes of hyperkinesis in other instances (Ross & Ross, 1976).

Definition of Hyperactivity. Although many different subclasses appear to exist among the hyperactive population in terms of etiological factors, there exists a common cluster of behaviors regardless of subclass—similarities that have lead to the treatment of hyperactivity as a single behavioral phenomenon. These behaviors include short attention span, distractibility, restlessness, overactivity, poor judgment, impulsive action, low tolerance of frustration, irritability, poor perceptual and conceptual abilities, serious academic and social difficulties, and defective memory (Burks, 1960). Whereas the activity level *per se* does tend to be high for children exhibiting the hyperkinetic syndrome, it is the qualitative dimension of the behavior—and its purposelessness and/or situational inappropriateness—which is most apt to lead to a clinical referral (Cromwell, Baumeister, & Hawkins, 1963; Douglas, 1972; Werry & Sprague, 1970).

Consequences for the Afflicted Child. Because these symptomatic behaviors are judged inappropriate and annoying by others and because these behaviors also do not allow adequate academic progress and social development, the hyperactive child tends to develop a negative self-image. Although distractibility and compulsivity may decrease over time, longitudinal studies have indicated that as teenagers those children who had been classified as hyperactive continued to be more distractible than controls (Weiss, Minde, Werry, Douglas, & Nemeth, 1971), to have academic difficulties and to be disobedient at home and school (Mendelson, Johnson, & Stewart, 1971), and to exhibit generally low self-esteem (Stewart, 1973). Thus, this syndrome appears to have long-lasting consequences for the child—it is not just a problem of middle childhood which will disappear without leaving serious aftereffects. Because of the severity and long-term course of the hyperactive syndrome, hyperactivity poses serious problems for the families of these children.

Management of Hyperactivity and Consequences for Families

When the child is referred to a clinic, treatment may involve management of the hyperactive behaviors through the use of one of a number of drugs—most commonly the dextroamphetamines or methylphenidate (Sleator, von Neumann, & Sprague, 1974). Ellis, Witt, Reynolds, and Sprague (1974) reported that the benefits of the latter appear to be related to formal classroom settings involving clear-cut demands and tasks requiring high levels of attention. The drug did *not* appear to reduce activity in less structured settings, such as those that would exist in the home environment.

Behavior modification also has been widely used to eliminate hyperactive behaviors and to substitute more appropriate behaviors. As Werry and Sprague (1970) noted,

This combined conditioning-extinction procedure . . . is, of course, the one that is ordinarily used, if somewhat haphazardly, by parents and educators. The hyperactive child, however, is very often the victim of environmental expectations in excess of his actual behavioral function, so that a vicious-cycle effect obtains. "Good" (for him) behavior is viewed as below the norm for his age and hence, at best, it goes unrewarded, whereas deviant behavior receives fairly regular punishment. (p. 410)

For behavior modification techniques to operate effectively, rewards and punishments must be meted out immediately after the behavior occurs. A great deal of consistency in the reinforcement must be maintained by the parent or teacher who must, also, be very aware of exactly what behaviors are to be considered "good" for the individual child. Behavior modification alone has been found to produce improvement in the behavior of hyperactive children by some researchers (Christensen, 1975; O'Leary & Pelham, 1978; Walter & Gilmore, 1973).

Werry and Sprague (1970) raised the question of whether or not gains made with the use of drugs are permanent, and suggested that the effects of behavior modification were probably more enduring and beneficial to the child. However, others have indicated that a combination of behavior modification and drug therapy may be most effective (Gittelman-Klein, Klein, Abikoff, Katz, Gloisten, & Kates, 1976; Wolraich, 1979; Wolraich, Drummond, Salomon, O'Brien, & Sivage, 1978). Although Edelson and Sprague (1974) have devised means by which it is possible to mechanize some behavior modification techniques in an institutional setting and Meichenbaum and Goodman (1971) have described a self-instructional program that may be effective in slowing impulsive behavior, the important point to emphasize is that the hyperactive child probably will require a heavy investment of both time and energy from adults if appropriate behaviors are to be developed and maintained. Even in those few cases where the child's behaviors may be managed adequately by eliminating allergens from the diet, a great deal of special planning of menus and change in the diet of the entire family may be necessary in addition to extensive supervision of the eating habits of the child.

It should be apparent that effective management of a child's hyperactive behaviors will necessitate major modifications in a family's life style. Dealing with hyperactive children, of necessity, requires time and energy from all members of the family. Such modifications in the family's functioning *may* generate stresses and conflicts within the family.

Sources of Stress for Parents of Hyperactive Children

Conflicts can occur between the parents if they disagree on childrearing practices in general and particularly if they disagree on the proper management techniques for dealing with the hyperactive behaviors. If the assumption is made that one caregiver is responsible for the child, little time or energy will be left to devote to the spouse; stresses are likely to arise. In those cases where the child is so severely hyperactive that constant supervision is essential, the parents may be forced to engage separately in family activities that otherwise they would choose to share. One parent might have to watch the child while the other does the shopping, runs errands, and represents the family at formal social activities.

In addition, family activities that might provide too much stimulation for the hyperactive child are proscribed. Willing babysitters may be difficult to find; and, when located, without special training or extensive instructions, babysitters may not be able to control the child's behavior.

Resources that usually are available to families through informal helping networks may not be so available to a family with a hyperactive child. For example, friends, relatives, and neighbors may be less willing to exchange such services as keeping children overnight if one child is difficult to manage.

Thus, parents may be forced to rely exclusively on each other in dealing with their "problem" child, a situation which may generate a great deal of stress. This may ultimately lead to resentment, which is expressed toward the child or toward one's spouse if s/he is perceived as "responsible" for the child's management (and perceived lack of progress in treatment). In addition, social outlets that provide variety to daily life may rarely be available for parents who need a respite from the demands of rearing an unusually difficult child.

Sources of Stress for Siblings of Hyperactive Children

Problems centered around sibling conflicts may also arise in the family with a hyperactive child. Campbell (1975) found that mothers of hyperactive children interacted more frequently with hyperactive children than did mothers of either normal or learning-disabled children. One reason for this high level of interaction stemmed from the mothers' efforts to keep the children's attention focused on the relevant task; another came from the children's requests for maternal feedback. Halverson and Waldrop (1970) found that mothers of hyperactive, impulsive children spent more time managing their children in an interaction situation and gave many more controlling and negative statements than when interacting with non-hyperactive children. These parents were "set for trouble" even when no misbehavior occurred.

If the parents' attention is directed toward the management of one difficult child, other children in the family may come to resent the fact that they do not receive as much time and/or care. Also, if the hyperactive child is rewarded for behavior which would not be considered appropriate for a normal sibling of the same age, stresses and resentments may develop. Because the hyperactive child tends to be impulsive and destructive, conflicts with siblings may arise if shared toys are broken— or even if the possessions of the hyperactive child are replaced more frequently than are those of the siblings. Furthermore, if the family's social activities (such as vacations, traveling, having friends over for dinner, or attending formal events together) have to be restricted because of the presence of a severely hyperactive child, the siblings may come to feel deprived and resentful. Embarrassment over the unpredictable behavior of a hyperactive child may affect the peer relationships and interactions of the siblings. In addition to generating stress and conflict within the family system, such resentment may further compound the negative self-feelings that the hyperactive child is likely to experience.

Extra-Familial Sources of Stress for Families of Hyperactive Children

Interactions with members of the larger community may prove difficult for the family with a hyperactive child. Complaints about the child's annoying behaviors may come from officials of the school system or from neighbors who come into contact with the child. To control the behavior of their hyperactive children, some parents have had to resort to techniques that others in the community might define as neglectful or abusive. Thus, parental behavior as well as the child's behavior may be criticized by persons with whom the family interacts.

In a report on overactive, brain-damaged children, Ingram (1956) cited cases in which it was impossible to keep clothing on the children or bedclothing on their beds. One family handled this problem by placing the naked child on the bare springs of a mattress and kept the room warm by means of an electric wall heater which was out of the child's reach. Woodard and Brodie (1974) cited the case of a family which placed a lock on the child's bedroom door so that they could enforce the punishment of social isolation when the child exhibited misbehavior. Both forms of management could be judged negatively by many community members and child-welfare professionals in contemporary American society. These parents would be made to feel that they lack the support of others, that they are under direct pressure from others, and/or that their behavior is considered deviant or improper by others—even though the techniques they use (or are forced to use) may be the most effective ways of managing their child and may be employed in a spirit of genuine concern for the welfare of the child.

Parents who choose to control their child's behavior through the use of stimulant drugs may find themselves and their child stigmatized by others who fear the illegal use of such drugs (Cole, 1975). Even the parent who places the child on an allergen-free diet to, control the hyperactive symptoms may be exposed to harsh, negative judgments from friends and relatives who may believe that the child is being unduly restricted and that the "real" problem somehow lies in the parental treatment of the child.

Suggestions for Intervention by Helping Professionals

Because these families not only face internal stresses, but may also receive a great deal of negative feedback and unsolicited advice from others, helping professionals should be especially sensitive to any feelings of resentment toward the child and the concomitant guilt and fear that family members may have caused the child's condition. Our culture tends to place the burden of the child's outcome squarely on the parents' shoulders. Thus, feelings of parental responsibility for the child's behavior may lead to self-castigation and self-doubts about one's own (or one's spouse's) parenting skills. Helplessness and despair can be generated by the difficulties experienced in handling the hyperactive behaviors of the child; cultural tendencies to hold parents responsible for the behaviors of their children serve to increase the likelihood that these emotions will be felt by the parents of hyperactive children.

In some instances, the actions of professionals may have exacerbated these feelings rather than alleviated them. Clements and Peters (1962) maintained that in dealing with the causes of hyperactivity

> . . . lip service is often given to "constitutional factors," temperament, heredity, and "possible organicity," [but] the overwhelming tendency has been to weave a complete causative fabric out of the fragile threads of stereotypes such as sibling rivalry, rejecting parents, repressed hostility, oedipal conflict, repressed sexuality, etc. . . . (p. 185)

Parents, particularly those who have been exposed to the popularized versions of psychological concepts and theories, may be quite sensitive to the fact that they are being blamed for their child's problem, even though some mildly stated euphemism is offered that they are not responsible. (For example, Bettleheim [1973], writing in a popular magazine, suggested that children who are constitutionally predisposed to hyperactivity come to exhibit the behavior *because of the mother's lack of tolerance for the restlessness of the infant* [italics ours].) Bakwin and Bakwin (1966) had maintained that the parents should be assured that the child's hyperactivity is not due to parental mismanagement, yet advised the clinician to review the family situation in order to make corrective suggestions—indicating an underlying belief that better methods of management than those employed by the family can surely be found and implicitly communicating the belief that the parents are at the heart of the problem. The apparent contradiction between being told that the family situation did not cause the child's behavior and being given suggestions for changing the family situation will not go unnoticed by parents who already may be burdened with guilt over negative feelings that they may have toward the child or over ways in which they feel that their childrearing practices may have contributed to the child's affliction.

Professionals may have unwittingly compounded any feelings of resentment toward the child and of helplessness on the part of the family by making suggestions for the management of the child without giving sufficient attention to the effects that these management techniques may have on the family. Behavior modification programs require great investments of time and effort, but also may subtly communicate to the parents that their own forms of management were inferior and inadequate. Suggestions that potentially embarrassing situations (such as visits to stores and participation in formal social gatherings) be avoided impose restrictions on the family that may lead to feelings of antagonism toward the child and an increased sense of helplessness and despair. Helping professionals must be conscious of the possibility that the methods used to improve the hyperactive behaviors, thereby eliminating one source of tension in the family, may lead to equally severe tensions. Even if the outcome of the management practices is a dramatic improvement in the child's behavior, the changes in interaction patterns that such improvement induces may be a source of stress for the family—a possibility to which helping professionals must be sensitive. The commitment to help a family should be a continuing one and should not end with the development of a program to manage the child's impulsivity. Concern must be given to the entire situation of the family—not just to alleviating the hyperactive symptoms of one of its members.

Interventions that may improve the situation of the entire family include care for the severely hyperactive child which would provide occasional relief for the family from the burdens of constant supervision and management of the hyperactive behaviors. This care must be made available in a way which communicates concern for the unusual problems of the family *and* of the child and not in a way that suggests that the family has been ineffective in its management or that the child is being punished for his misdeeds. Drop-off babysitting services staffed by individuals who have been trained in relevant management techniques may allow the family to engage in needed recreation, run errands, accept or return social invitations, or perform household chores without having to supervise the hyperactive child. If services are staffed by people who are sensitive to the needs of impulsive children with generally low self-esteem, opportunities for positive, ego-enhancing experiences may be made available to children who are desperately in need of them.

The most critical need for these services exists among single-parent families and families in which both parents are employed. For example, after-school care for the child could allow the primary caregivers to take jobs that might otherwise have to be turned down.

Constant supervision and management of impulsive behavior can be a draining experience for even the strongest individual. Occasional relief from these tasks must be provided especially for parents with children who exhibit the more extreme forms of hyperactivity.

Implications

The present review has led us to the conclusion that helping professionals must be even more sensitive to the guilt which may be experienced by parents of hyperactive children than they have been in the past. When such guilt is worked through constructively, parents can be most helpful in meeting the needs of their child and most successful in coping with the behaviors of their child. Parents must be helped to handle this guilt in a supportive environment which, at the same time (and most importantly), provides *concrete* assistance in handling the tensions generated by living with an impulsive child, including occasional relief for the family. Lip-service acknowledgment that the family is not the cause of the child's hyperactivity is not sufficient. Too often, lip-service is all that has been offered to troubled, guilt-ridden, and "burned out" parents.

Educators can assist hyperactive children and their families by disseminating information about the biological mechanisms that likely are involved in the hyperkinetic syndrome. When the general public understands that the behaviors are the result neither of willful wrongdoing on the part of the child nor of ineffective parenting, unjustified castigation of the child and/or the parents will be minimized, thereby reducing feelings of guilt on the part of the child or his family. Those educators who come into direct contact with hyperactive children may have a positive effect on the self-esteem of these children, if they are sensitive to their special needs and the nature of their behavioral problems.

Researchers may assist families with hyperactive children by exploring the effects of living with an afflicted child (and of employing various management techniques) on his/her parents and siblings. Indeed, a review of the available research literature reveals relatively little emphasis on the possible stresses generated in families from living with children with serious behavior problems. The research that is reported concerning families deals almost exclusively with assessments of the effectiveness of parental management strategies on the affected *child*. Little attention, except anecdotally, has been focused on how implementation of various management strategies affects family members (Dubey & Kaufman, 1978; Prout, 1977; Varga, 1979). Research studies most certainly are needed in which the type of family (e.g., social class, single-parent, number and sex of siblings, etc.) is assessed relative to various types of management strategies. Research of this nature will allow helping professionals to make better and more informed decisions when working with families.

Although the emphasis throughout this paper has been on hyperactivity, much of what has been said is also relevant to other behavioral problems of children. Organic brain damage, certain types of mental retardation, autism, childhood schizophrenia, and other conditions in which severe behavioral manifestations are involved may create similar problems of management, sources of tension, and feelings of guilt for families. Professionals must be sensitive to these factors if they are to be able to offer effective help to families who are experiencing these difficulties. Through education of the general public about the nature of the behavioral problems, counseling of the families, *and* occasional relief for the family, helping professionals may serve to alleviate stresses and enhance the coping abilities of the families of children who exhibit severe behavioral disorders.

REFERENCES

Bakwin, H., & Bakwin, R. M. *Clinical management of behavior disorders in children* (3rd ed.). Philadelphia: Saunders, 1966.

Bettleheim, B. Bringing up children. *Ladies' Home Journal*, 1973, **90**, 28.

Burks, H. F. The hyperkinetic child. *Exceptional Children*, 1960, **27**, 18-26.

Campbell, S. B. Mother-child interaction: A comparison of hyperactive, learning disabled, and normal boys. *American Journal of Orthopsychiatry*, 1975, **45**, 51-57.

Christensen, D. E. Effects of combining methylphenidate and a classroom token system in modifying hyperactive behavior. *American Journal of Mental Deficiency*, 1975, **80**, 266-276.

Clements, S. D., & Peters, J. E. Minimal brain dysfunctions in the school-age child. *Archives of General Psychiatry*, 1962, **6**, 185-197.

Cole, S. O. Hyperkinetic children: The use of stimulant drugs evaluated. *American Journal of Orthopsychiatry*, 1975, **45**, 28-37.

Cromwell, R. L., Baumeister, A., & Hawkins, W. F. Research in activity level. In N. R. Ellis (Ed.), *Handbook of mental deficiency*. New York: McGraw-Hill, 1963.

Douglas, V. I. Stop, look and listen: The problem of sustained attention and impulse control in hyperactive and normal children. *Canadian Journal of Behavioral Science*, 1972, **4**, 259-282.

Dubey, D. R., & Kaufman, K. F. Home management of hyperkinetic children. *Journal of Pediatrics*, 1978, **93**, 141-146.

Edelson, R. I., & Sprague, R. L. Conditioning activity level in a classroom with institutionalized retarded boys. *American Journal of Mental Deficiency*, 1974, **76**, 384-388.

Ellis, M. J., Witt, P. A., Reynolds, R., & Sprague, R. L. Methylphenidate and the activity of hyperactives in the informal setting. *Child Development*, 1974, **45**, 217-220.

Feingold, B. F. Hyperkinesis and learning disabilities linked to artificial food flavors and colors. *American Journal of Nursing*, 1975, **75**, 797-803.

Gittleman-Klein, R., Klein, D. F., Abikoff, H., Katz, S., Gloisten, A. C., & Kates, W. Relative efficacy of methylphenidate and behavior modification in hyperactive children. *Journal of Abnormal Child Psychology*, 1976, **4**, 361-379.

Halverson, C. F., Jr., & Victor, J. B. Minor physical anomalies and problem behavior in elementary school children. *Child Development*, 1976, **47**, 281-285.

Halverson, C. F., Jr., & Waldrop, M. F. Maternal behavior toward own and other preschool children: The problem of "owness." *Child Development*, 1970, **41**, 839-845.

Harley, J. P., Matthews, C. G., & Eichman, P. Synthetic food colors and hyperactivity in children: A double-blind challenge experiment. *Pediatrics*, 1978, **62**, 975-983.

Harley, J. P., Ray, R. S., Tomasi, L., Eichman, P. L., Matthews, C. G., Chun, R., Cleeland, C. S., & Traisman, E. Hyperkinesis and food additives: Testing the Feingold hypothesis. *Pediatrics*, 1978, **61**, 818-828.

Ingram, T. T. S. A characteristic form of overactive behavior in brain damaged children. *Journal of Mental Science*, 1956, **102**, 550-558.

Laufer, M. W., Denhoff, E., & Solomons, G. Hyperkinetic impulse disorder in children's behavior problems. *Psychosomatic Medicine*, 1957, **19**, 38-49.

Meichenbaum, D. H., & Goodman, J. Training impulsive children to talk to themselves: A means of developing self-control. *Journal of Abnormal Psychology*, 1971, **77**, 115-126.

Mendelson, W., Johnson, N., & Stewart, M. A. Hyperactive children as teenagers: A follow-up study. *Journal of Nervous and Mental Disease*, 1971, **153**, 273-279.

Minde, K., Webb, G., & Sykes, D. Studies on the hyperactive child VI: Prenatal and paranatal (sic) factors associated with hyperactivity. *Developmental Medicine and Child Neurology*, 1968, **10**, 355-363.

Morrison, J. R., & Stewart, M. A. A family study of the hyperactive child syndrome. *Biological Psychiatry*, 1971, **3**, 189-195.

Morrison, J. R., & Stewart, M. A. Bilateral inheritance as evidence for polygenicity in the hyperactive child syndrome. *Journal of Nervous and Mental Disease*, 1974, **158**, 226-228.

O'Leary, S. G., & Pelham, W. E. Behavior therapy and withdrawal of stimulant medication in hyperactive children. *Pediatrics*, 1978, **61**, 211-217.

Prechtl, H. F. R., & Stemmer, C. J. The choreiform syndrome in children. *Developmental Medicine and Child Neurology*, 1962, **4**, 119-127.

Prout, H. T. Behavioral intervention with hyperactive children: A review. *Journal of Learning Disabilities*, 1977, **10**, 141-146.

Quinn, P. O., & Rapoport, J. L. Minor physical anomalies and neurologic status in hyperactive boys. *Pediatrics*, 1974, **53**, 742-747.

Rapoport, J. L., Quinn, P. O., & Lamprecht, F. Minor physical anomalies and plasma dopamine-beta-hydroxylase activity in hyperactive boys. *American Journal of Psychiatry*, 1974, **131**, 386-390.

Ross, D. M., & Ross, S. A. *Hyperactivity: Research, theory, action*. New York: Wiley, 1976.

Satterfield, J. H., Cantwell, D. P., Saul, R. E., Lesser, L. I., & Podosin, R. L. Response to stimulant drug treatment in hyperactive children: Prediction from EEG and neurological findings. *Journal of Autism and Childhood Schizophrenia*, 1973, **3**, 36-48.

Silver, L. B. A proposed view on the etiology of the neurological learning disability syndrome. *Journal of Learning Disabilities*, 1971, **4**, 123-133.

Sleator, E. M., von Neumann, A., & Sprague, R. L. Hyperactive children: A continuous long-term placebo-controlled follow-up. *Journal of the American Medical Association*, 1974, **229**, 316-317.

Stewart, M. A. Hyperactive children as adolescents: How they describe themselves. *Child Psychiatry and Human Development*, 1973, **4**, 3-11.

Varga, J. The hyperactive child—Should we be paying more attention? *American Journal of Diseases of Children*, 1979, **133**, 413-418.

Waldrop, M. F., & Halverson, C. F., Jr. Minor physical anomalies: Their incidence and relation to behavior in a normal and a deviant sample. In M. S. Smart & R. C. Smart (Eds.), *Readings in development and relationships*. New York: MacMillan, 1971.

Walter, H. I., & Gilmore, S. K. Placebo versus social learning effects in parent training procedures designed to alter the behavior of aggressive boys. *Behavior Therapy*, 1973, **4**, 361-377.

Weiss, G., Minde, K., Werry, J. S., Douglas, V., & Nemeth, E. Studies on the hyperactive child: VIII. Five-year follow-up. *Archives of General Psychiatry*, 1971, **24**, 409-414.

Werry, J. S., & Sprague, R. L. Hyperactivity. In C. G. Costello (Ed.), *Symptoms of psychopathology: A handbook*. New York: Wiley, 1970.

Williams, J. I., Cram, D. M., Tausig, F. T., & Webster, E. Relative effects of drugs and diet on hyperactive behaviors: An experimental study. *Pediatrics*, 1978, **61**, 811-817.

Woodard, P. B., & Brodie, B. The hyperactive child: Who is he? *Nursing Clinics of North America*, 1974, **9**, 727-745.

Wolraich, M. L. Behavior modification therapy in hyperactive children. *Clinical Pediatrics*, 1979, **18**, 563-570.

Wolraich, M., Drummond, T., Salomon, M. K., O'Brien, M. L., & Sivage, C. Effects of methylphenidate alone and in combination with behavior modification procedures on the behavior and academic performance of hyperactive children. *Journal of Abnormal Child Psychology*, 1978, **6**, 149-161.

Family Adaptation to Traumatic Spinal Cord Injury: Response to Crisis

MARTHA CLEVELAND*

This exploratory study examines family adaptation to stress induced by the traumatic spinal cord injury of a son or daughter. Questionnaire and interview data gathered from family members soon after the stressor event and one year post trauma describe post injury changes in family task, affection, communication, and power structures. The study focuses on the patterns of these changes and also discusses the effect of the injury on specific intrafamily relationships. Suggestions for clinical intervention are presented.

An important effect of the application of systems theory to families is the increasing interest of both family academicians and practitioners in the response of the family unit to crisis situations. To date, family stress and adaptation literature seems to have been focused on families' response to traumatic natural and/or social disaster such as economic depression or war (McCubbin, 1979). Families suffering from these kinds of stressors share their trauma with many other families, their circumstance is socially common rather than socially isolated, and they receive much social support. Other than Farber's (1959) work on families of retarded children, little systematic research attention has been directed toward families suffering from traumatic events which occur randomly to individual families. These families are socially isolated and receive little social support. The research described in this article focuses on a socially isolated crisis, that is the traumatic physical disablement of a family member.

In terms of family reaction to a stressor event, traumatic spinal cord injury to a son or daughter can be considered to produce a severe crisis. It meets Hill's definition of crisis as a "sharp or decisive change for which old, or ongoing, roles are inadequate" as well as Burr's "situation in which a change has brought about disruption in the family system" (Burr, 1973:199,201). By Hill's criteria this stressor yields a high potential for family vulnerability: all families define the event as producing an extreme crisis; it is very difficult to externalize blame for the stressor; the family has not time to anticipate the change; there are no norms allowing for anticipatory socialization; the crisis producing stressor is permanent; and there are, in general, no collective support groups with which the family may identify or become involved (Hill, 1958). In addition to fulfilling the criteria for a high degree of family vulnerability to crisis, traumatic spinal cord injury families fit the classification which Hill reports to be most difficult of crisis resolution: Dismemberment ("death" of the uninjured family member as s/he normally was), plus Accession ("birth" of the injured family member as a disabled person), plus Demoralization (the culture's strong negative view of disabled persons). Finally, there are no clear normative guidelines or expectations for a family in which a person becomes traumatically paralyzed, these fam-

*Martha Cleveland is a family therapist and researcher, 6185 Apple Road, Excelsior, Minnesota 55331. Research on which this article is based was done for the author's doctoral dissertation, Department of Family Social Science, University of Minnesota, Dr. Paul Rosenblatt, major advisor.

(*Family Relations*, 1980, 29, 558-565.)

ilies must find their way out of the crisis alone. Traumatic spinal cord injury to a family member is an extreme stressor, which strikes isolated families and, as such, may provide a prototype for the examination of family adaptation to crisis.

It is becoming increasingly clear that stress is a very complex factor, made up of physiological, emotional, and behavioral components. Studies of family stress need to consider the impact of the stressor on an incredibly enmeshed system of individual and family processes. As we attempt to describe and explain family stress we need to examine how the stressor affects many different aspects of the family system. The following study attempts to analyze the impact of traumatic spinal cord injury first on family structures and second, on specific interpersonal relationships of family members.

Method

Sample

The sample consisted of families of traumatically spinal cord injured young people who were unmarried and for whom their family of orientation took primary responsibility. All families were intact at the time of the injury, husband, wife, and children residing together. The group contained families of the entire population of patients who met the criteria and were treated at the most extensive rehabilitation facilities serving Minnesota and North and South Dakota.[1] Data were gathered from April of 1975 through November of 1976. Seventeen of 19 injured were male and 17 of 19 families had more than three children. Consequently, family adaptation to the injury of a son could not be compared with that of injury to a daughter, nor could adaptation patterns of large families be compared with those of families with less than four children. Statistical breakdown of the sample in terms of residence, socio-economic status, and age at injury showed no significant differences between adaptation patterns of rural and urban families, families with high or low socioeconomic status. or families in which the young person was injured before or after

[1]Sister Elizabeth Kenny Institute, Minneapolis, MN.; University of Minnesota Hospitals.

Table 1. Demographic Description of Sample

Case	Number of Children	Occupation of Husband	Occupation of Wife	Education of Husband	Education of Wife	Religion	Age: Injured	Rural/Urban/ Suburban	Residence Injured	Extent of Injury
011	5	Janitor	Factory	8	High School	Baptist	22	Urban	Home	Quadriplegic
012	3	Executive	Housewife	College	College	Lutheran	17	Urban	Home	Quadriplegic
013	7	Farmer	Housewife	8	8	Evangelical	18	Rural	Home	Paraplegic
014	12	Farmer	Factory	10	10	Catholic	21	Rural	Home	Quadriplegic
015	6	Factory	Housewife	8	8	Catholic	19	Rural/Urban	Home	Paraplegic
016	4	Electrician	Housewife	High School	9	Lutheran	18	Rural/Urban	Home	Paraplegic
017	9	Farmer	Housewife	9	8	Catholic	18	Rural	Home	Quadriplegic
018	5	Architect	Housewife	College	High School	Lutheran	16	Urban	Home	Paraplegic
019	4	Post office worker	Housewife	Junior College	High School	Evangelical	20	Rural/Urban	Home	Walker
020	5	Salesman	Housewife	High School	8	Catholic	18	Rural/Urban	Hospital	Quadriplegic
021*	5	None	Post office worker	8	8	Lutheran	17	Rural	Residential facility	Paraplegic
022	9	Farmer	Housewife	8	8	Catholic	19	Rural	Home	Quadriplegic
023*	5	Farmer	Housewife	High School	High School	Catholic	16	Rural	Home	Paraplegic
025	5	Teacher	Teacher	College	College	None	16	Rural/Urban	Home	Walker
026	13	Farmer	Housewife	8	High School	Lutheran	16	Rural	Home	Quadriplegic
027	7	Construction worker	Housewife	High School	High School	Catholic	18	Urban	Home	Quadriplegic
028	6	Factory	Housewife	8	8	Catholic	18	Rural/Urban	Home	Paraplegic
029	2	Executive	Housewife	College	High School	Catholic	15	Urban	Home	Quadriplegic
030	4	Salesman	Housewife	High School	High School	Catholic	17	Urban	Home	Quadriplegic

*Indicates female injured.

graduation from high school. A demographic breakdown of the sample is presented in Table 1.

Data Collection

Data were collected in two phases, Phase I, at the beginning of rehabilitation treatment, and Phase II, six months following the injured's release from the rehab institution. The Phase I contact was carried out at the hospital or the rehabilitation facility, the Phase II contact in the family home. The length of time between Phase I and Phase II was between nine and twelve months. This range, which was based on variations in length of rehabilitation treatment, did not appear to affect the findings. At the time of each contact conjoint family and individual interviews were held, based on structured interview schedules. In addition, fathers, mothers, the injured, and siblings completed lengthy questionnaires. All instruments were developed by the author for the study. Comparison of data from the families of quadriplegics with data from families of paraplegics indicated no significant differences. Therefore, the results and discussion below include data from both groups. groups.

Results

Impact on Family Structure

Task Organization. Following the injury mothers spent most of their time at the hospital, which significantly disrupted family task organization. Families coped with this problem in one of two ways. Fourteen families reallocated household tasks within the residential nuclear unit, five brought in an outside female relative to take on the role of mother substitute. In general, fathers were not incorporated into the reallocation of household tasks, rather, they acted as general overseer while siblings carried out mothers' duties.

Following the injured child's return home from rehabilitation there was almost no change in the distribution of pre-injury tasks. However, there were major increases in the overall task repetoire of each family member. The new tasks which resulted from the condition of the injured were allocated within the previously existing conceptual framework of appropriate Mother, Father, and Sibling roles.

Mothers were physical/emotional caretakers of the injured, fathers helped with heavy lifting and did remodeling tasks to make the house more accessible to the wheelchair. Most siblings carried on household tasks, and also carried out newly derived tasks oriented toward helping the injured.

In looking at the effect of post-injury task organization on the family, an important question concerns whether this organizational adaptation results in any family members experiencing what Goode (1960) defines as "role strain," a felt difficulty in fulfilling role obligations. Across time fathers and siblings reported a relative lack of role strain, however, mothers experienced such strain as continual and increasing. Maternal involvement with the injured resulted in reported wife/mother role strain for all women. In addition they suffered severe role strain within the maternal role cluster itself. The nurturant maternal role prescription to care for their dependent offspring conflicted with the cultural maternal role prescription to help their child toward independence. Role strain was also reported by the injured son or daughter, most of whom felt they had lost all of their pre-injury roles and expressed feelings of helplessness and powerlessness.

Affection Structure. Traumatic spinal cord injury to a child had a significant impact on family affection structure, and a clear adaptation pattern emerged. Following the injury there was an immediate upsurge in feelings of intrafamily closeness. Fifty percent or more of all respondents reported themselves as feeling closer to each of the other members of their family. In addition, over 50% perceived other family members as having closer relationships since the injury. Gradually, across time, the affection structure became more complex and discriminate in terms of developing specific "close" dyadic relationships. Individual family members tended to feel "close to" those for whom they held specific responsibility or on whom they felt particularly dependent. Mothers and fathers reported feeling closer to the injured, sibs to mother and father, and injured to the entire family.

A discrepancy in post injury adaptation of the affection structure was that although family members reported increased feelings of closeness following the stressor, they reported no change in the affectional behavior of the family. There was no report of post injury increase in physical or verbal affection, nor did family members perceive themselves as "getting along better" with each other.

Communication Structure. Following the stressor, communication became centered on the injured, and Mother took on the role of interpreter between injured and the family. When the injured returned home this interpreter role was generally taken over by an older sib. Both injured and noninjured sibs reported more post injury openness among themselves. For example, they said they discussed the crisis situation with each other rather than with their parents. Several siblings spontaneously mentioned that these were such hard times for Mother and Dad that they, the sibs, had an obligation not to upset their parents with the sibs' own difficulties. Intra-sib openness seemed to be the only significant change in the family communication structure.

Analysis of communication data made it possible to examine husbands', wives', and disabled childrens' empathy concerning levels of adjustment to the injureds' condition. Table 2 reveals how each person's reported perception of another's adjustment level was associated with the other's reported perception of his own. Across time mothers' empathy remained relatively stable, showing moderate empathy for the injured, and very low empathy for father. From Phase I to Phase II fathers' empathy for the injured's feelings of adjustment dropped radically, as their empathy for mothers' rose dramatically. The injureds' empathy for their parents' adjustment rose over time. Phase II empathy may be an indicator of conflicted relationships among Husband, Wife, and Injured Child. Mother and Injured share a fair amount of reciprocal empathy for each others' feelings of adjustment; Father and Injured report lower reciprocal empathy; fathers' empathy for mothers is moderate, mothers' for fathers is very low.

Power Structure. At the Phase I contact no respondent reported the injured to hold excessive power in the family system; all reported father and/or mother to be the most powerful family figures. By Phase II there was

Table 2
Rank Correlation Coefficients
of Empathy[a] at Phases I and II

	I	II
F/M	.03	.46
M/F	.18	.03
F/X	.71	.24
X/F	.08	.33
M/X	.57	.45
X/M	.10	.52

[a]Empathy: Correlation of ego's reported perception of another's adjustment level with the other's reported perception of his own adjustment.

a change in the family power structure, a clear conflict had developed between father and injured. Although the father continued to be perceived by family members as having the "most power," the injured was reported to be struggling with him for this position. With only two exceptions (both female) the injured reported themselves as holding the most power within the family.

Study results indicated that across time injured sons and daughters came to hold an extraordinary amount of control within the family unit. Perhaps the most critical was the emotional power which they developed over non-injured family members. Most of the injured had the ability to cause emotional suffering in their parents and siblings and to ease that suffering whenever they wished. They did this by selectively activating and deactivating parental or sibling guilt. As Phase II interviews and family contacts were conducted it became clear that the major mechanism used by the injured to activate parental guilt was manipulation of his or her own mood. If parents, brothers, or sisters didn't respond to the wishes of the injured s/he would become angry, or more often depressed, which had the effect of making parent or sibling feel guilty. When questioned about their guilt, non-injured family members expressed the feeling that they must do everything in their power to help the injured and "keep him happy."

Family Unity. Data gathered at the first contact indicated that although families perceived the situation brought about by the child's disablement to be a serious crisis, they also saw themselves as integrated units able to deal with the problem. By the time of the Phase II contact, the realities of living with a physically disabled person were reflected in a lowered feeling of family unity. Two-thirds of the fathers and sibs and one-half of the mothers reported that this kind of situation caused significant problems in terms of "holding the family together." They also reported a sharp decrease in the "closeness" of the family as a whole. Behavioral data from family members reflected the decrease of family closeness. At Phase I most respondents felt unable to maintain social contacts outside the home. They reported anxiety, and even fear, at exposing themselves to the community and turned to each other for support. Nine months later this pattern had changed, and siblings (but not husbands and wives) reported turning outward to peers for relief from the pressures and tensions at home.

There is some literature to suggest that in this type of situation family unity might be maintained by scapegoating the injured (Vogel & Bell, 1960). It was the author's judgment that this process did not occur to any significant degree, families did not mask other relationship problems by focusing on the injured's condition. Respondents recognized "non-injury" related family problems, but indicated that those problems must be dealt with in the context of a reality which demanded excessive physical and emotional involvement with the injured at this point in the family's career.

*Impact on Specific
Interpersonal Relationships*

An important question concerning post injury adaptation patterns concerns the effect of the injured's condition on specific interpersonal relationships within the family. The situation did not seem to have a significant impact on relationships between parents and non-injured sibs, and, in fact, sibs indicated more open communication among themselves following the injury. The most significant changes in interpersonal relationships occurred between the injured and each parent and in the husband/wife relationship.

Father/Injured. Most fathers and sons reported that the injury had led to a closer relationship between them. Sons said their fathers were more nurturant than in the past,

and that they, the sons, enjoyed this nurturance. Data also indicated two significant problem areas for fathers and their injured sons.

The first problem area concerned our cultural definition of "male." Fathers in the sample were reared within the traditional value structure of the 1930s, believing that their job as fathers was to teach their sons to "become men." To become men meant to learn to hunt, to fish, to participate in sports, to date girls, and to be stoic in the face of hurt. Following the injury most of these values were incompatible with the injureds' physical condition. Consequently, fathers reported being confused and frightened about their sons' overall sexual identity. Injured sons faced the same dilemma, yet "male" values for stoicism and repression of feelings stood between father/son discussion of their mutual fears and confusions.

A second problem area for fathers and sons centered around mother. All fathers reported that mother's involvement with the injured interfered with her role as wife. They believed that their sons deliberately intensified this problem by making excessive demands which took mothers' time and emotional energy. This often resulted in fathers feeling serious resentment toward the needs of their injured sons.

Mother/Injured. The relationship between mothers and injured seemed to be the critical focus of the post injury family system. It was around this dyad that the family organized itself. Mother and injured were forced into a close relationship, both physically and emotionally. Mothers were physical caretakers for the injured, and as culturally designated "guardians of affective needs" they took on primary responsibility for the injured's emotional adjustment.

Given this situation, it is not surprising that although over 70% of mothers and sons reported a closer post injury relationship, major mother/injured problems arose in the area of mother's overprotectiveness. Data indicated that mothers did not underestimate the physical capabilities of the injured, but were unable to allow them to function to their maximum potential. The injured added to this problem by frequently asking for help or support and then criticizing mothers for giving it. On the other hand, if mothers refused to help the injured would become angry or depressed. Mothers responded to the anger/depression by solicitating or cajoling which, in turn, gave positive reinforcement to the injured's use of his own mood as a mechanism of control.

Husband/Wife. Data showed the post injury marital relationship to be significantly affected by mothers' involvement with the injured. Her physical involvement decreased the time she had to spend with her husband, and her emotional involvement resulted in a decreased ability to make an active investment in her marriage. As a result of this situation, husbands became angry with wives, and wives reciprocated that anger for husbands' "lack of understanding."

Husbands and wives also reported ongoing tension between them in terms of mothers' protectiveness toward the injured. Typically, fathers reported that mothers' overprotectiveness impeded both the physical and emotional adjustment of their injured sons.

In general, both husbands and wives reported that marriage had been neither improved nor harmed by the injury, and expressed a deep regret that due to their child's condition they would never feel free from parenthood. Many reported feeling that plans for themselves as a couple would always be contingent on the injured's life situation.

Discussion

In adapting to the stressor, family tasks and organization were not renegotiated in a load equalizing way. Consequently, mothers in the sample experienced continuing and increasing role strain across time. This tended to decrease her effectiveness as a mother to non-injured children, as wife to husband, and as individual to self. Changes in family affection structure which occurred on a feeling level were not reflected in behavior. This seemed to result in confusion and discomfort in affective relationships. Also, the differentiating of "close" dyads on the basis of dependency/responsibility seemed to isolate some family members from each other. Changes in communication structures tended to separate parents from children, rigidifying boundaries between generations. In terms of power, the

father/injured struggle for dominance apparently resulted in ambiguity and confusion. In addition, the power of the injured to control through the manipulation of his own mood can be described as destructive. It was destructive for the entire family because the power structure was not an equitable one, the injured held excessive control in many areas of family life.

Marris (1974) claims that people can adjust to life change only when they are able to find meaning in, to make sense of, the change. During the course of this study each respondent in the sample came to rationalize the situation in terms of his or her previous life philosophy, none reported any basic change in attitudes toward God, fate, or the meaning of life. Under the severe stress of traumatic spinal cord injury to a family member, the great majority of respondents in this sample maintained their previous coping behaviors, as well as the philosophies and attitudes underlying these behaviors.

Implications for Intervention

As a practitioner, the author has determined several goals which she has found useful when working with families of spinal cord injured young people.

Minimize Involvement Between Mother and Injured

In a family facing this situation it is crucial to their long term post injury adjustment that the physical and emotional enmeshment between mother and injured be untangled. The author has found it helpful to explore with the mother and her injured son or daughter the symbiotic nature of their relationship and the part each plays in maintaining it. Once the pattern of interaction is recognized, the enmeshment can be broken down. When the mother/child system begins to change, the mother may feel guilty and useless, as though she is somehow not fulfilling the duties expected of her. The practitioner plays an important role is supporting the mother toward a realistic appraisal of the situation and of the part she can play in her injured child's life.

One of the things that can be most helpful in working with mothers through this process is their own recognition that fathers may be as important to the injured's adjustment as are mothers. Mothers almost invariably recognize that their son or daughter responds more maturely, more at their age level, with their father. Practitioners can utilize this understanding on the part of mothers to help de-intensify the mother/injured relationship while encouraging increasing father/injured involvement.

Maximize Involvement Between Father and Injured

The relationship between father and injured is often a potentially strong element in the post injury family system. They feel closer to each other, and tend to "get along better." A major obstacle to the development of their relationship is their problem in communicating, particularly about affective or relationship issues. The practitioner can serve a valuable function by facilitating communication between them concerning their fears about sexuality, their conflict over Mother, and specific expectations each has for the future independence of the injured. Each of these topics is important in the development of a mature relationship between father and son, and each, if ignored, has the potential to be destructive to their relationship. Skillful facilitation can bring the issues into clear focus and set the pattern for an ongoing rational dialogue between father and son.

Maximize the Relationship Between Husband and Wife

A way to help mothers break out of enmeshed relationships with their injured child is to work with them toward an improved marital relationship and increasing marital involvement. Satir (1967) calls parents the "architects of the family" and claims that as the marriage goes, so goes the family system. Focusing on the marital relationship in a family with a cord injured child seems to have three important results. First, husbands and wives come to see their marriage as an avenue of emotional support and personal development and as a viable alternative to a stultifying overinvolved parental relationship. Second, when a couple consciously focuses on their relationship as husband and wife they are not apt to displace their interpersonal problems onto the condition of their injured son or daughter. Finally, the couple's involvement with each other allows the injured the psychological room he or she needs to face the situation of physical disability, to grow into that situation, and to reach his or her potential of physical and emotional independence.

Through contact with families of traumatically disabled young people it has become clear to the author that without clinical intervention the great majority of these families do not move toward goals which have been suggested as important to post trauma functioning. Typically, grief is dealt with intrapersonally, fear of depression becomes a powerful factor in family relationships, mothers remain enmeshed with disabled children, and husbands and wives remain conflicted in areas concerning the injured.

Conclusion

The above discussion of families which experience traumatic spinal cord injury to a son or daughter is necessarily brief. However, the results of the study clearly show that following this particular stressor event families are in crisis, and that family systems adapt to the crisis by making structural change. A fascinating, and unanswered, question growing out of this study relates to the rigid application of pre-injury family principles to post injury adaptation. Is post injury family dysfunction due to the reliance on previous coping strategies? Beyond this: Do families experiencing other severe stressors typically respond in this way? Are less severe stressors, or those which are "socially common," more apt to be dealt with creatively? Is it the nature of the stressor event, or the type of pre-stressor family structure which most influences post stressor adaptation patterns? Many such questions exist. Unfortunately, the present study can only lead to speculation, perhaps further research may lead to answers.

REFERENCES

Burr, W. *Theory construction and the sociology of the family.* New York: Wiley, 1973.

Farber, B. Effects of a severely mentally retarded child on family integration. *Monograph of the Society for Research in Child Development*, 1959, **71**, 24(2).

Goode, W. A theory of role strain. *American Sociological Review*, 1960, **25**, 488-496.

Hill, R. Social stresses on the family. *Social Casework,* 1958, **39**. 139-150.

Marris, P. *Loss and change*. New York: Pantheon, 1974.

McCubbin, H. I. Integrating coping behavior in family stress theory. *Journal of Marriage and the Family*, 1979, **41**, 237-244.

Satir, V. *Peoplemaking*. Palo Alto: Science and Behavior Books, 1967.

Vogel, E., & Bell, N. The emotionally disturbed child as the family scapegoat. In E. Vogel & N. Bell (Eds.), *A modern introduction to the family*. New York: Free Press, 1960.

Supporting Families Under Stress: The Role of Social Networks

DONALD G. UNGER AND DOUGLAS R. POWELL*

The role of family social networks in mediating the effects of stress has been underscored in the literature. Drawing from sociological and psychological studies, this paper examines the strong positive relationship between social networks and a family's adaptation to societal crises, life transitions and family conflicts. Who helps and when, the types of support offered and given, the conditions influencing the use and effect of networks, and the implications for professional intervention are discussed.

Interest in factors that influence a family's ability to cope with normative stress and crisis situations largely has focused on attributes of a family and its members. Practitioners and researchers have given attention to the personal characteristics of family members, the structure of a family and the amount of existing stress within a family. Although these variables are of extreme importance in understanding adaptation to stress, they contribute to a "closed system" view of families if considered as the exclusive or primary determinants of a family's response to stress.

A factor external to the family which plays a critical role in facilitating adaptation to stress is emotional and material support from formal and informal sources. An "open systems" perspective of the family emphasizes the embeddedness of a family in a social environment that has a major influence on family functioning. It has been suggested in the research literature that informal social networks provide a considerable amount of support to families experiencing stress. An alternative perspective of

a family's ability to cope with stress, then, is focused on the quality of support received from the family's social network.

The purpose of this article is to examine the role of family social networks in mediating the effects of stress caused by everyday situations, crises, and developmental change. Research evidence is reviewed indicating a strong relation between a family's response to stress and the aid received from an informal network of relatives, friends, neighbors, and acquaintances. Attention is given to differences among network members in responding to varied stress situations, the types of aid provided by social networks, and factors that influence the use of a social network to deal with stressors. Implications of the relation between family stress and social networks also are discussed for professional practices and programs that seek to support families under stress.

Social Networks and Family Stress

A social network consists of a person's relationships with relatives, friends, neighbors, coworkers, and other acquaintances who interact with the person. Each member of a family, including children, has a personal network and collectively these networks comprise the family social network. Each member of a network does not necessarily know or interact with every other member, and networks do not have

*Donald G. Unger is a Ph.D. student in clinical-community psychology at the University of South Carolina. Douglas R. Powell is Associate Professor of Human Development and Relationships, Department of Family and Consumer Resources, Wayne State University, Detroit, Michigan 48202.

(*Family Relations*, 1980, **29**, 566-574.)

clear boundaries. The common characteristic of members of a network is their relationship to the family (Sarason, Carroll, Maton, Cohen, & Lorentz, 1977).

Network Support and Adaptation

A strong relation between social networks and a family's adaptation to stress is suggested in findings of studies dealing with societal crises, personal health, life transitions, and family interaction. Apparently, during the Great Depression, World Wars, and disasters, families who had contact with and pooled resources with friends, relatives, and neighbors coped better than isolated families (Drabek & Boggs, 1968; Hill, 1949; Koos, 1946; Stouffer & Lazarsfeld, 1937; Young, 1937). Relationships with friends, relatives, and neighbors also relate significantly to personal health conditions. Cobb (1976) has reviewed research data and concluded that supportive interactions among individuals are protective against health consequences of life stress and may facilitate recovery from illnesses. Further, social network support has been reported to help a person's ability to cope with job loss (Gore, 1974), life and job stressors impacting upon a marriage (Burke & Weir, 1977), and life transitions (Hamburg & Adams, 1967; Hirsch, 1980).

Interaction between family members under stress also may be influenced by social networks. For example, it has been found that families who abuse their children are characterized by high levels of stress, social isolation and inadequate support systems (Garbarino & Crouter, 1978; Garbarino & Sherman, 1980; Gottlieb, 1979; Polansky, Chalmers, Buttenweiser, & Williams, 1979). Wandersman, Wandersman and Kahn (in press) have suggested that network social support for parents during the postpartum period facilitates their adjustment to parenthood. Hetherington, Cox, and Cox (1977) also have indicated that during the first two years of divorce, a mother's contact with relatives and close friends may enhance her effectiveness with her children.

Unger (1979) further investigated the influence of social networks on mother-child interaction under stressful life conditions. In his study, 18 white low-income mothers with infants under six months of age were interviewed in their homes to determine characteristics of the informal networks that they were using. Both stressful life events and everyday, current stressors that occurred during the mother's past year also were measured. Two subscales from the Home Observation for Measurement of the Environment Inventory (HOME) (Note 1) were used as measures of mother-child interaction: (a) emotional and verbal responsivity of mother and (b) maternal involvement with child. Parents were found to have face-to-face contact with an average of 11.4 kin, 6.7 friends and 7.8 neighbors during the past year. Mothers who experienced high levels of stress were found more likely to be actively involved with their infant when they had weekly contact with kin and friends than when they were infrequently in contact. Parents also appeared more responsive to their children if they were receiving material resources from their network members.

Utilization of Informal Aid

An examination of family help-seeking behaviors during times of stress underscores the salience of family social networks when compared to the use of formal institutions. When families are in need of help they typically do not seek initial aid from formal organizations even if the organization is designed to serve the individual's presenting problem. In 1940-43, Koos (1946) interviewed 62 low-income urban families in New York City about their "troubles" and how they solved them. Koos reported that families had little knowledge of and contact with family service agencies. Moreover, when families needed advice in emergencies, they typically went to relatives, the local druggist, bartender, or priest. Formal agencies were not utilized by families in trouble.

The preference for informal as opposed to formal sources of aid still appears prevalent, even with increases in services potentially available to families. For instance, Eddy, Paap, and Glad (1970) asked 100 adults in a metropolitan area to list and rank persons and organizations that they felt were valuable sources of aid. Family was mentioned more frequently followed by clergymen and physicians. Friends and mental health centers were ranked with the same frequency as a source of aid (tenth).

Although some formal organizations were cited as useful (e.g., welfare agency, hospital, family service), informal sources were utilized just as or more frequently than agencies.

A study by Turner, Kimbrough, and Traynhan (1977) adds further support. Persons (277) from two rural communities were asked to rank the usefulness of referral sources for each of 21 critical life situations that were endemic to the population and could have been handled by a community mental health center. The center ranked fifth as an overall helping source with relatives and friends, physicians, pastors, and teachers being the primary sources of aid. Rosenblatt and Mayer (1972), moreover, interviewed 5,600 women throughout the U.S. and asked who they had contacted in the past for family troubles. Relatives, friends, and neighbors were more likely to be consulted than professionals. In an interview study of 305 middle-class, urban and suburban black parents, McAdoo (1978) also found that kin provided the most support for a family with 20% viewing friends to be of secondary importance. Very few (2%) felt community agencies were a source of help to them.

A further argument for considering the importance of informal sources of aid for families under stress comes from a study by Croog, Lipson, and Levine (1972). The patterns of support (including kin, non-family resources, and institution) utilized by men who had experienced their first myocardial infarction were investigated. These 293 men were interviewed over three periods—when still in the hospital, one month after discharge, and one year after the occurrence of the infarction. Kin, friends, and neighbors provided much support and aid for the respondents. Parents were rated very helpful by 43.6% of the patients, in-laws by 43.3%, friends by 38.3%, and neighbors by 29.4% of the patients. During the third interview, respondents were given a list of institutions, agencies, and categories of professionals to indicate those that they had contacted for aid. Of the 293 men, 72% reported they had contacted no institution or professional person listed, 15.3% had contacted one and only 12.7% had contacted two or more. Thus, the primary sources of support were from friends and family, along with contacts with the patient's physician, of course.

There is one important qualification, however. The importance of informal support systems may vary according to the level and type of stress being experienced. Lindenthal, Thomas, and Myers (1971), for example, suggested that psychological impairment predisposes persons to perceive formal, organizational supports as more helpful than family and friends. Lindenthal et al. interviewed 720 individuals and classified them into three categories: (a) very impaired psychologically, (b) moderately impaired, and (c) unimpaired. Of the very impaired, 72% perceived secondary sources of aid (professional and organizational) to be useful as compared to only 44% of the unimpaired and 51% of the semi-impaired.

Who Helps and When?

Kin, friends, and neighbors provide unique resources to a family under stress, varying, for example, in the degree of intimate contact and type of help provided (Bell & Boat, 1957). Litwak and Szelenyi (1969) studied the explicit differences in these primary group structures from data gathered in Detroit in 1961 and two Hungarian cities in 1966. Differences in the groups predisposed them to performing certain tasks better than others. The neighborhood, characterized by face-to-face contact and high membership turnover, tended to be best suited to help with short-term immediate emergencies. Kin groups, although often mobile, had permanent membership and were able to maintain contact due to modern means of communication. Consequently, the kinship group seemed best able to handle long-term commitments. The friendship peer group, though characterized also by differential mobility, had affectivity and free choice as the ties holding friendship together. Friend groups therefore were able to deal best with heterogeneity, helping with fluctuations and changes in a network member's life.

It appears, then, that families utilize different social network members for different needs. Each of these primary groups provide unique types of aid and seem to "supplement" each other's services or exchanges of aid. This is in contrast to a compensatory view wherein one group makes up for the *lack* of help provided by another group. This model of supplementary relationships between primary groups frequently has been suggested and supported in the research literature (Croog et al., 1972; Litwak & Szelenyi, 1969; Rosow, 1967; Unger, 1979).

Types of Support

Social networks provide essentially three types of aid: (a) instrumental support, (b) emotional or social support, and (c) referral and information. The first two have been discussed and reviewed elsewhere (Lee, 1979; Dean & Lin, 1977; Unger, 1979) and will be mentioned here briefly.

Instrumental support consists of material goods and services to an individual to alleviate financial and economic situations or crises. For low-income families and those living in crisis conditions, it appears there is a heavy reliance on material support from social network sources. For instance, an important study by Stack (1974) found social networks to be an exceedingly critical support system for low-income black families.

Emotional support involves the communication of information to an individual that s/he is loved, esteemed, and mutually obligated to members of his/her network (Cobb, 1976). For example, in a study of women who had experienced high levels of stress before and during their pregnancies, it was found that women with high amounts of emotional support had considerably fewer medical complications during pregnancy than women with low levels of social support (Nuckolls, Cassel, & Kaplan, 1972).

Social networks also may influence family members' interactions with formal systems and may play a major role in helping an individual locate other sources of aid. The effect of a social network on an individual's relations with a formal organization is suggested in a study by Powell (1978) of interactions between parents and staff in group child care centers. It was found that a greater frequency and diversity of parent-staff communication existed among parents who maintained friendship-type relationships with other parents using the same child care center than among parents who did not include other parents in their network of friends and acquaintances. A study by Hamburg and Adams (1967) of students entering their freshman year at a university found

that students who effectively coped with their stressors (as determined by interpersonal and academic effectiveness) reportedly utilized informal social networks. Friends, parents, siblings, and peers were contacted by students before entering college for information about what the new situation would be like and how they could prepare. When attending the university, establishing friendships and utilizing these for information proved useful. New friendships, for example, helped the student to clarify career possibilities, find necessary resources, and learn effective coping strategies. Informal social networks helped to "prepare and support" involvement in an organization outside of the family system.

Social networks may be used by persons to help find resources that transcend the aid provided by social network members. Lee (1969) gave a detailed account of how women seeking an abortion consistently utilized their "acquaintance networks" in the search process. Seventy-seven percent of their first contacts were with relatives and friends, and only 15% were with doctors or formal "abortion specialists."

Freidson (1960) has developed the notion of a "lay referral system" in which members of a social network are consulted about health problems and the advisability of obtaining formal medical services. Network members most often refer first to the diagnostic resources of family, friends, neighbors, and the local druggist until possibly the person is advised and referred to a professional doctor. Whereas this lay referral system may help an individual reach appropriate services, it may also inhibit an individual from ever having contact with a professional practitioner. For instance, if the lay referral system does not support the professional culture, solutions more germane to one's culture will be encouraged.

The ability of social networks to inhibit use of formal services is pointed out in a rather extensive study done in Scotland in which 87 women were selected randomly from a maternity clinic and classified as "utilizers" or "underutilizers" of prenatal care (McKinlay, 1973). Utilizers were found to visit relatives less frequently than underutilizers. There also was a tendency for underutilizers' friends to be closely interlocked with their kinship network (i.e., friends were "family friends" as opposed to exclusively personal friends). Moreover, underutilizers relied heavily on their relatives and friends as lay consultants while utilizers tended to make greater use of their loose-knit, more differentiated networks, using friends and husbands more, and depending less on relatives in the process of solving problems (e.g., whether to consult a family doctor concerning health of baby). McKinlay (1973) suggested that the utilizer's close-knit networks may be operative in a form of social control such that underutilizers must accommodate to the advice and wishes of members of her network and conform to expectations. An inevitable consequence of this lay consultation for underutilizers appears to be a delayed use or no use of formal services.

Conditions Influencing the Use and Effect of Networks

When and under what conditions are social networks operative? What factors determine which social network members will be useful to a family member? What aspects of social networks seem to be related to their utilization? These questions have not been answered in previous anthropological accounts (Whitten & Wolfe, 1973) and the classic studies of social networks (e.g., Bott, 1957), but are critical to future research and considerations of the use of social networks as a component of professional intervention strategies. The following discussion is a consideration of some of these issues; the purpose is to generate ideas.

There may be a "situation specificity" which determines when and how networks will be used. For example, co-workers may support each other exclusively at work whereas neighbors act as a leisure-time network after work hours. Depending upon the situational crisis, a certain network potentially can be mobilized. Networks, then, might be viewed "as representing a series and an ongoing set of social relationships" (Boswell, 1969, p. 294). A person's social network evolves throughout his life and potentially is very large. Not all members, of course, remain active. Most of the network may be dormant. With the advent of a stressful situation, however, different members may rally or become mobilized to provide aid. After the stress is over, they may once again become dormant. Boswell suggested that this happens upon death. As this stress subsides, the extent of aid to the family from certain groups also subsides.

The cultural values of the person's environment may influence the type of networks utilized. Gottlieb (1975) found that the subgroups of which adolescents were members determined what social networks the adolescents would utilize for help. This also was suggested by the restrictive networks for utilizers in the McKinlay study discussed above. Each group had specific preferences for resources within the environment. Westbrook (1979) further supported this by suggesting that socioeconomic status differences influence the mode of coping a person employs.

The availability of network members (related to density or the interconnectedness of a network) and their frequency of contact with persons in need appear to affect the provision of aid by network members. Hirsch (1979) has suggested that density is positively related to the effectiveness of a helping network, and Litwak and Szelenyi (1969) showed that differences in structures of primary groups were related to whether they were available and able to respond to crises. Moreover, Wellman (1979) and Unger (1979) both found a high positive correlation between the frequency of contact with network members and the extent of help received.

The costs involved in and the reciprocal nature of informal social networks may at times actually serve as an additional source of stress, influencing the potential beneficial impact of network involvement. For instance, Ackerman (1959) emphasized that the extended family can incite stress, stimulate family conflict, and add undue influential power over family members. Lee (1979) suggested that conjugal power and marital solidarity may be influenced by social network participation leading to marital conflict. For example, when one spouse has a higher rate of participation in extra-family social networks, this may lead to an increase in the spouse's status in the community as well as a reduction in the dependence on the other spouse. Hence, an increase in power may lead to conflict within the marital relationship. Furthermore, primarily based upon Ackerman's (1963) work, Lee reported that marital stability may be related positively to the extent to which spouses' networks are similar and overlapping, consequently leading to group pressure for marital conformity and stability. However, spouses having diverse characteristics and different friends and associates may experience greater instability and conflict and may be prone to divorce.

Networks, typically, are characterized by reciprocity such that one favor is exchanged in return for another; reciprocity has been noted as highly associated with network stability and effective functioning (Garigue, 1956; Nett, 1952). Stack (1974), however, has shown that the reciprocal nature of informal social networks which makes them effective also results in many demands involving much time and responsibility that can cause networks themselves to become a source of stress. When goods and services are exchanged, a condition of dependency can develop which also might lead to stress. Muir and Weinstein (1962) noted that exchanges may result in a person feeling "grateful" or "obligated." If the process of exchanging aid with network members becomes aversive, i.e., requires too much obligation, a person may forfeit the use of the network. It seems, however, that social networks prompt family stress in atypical cases where individuals have extreme or excessive involvement in a social network (see Blood, 1969).

In summary, an understanding of the use of social networks in coping with stress should include the interactive process of the family member in need of aid (i.e., cultural values, view of costs) in relation to social networks (i.e., availability and frequency of contact, reciprocal relations) and the situation involved (i.e., type of crisis, aid needed). Thus, the key question is not whether social networks provide support, but when and under what conditions are social networks a means of support?

Implications for Professional Intervention

The relation between social networks and a family's adaptation to stress has major implications for the design and delivery of services to families under stress. At a general level the findings imply a need for family counselors, educators, medical professionals and policymakers to consider the social contexts in which families function when designing and providing professional services. This implication is consistent with an emerging paradigm in the social sciences and human services. The paradigm reflects a socio-ecological perspective of services within a family and community context as contrasted to an individualistic, professional-institutional perspective of services to isolated individuals by a professional in an institutional setting (Schaefer, Note 2). In terms of specific implications for professional intervention, three nonexclusive ways that social networks may be utilized to assist families experiencing stress are suggested.

First, it might be beneficial to form complementary linkages between human service organizations and social networks (Tiejen, 1980). Formal organizations and families have important structural differences and are best suited to perform specific functions. Organizations deal with large numbers of individuals and approach problems in a uniform manner. Families, in contrast, deal with diversity, adjust to problems in unique ways, and provide a supportive emotional environment (Litwak & Figureira, 1970). By linking these two approaches, a family member could optimize his coping strategies. For instance, Sussman (1977) suggested that the elderly would benefit from a family-bureaucracy linkage approach such that the elderly member's kin network could bridge the gap between him and the organization to provide needed resources.

The Prenatal/Early Infancy Project (PEIP) (Olds, 1980), an ongoing demonstration and research project in New York state, utilizes nurses to "link" high-risk parents bearing their first child and formal health care services. Nurses work in the home and community to improve conditions for childbearing and childrearing. They provide home-based education concerning pregnancy and infancy, act as a referral agent for community resources, and help the parent identify and mobilize their social networks. PEIP also provides free transportation for prenatal and well-child care at a physician's office or health department. Utilization of informal and formal support systems is hoped to be optimized through this linkage approach.

Another form of social network-organization linkages might be the use of social networks to disseminate information about agency services. Because networks serve as major sources of information about and referral to professional services, organizations could supplement their formal channels of communication to prospective clients with the use of local community gatekeepers, neighborhood leaders, and grassroots community organizations to disseminate information. Leutz (1976), for example, found that informal caregivers such as clergy, bartenders, and merchants are likely to refer a person who approaches them about a problem when they are aware of a social service program that meets the need.

Second, professionals and agencies wishing to help families under stress might provide services that strengthen a family's use of social network ties in coping with stress. Instead of attempting to meet a family's needs directly through professional services, this approach would focus on the development and maintenance of a resourceful family social network. The Merrill-Palmer Institute is experimenting with this treatment strategy in a neighborhood-based program for families with children between the ages of 0 and 3 years. One purpose of the project is to strengthen families' use of social networks in dealing with stressful situations by encouraging the development of an active mutual aid system among the families participating in the program. Project activities also emphasize skills required to develop and sustain a significant social relationship; these include listening, respecting another's opinions, cooperation, reciprocity, and the value of mutual help as opposed to self help (Powell, 1979). A similar strategy that has been attempted is the development of "support groups." Persons experiencing similar stressful life transitions provide each other with emotional social support, enhancing their willingness and ability to supplement and/or change the resources provided by their present social network (McGuire & Gottleib, 1979; Wandersman et al., in press).

Third, existing networks may be mobilized to help a family member cope with crisis situations. Speck and Attenave (1973) and Rueveni (1979), for instance, have suggested detailed methods and strategies for network interven-

tion in emotional crises. Generally, family, friends, and neighbors are contacted and encouraged to increase their involvement in the family problem, share their concerns, and generate and implement solutions—including the formation of temporary support groups for the family members under stress. When working with handicapped children, Berger and Fowlkes (1980) have suggested that network member involvement is essential for successful intervention. Network members can provide support for the parents as well as take an active role in implementing the treatment programs for the child. Actively involving persons who care about the family member under stress and who are influential in his life increases the amount of support and resources available for effective family coping strategies.

In conclusion, networks may provide needed emotional and material support as well as help in finding infomation and services. Professional intervention efforts aimed at utilizing social networks should include careful consideration of the form of aid needed, types of network members most appropriate for providing the aid, and the life circumstances of the person needing assistance.

REFERENCE NOTES

1. Caldwell, B., Heider, J., & Kaplan, B. *Home observation for measurement of the environment.* (Available from the Center for Early Development and Education, University of Arkansas at Little Rock, Little Rock, Arkansas.)
2. Schaefer, E. S. *Professional paradigms in programs for parents and children.* Paper presented at the annual meeting of the American Psychological Association, San Francisco, August, 1977.

REFERENCES

Ackerman, C. Affiliations: Structural determination of differential divorce rates. *American Journal of Sociology*, 1963, **69**, 13-20.
Ackerman, N. Emotional impact of in-laws and relatives. In S. Liebman (Ed.). *Emotional forces in the family.* Philadelphia: Lippincott, 1959.
Bell, W., & Boat, M. D. Urban neighborhoods and informal social relations. *American Journal of Sociology*, 1957, **63**, 391-398.
Berger, M., & Fowlkes, M. A. Family Intervention project: A family network model for serving young handicapped children. *Young Children*, 1980, **51**, 188-198.
Blood, R. O. Kinship interaction and marital solidarity. *Merrill-Palmer Quarterly*, 1969, **15**, 171-184.

Boswell, D. M. Personal crisis and the mobilization of the social network. In C. Mitchell (Ed.), *Social networks in urban situations*. Manchester: Manchester University Press, 1969.

Bott, E. *Family and social network*. London: Tavistock, 1957.

Burke, R. J., & Weir, T. Marital helping relationships: The moderators between stress and well-being. *Journal of Psychology*, 1977, **95**, 121-130.

Cobb, S. Social support as a moderator of life stress. *Psychosomatic Medicine*, 1976, **38**, 300-314.

Croog, S. H., Lipson, A., & Levine, S. Help patterns in severe illnesses: The roles of kin network, nonfamily resources and institutions. *Journal of Marriage and the Family*, 1972, **34**, 32-41.

Dean, A., & Lin, N. The stress-buffering role of social support: Problems and prospects for systematic investigation. *Journal of Nervous and Mental Disease*, 1977, **165**, 403-417.

Drabek, P. E., & Boggs, K. S. Families in disaster: Reactions and relatives. *Journal of Marriage and the Family*, 1968, **30**, 443-457.

Eddy, W. B., Paap, S. M., & Glad, D. M. Solving problems in living: The citizen's viewpoint. *Mental Hygiene*, 1970, **54**, 64-72.

Freidson, E. Client control and medical practice. *American Journal of Sociology*, 1960, **56**, 374-382.

Garbarino, J., & Crouter, A. Defining the community context for parent-child relations: The correlates of child maltreatment. *Child Development*, 1978, **49**, 604-616.

Garbarino, J., & Sherman, D. High-risk neighborhoods and high-risk families: The human ecology of child maltreatment. *Child Development*, 1980, **35**, 22-32.

Garigue, P. French Canadian kinship and urban life. *American Anthropologist*, 1956, **58**, 1090-1101.

Gore, S. The influence of social support and related variables in ameliorating the consequences of job loss. *Dissertation Abstracts International*, 1974, **34**, 5330A-5331A.

Gottlieb, B. H. The contribution of natural support systems and primary prevention among four social subgroups of adolescent males. *Adolescence*, 1975, **10**, 207-220.

Gottlieb, B. H. Social networks, social support, and child maltreatment. In J. Garbarino & S. H. Stocking (Eds.), *Supporting families and protecting children*. Nebraska: Boys Town, 1979.

Hamburg, D. A., & Adams, J. E. A perspective on coping behavior. *Archives of General Psychiatry*, 1967, **17**, 277-284.

Hetherington, E. M., Cox, M., & Cox, R. The aftermath of divorce. In J. H. Stevens, Jr., & M. Matthews (Eds.), *Mother-child, father-child relations*. Washington, DC: National Association for the Education of Young Children, 1977.

Hill, R. *Families under stress*. New York: Harper, 1949.

Hirsch, B. J. Psychological dimensions of social networks: A multi-method analysis. *American Journal of Community Psychology*, 1979, **7**, 263-277.

Hirsch, B. J. Natural support systems and coping with major life changes. *American Journal of Community Psychology*, 1980, **8**, 159-171.

Koos, E. L. *Families in trouble*. New York: King's Crown Press, 1946.

Lee, G. R. Effects of social networks on the family. In W. R. Burr, R. Hill, F. I. Nye, & I. L. Reiss (Eds.), *Contemporary theories about the family* (Vol. 1). New York: Free Press, 1979.

Lee, N. H. *The search for an abortionist*. Chicago: University of Chicago Press, 1969.

Leutz, W. N. The informal community caregiver: A link between the health care system and local residents. *American Journal of Orthopsychiatry*, 1976, **46**, 678-688.

Lindenthal, J. J., Thomas, C. S., & Myers, J. K. Psychological status and the perception of primary and secondary support from the social milieu in time of crisis. *Journal of Nervous and Mental Disease*, 1971, **153**, 92-98.

Litwak, E., & Figueira, J. Technological innovation and ideal forms of family structure in an industrial democratic society. In R. Hill & R. Konig (Eds.), *Families in east and west*. Paris: Mouton, 1970.

Litwak, E., & Szelenyi, I. Primary group structures and their functions: Kin, neighbors and friends. *American Sociological Review*, 1969, **34**, 465-481.

McAdoo, H. P. Factors related to stability in upwardly mobile black families. *Journal of Marriage and the Family*, 1978, **40**, 761-778.

McKinlay, J. B. Social networks, lay consultation and help-seeking behavior. *Social Forces*, 1973, **51**, 275-292.

Muir, D. E., & Weinstein, E. A. The social debt: An investigation of lower-class and middle-class norms of social obligation. *American Sociological Review*, 1962, **27**, 532-539.

Nett, B. R. Historical changes in the Osage kinship system. *Southwest Journal of Anthropology*, 1952, **8**, 164-181.

Nuckolls, C. B., Cassel, J., & Kaplan, B. H. Psychosocial assets, life crises, and the prognosis of pregnancy. *American Journal of Epidemiology*, 1972, **95**, 431-441.

Olds, D. Improving formal services for mothers and children. In J. Garbarino, S. H. Stocking, & Associates (Eds.), *Protecting children from abuse and neglect*. San Francisco: Jossey-Bass, 1980.

Polansky, N. A., Chalmers, M. A., Buttenwieser, C., & Williams, D. P. Isolation of the neglectful family. *American Journal of Orthopsychiatry*, 1979, **49**, 149-152.

Powell, D. R. Correlates of parent-teacher communication frequency and diversity. *Journal of Educational Research*, 1978, **71**, 333-341.

Powell, D. R. Family-environment relations and early child-rearing: The role of social networks and neighborhoods. *Journal of Research and Development in Education*, 1979, **13**, 1-11.

Rosenblatt, A., & Mayer, J. E. Help seeking for family problems: A survey of utilization and satisfaction. *American Journal of Psychiatry*, 1972, **128**, 1136-1140.

Rosow, I. *Social integration of the aged*. New York: Free Press, 1967.

Rueveni, U. *Networking families in crisis*. New York: Human Services Press, 1979.

Sarason, S. B., Carroll, C. F., Maton, K., Cohen, S., & Lorentz, E. *Human services and resource networks*. San Francisco: Jossey-Bass, 1977.

Speck, R. V., & Attenave, C. *Family networks*. New York: Vintage, 1973.

Stack, C. B. *All our kin: Strategies for survival in a black community*. New York: Harper & Row, 1974.

Stouffer, S. A., & Lazarsfeld, P. F. *Research moratorium on the family in the depression* (Bulletin 29). New York: Social Science Research Council, 1937.

Sussman, M. B. Family, bureaucracy and the elderly individual. An organization/linkage perspective. In E. Shanas & M. B. Sussman (Eds.), *Family, bureaucracy and the elderly.* North Carolina: Duke University Press, 1977.

Tiejen, A. Integrating formal and informal support systems: The Swedish experience. In J. Garbarino, S. H. Stocking, & Associates (Eds.), *Protecting children from abuse and neglect.* San Francisco: Jossey-Bass, 1980.

Turner, J. T., Kimbrough, W. W., & Traynhan, R. N. A survey of community perceptions of critical life situations and community helping sources as a tool for mental health development. *Journal of Community Psychology*, 1977, 5, 225-230.

Unger, D. G. *An ecological approach to the family: The role of social networks, social stress, and mother-child interaction.* Unpublished Master's thesis, Merrill-Palmer Institute, Detroit, 1979.

Wandersman, L. P., Wandersman, A., & Kahn, S. Social support in the transition to parenthood. *Journal of Community Psychology*, 1980, in press.

Wellman, B. The community question: The intimate networks of East Yorkers. *American Journal of Sociology*, 1979, **84**, 1201-1231.

Westbrook, M. T. Socioeconomic differences in coping with childbearing. *American Journal of Community Psychology*, 1979, **7**, 397-412.

Whitten, N. E., & Wolfe, A. W. Network analysis. In J. J. Honigman (Ed.), *Handbook of social and cultural anthropology.* Chicago: Rand McNally, 1973.

Young, D. *Research moratorium on minority peoples in the depression* (Bulletin 31). New York: Social Science Research Council, 1937.

Family Stress and the Effectiveness of In-Home Intervention*

PATRICIA W. CAUTLEY**

A research and demonstration project, this study was focused on the effectiveness of in-home intervention in facilitating permanency planning for children. Data obtained were examined in terms of the relationships between the degree of stress and the extent of social support experienced, and the outcome of the intervention. Consistent differences, some significant, were found between the mothers in the two groups whose treatment was judged "effective" and "ineffective." Analysis suggests that those experiencing internal stress, as contrasted with external stress or pressure, and having an adequate social support system, are more likely to respond positively to the kind of intervention offered.

In this paper the relationship between characteristics of families under stress and the outcome of intensive in-home treatment will be examined. The data are based on work with 32 families referred by a helping professional because of problems in parent-child interaction. In the majority of cases, there was a possibility of later removal of the child or children to substitute care if the interaction did not improve.

Drawing from Lazarus' (1966) conceptualization, we define stress as a perception of additional strain on the family system, produced by persons or events within or outside the family, which upsets the "balance" of the family system. Stress is experienced as "anticipatory threat" (Lazarus' term), that is, the fear that something will happen in the future. Such fear may be very explicit, as a social

worker's threat to remove the child, or it may be more general, as the fear of still more difficult behavior on the part of the child, or increasingly unpleasant interchanges within the family.

It is important to note that it is the individual's *perceptions* of the persons or events which produce the stress. Parents may react very differently to a report from an early childhood program that their child shows signs of developmental delay; one may experience considerable stress, while another may regard the school as "meddling." Both of these responses represent a type of coping with the threat, that is, the implicit prediction that the child will develop more slowly than others and may be "different" or possibly "inferior" in some respect. Although both children and parents cope with stress, we will look primarily at the coping skills shown by the parents during the course of the intervention with them. A primary hypothesis to be tested is that the coping skills developed by parents depend substantially upon their view of themselves and of their relationships with others.

Cobb (1976) describes both view of self and relationships with others as aspects of "social support," and has presented a variety of evidence that individuals cope with life crises more effectively if they experience such support. He defines "social support" as based

*This paper is based on research conducted as part of "Facilitating Long-term Optimal Planning for Children (OPT)," supported by Grant 90-C-996 from the Center for Child Advocacy, Children's Bureau, Administration for Children, Youth and Families, Department of Health, Education, and Welfare, to the Division of Community Services, Wisconsin Department of Health and Social Services.

**Patricia Cautley is a social psychologist and former director of project OPT, on which this article is based.

(Family Relations, 1980, 29, 575-583.)

upon information available to the subject and "leading the subject to believe" that s/he:

    a. is cared for and loved,

    b. is esteemed and valued,

    c. belongs to a network of communication and mutual obligation (Cobb, 1976, p. 300).

It is notable that these three characteristics, stated in negative rather than positive terms, are among five found by Helfer (Note 1) to indicate a potential for child abuse. He also included a lack of understanding of child development, such as unrealistic expectations of a child, and a likelihood of selecting a spouse unable to give emotional support. In the work reported here, however, data pertaining to only the first three characteristics are available.

Overview of Approach and Outcome

The purpose of this work was to test the effectiveness of short-term intervention in bringing about significant change in families with problems in parent-child interaction, and in which the targeted child or children were 11 years of age or younger (Cautley, in press). The focus of treatment was on the "family system," that is, on the contribution of each member to the kinds of interaction occurring and on ways in which this interaction might be shifted to be more positive and mutually satisfying. It was assumed that the problems had developed because of the ways in which the parents and children were acting or responding, or failing to do so, to each other, and that changes in the behaviors of one would be reflected in changes in the other.

The principles involved are based on social learning theory: that most behavior is learned and is maintained because it brings certain dividends or "rewards," that it can be changed or replaced if more socially desirable ways of obtaining these dividends or rewards are identified and learned, and that the parent can be an effective change agent. Hence, primary attention was first given to teaching desirable child management methods to the parents, although considerable effort was also devoted to other relationships within the family system.

The staff of the project was first trained by two members of the Home and Community Treatment Program at Mendota Mental Health Institute (Note 2). The basic methodology had been developed there during an eight-year period, stemming initially from observations that significant gains made by emotionally disturbed children in an institutional setting were rarely maintained after the children returned home. This suggested that the problems lay within the family system and the community rather than solely within the child, and led to the development of methods of working within these systems rather than removing the child to an artificial environment (Fahl & Morrissey, 1979; Fahl, 1980).

One important aspect of this approach includes systematic observations of interaction within the family group, with all members present. These usually consist of at least three periods of one-and-a-half hours each, during which time two staff members observe what is going on, preferably at critical periods such as mealtime or bedtime. The rationale is that much more can be learned from such observations than from verbal descriptions. A team of two, following a pre-determined schedule of 5- or 10-minute segments, counts certain specific parent-and-child behaviors and also devotes some segments to recording qualitative descriptions of the behavior of each family member in turn. In addition, the project staff relied heavily on an initial tape-recorded interview with each member of the family individually in the presence of all the others. In this way the perceptions of each were gathered regarding various dimensions hypothesized to be pertinent, including the problems of the family and/or the children, possible causes of them, what had been tried, the sources of different kinds of social support, and each parent's perceptions of the characteristics of parenting experienced while growing up. Although further information was provided by the referring professional, main reliance in the analysis of data has been placed on the information obtained by use of these two methods.

The team assigned to a family would then review all the information obtained, and in a feedback session describe to the family both the strengths and the areas to be worked on. From this, definite plans for treatment were made, and an attempt made to schedule sessions three times a week with the family for a maximum period of 8 to 12 weeks.[1] Such a limitation was necessitated by the terms of the first grant, made for one year only with no likelihood of renewal. Butcher and Koss (1978) describe some advantages of time-limited therapy, however.

The Process of Treatment

The importance of helping the parents improve child management skills was emphasized in almost every feedback session, and received attention in the early treatment sessions. Work generally focused on giving positive feedback to the child, on using clear directions—as contrasted with unclear directions or threats—and expecting compliance to them, and on consistent expectations. The antecedents and consequences of difficult behaviors were examined as both contribute to maintaining the undesired behavior. Since many of the parents had little or no awareness that it could be fun to play with their children, activities enjoyable for both parents and children were introduced. As methods of discipline, "time-out" and "stop the world" were taught.

In many of the families it became clear that there were other problems affecting the ability of the parents to function adequately and appropriately. The approaches to these were of necessity more varied and also depended to a larger extent on the background and skills of staff members than the work on child management.[2] In both direct and subtle ways, the staff attempted to help each parent become more confident and more capable in interaction with the children, to bolster the self-esteem of each one, to help them resolve problems of relationship with the current spouse or mate or others, and to help them find small groups or other community resources which could continue to provide support after the project's involvement ended.

[1] The training provided by Mary Ann Fahl and Donna Morrissey is gratefully acknowledged. See *Home and Community Treatment Programs* (Note 2) for a detailed description of the methodology.

[2] The original design of the study specified a random assignment of families after the initial interview and observations to a control and a treatment group, but this was not possible as workers did not want to refer families unless they could receive treatment.

Other work included such areas as helping several single mothers become involved in psychotherapy—one with her family of origin, and the other in individual therapy—and helping several obtain the services of the Division of Vocational Rehabilitation for job counseling and possible job training.

Evaluation of Effectiveness

A variety of measures obtained at the end of treatment in order to evaluate its effectiveness include the following:

1. systematic observations of interaction within the family, following the same schedule used initially;
2. a questionnaire completed by the referring professional, or the one currently involved with the family;
3. an interview with the family, conducted by a staff member not involved in treatment with the family;
4. a detailed questionnaire and rating scale completed by the team which had worked with the family, in which each of the goals of treatment was listed and an appraisal made of the extent to which it had been achieved and the likelihood that any gains made would be maintained;
5. a judgment made by consensus of the entire staff, which had become familiar with every family through weekly staff meetings; this judgment, regarded as the best overall measure of the effectiveness of treatment, categorized the families in three outcome groups:

E. Treatment effective. Families made significant positive changes judged likely to be maintained. (Fourteen families were designated as "E" families.)

P. Treatment partially effective. Families made some significant positive changes judged unlikely to be maintained. (Ten families were designated as "P" families.)

I. Treatment ineffective. All but one of the families in this group withdrew before the agreed-upon period of treatment had ended; some had made very minimal gains, others none. (Eight families were designated as "I" families.) The one family that completed treatment made such limited changes that the project team cooperated with the agency in seeking out and obtaining termination of parental rights so that the two young children could be placed for adoption.

Although these staff judgments were made before any of the other outcome data were examined, they are for the most part supported by the others, although not necessarily at a statistically significant level (Cautley, in press).[3] The staff ratings indicate that permanent plans were facilitated for children in 47% of these families. Each family in the "E" and "P" outcome groups is being followed for 18 months after the end of treatment in order to learn more about the longer-term effects of the intervention.

Sources of Social Support

Data pertaining to the three dimensions of social support postulated by Cobb (1976) were obtained in the initial interviews with each family:

1. The extent to which each parent felt loved and cared for was assessed in the following ways:

a. The relationship each woman described with her own mother, and whether she would like it to be any different. (Three subjects whose mothers were no longer living were omitted from the analysis.) When the answers to these two questions were combined, the report of a close and satisfactory relationship or of a desire that it be closer was given by a significantly larger proportion of the "E" women than of the "I" women ($p < .05$).

b. The report of having received at least "some" affection from their fathers when growing up was made by significantly more of the "E" than of the "I" mothers.

c. When asked whether each parent had been "strict or lenient," significantly

more responses indicating that one or both parents were perceived as autocratic (for example, "We jumped whenever he spoke") were given by mothers in the "I" group than in the "E" group.

d. Since there were fathers or father figures in only 15 of the 32 families, data regarding them were examined in a qualitative way. All but one of the six families in which the father was the biological parent of all the children in the home were found in the "E" group, whereas all but one of the nine in which a father figure was present but not the biological parent of any or all the children were found in the "P" and "I" groups.

We interpret these findings as evidence that the mothers in the "E" group had more reason to feel "cared for and loved" during their growing up than those in the "I" group, and possibly more reason to feel secure in the greater commitment of their mate to the family.

2. The extent to which each mother felt "esteemed and valued" was assessed by use of a questionnaire developed to study self-esteem in college students, modified slightly to eliminate items concerning the student role. In the few instances in which it seemed likely that the respondent lacked the reading skill to complete it, each item was read aloud. Answers were in five categories: strongly agree, agree, uncertain, disagree, strongly disagree. Each mother was asked to indicate the extent to which the statement described her. Since some items seemed less pertinent to this population of women, a group of six items was selected for a sub-score.[4] The mean scores for the women in the "E" and "P" groups were very similar, regardless of whether the total score on all 23 items or the sub-score on 6 items was used, and they were higher than the mean scores for the

[3] I am greatly indebted to Suzanne Adelman, Julia Bonser, David Carson, Paula Elkins, Gary Howards, and Dottie Lambert Whisnant for their skills and commitment to the work. The death of Dottie Lambert Whisnant in a car accident when returning from work with a family was a great personal loss for each of us as well as for the professional field.

[4] The six items selected for the sub-score of self-esteem are the following:

I often wish I were someone else.

I always do the right thing.

There are a lot of things about myself I'd change if I could.

Most people are better liked than I am.

Things are all mixed up in my life.

My friends make me feel I'm not good enough.

women in the "I" group. Although not statistically significant, these differences suggest that the women in the more favorable outcome groups began treatment with slightly higher self-esteem than those in the least favorable outcome group.

3. The extent to which each mother felt she belonged to a "network of communication and mutual obligation" was assessed through three questions:

    a. Is there anyone outside this family that you like to talk with about things that are bothering you?

    b. Is there anyone you can depend on to help in a crisis?

    c. Is there anyone outside your family that you especially enjoy seeing?

A positive answer to each question was followed by questions about who the person was, how often s/he had been seen during the last month, and whether it was easy or difficult to get in touch with the person. When the answers to each question are compared, more of the women in the "P" group gave positive answers to the first two questions, and more of those in the "E" group than in the others gave positive answers to the third question. In each case, the women in the "I" group indicated less support than those in either of the other groups in answer to each question and in their overall average of answers.

From these three kinds of indicators of social support, it appears that the mothers in the "E" group were somewhat better equipped to handle stress than those in the "I" group, with those in the "P" group not showing a clear pattern. A relevant question which follows is whether the extent of stress differed for the families in these three outcome groups.

Sources of Stress in Client Families

Several different kinds of data pertain to the kind and extent of stress experienced by these families. In each case they are examined from the point of view of the families, primarily the mothers.

1. The primary reasons stated by the professional persons referring the families were nearly equally divided between problems in parenting behavior and problems in the child's behavior. However, considerably more of the families in the "I" and "P" groups than in the "E" group were referred because of problems in parenting behavior (62 and 50% as compared with 28%). If communicated to the clients, which generally occurred in the first meeting of the staff with the family and referring worker, this would suggest that the families in the "E" group had a better rationale or "excuse" for their problems than those in the other two groups. That is, if the problem is said to be mainly the child's behavior, the parents can believe that they simply have a very difficult child. They may be more willing to obtain help than parents who are told that the agency is concerned about the care they are giving their child.

2. Information in the initial interviews with the families also suggests some differences in the ways these three groups of families perceived sources of stress, both in their description of the "main problems of the family" and "problems with the children's behavior." Although the numbers are too small to show statistically significant differences, it is to be noted that half the families in the "I" group said they had "no main problems," but described only problems with their children, mainly lack of obedience or compliance. Families in the "E" group more frequently than in the "I" group mentioned problems of relationship with others in the family in answer to either question.

When asked "Why do you think (child) behaves in this way?" over half or more of the parents in the "P" and "I" groups naming problems had no idea of possible causes, while this was the case for only 25% of the "E" families. Of this latter group, 42% attributed the difficulties to their own child-rearing approach, including lack of skills. Such an attribution led to the question of whether the degree of stress experienced might depend in part on whether its source was perceived to be "internal" or "external," and whether this might be related to the outcome of treatment.

3. Two subjective ratings were made by the writer to examine such a possibility, although the limitations of such ratings are recognized:

a. One rating was based on whether the source of the immediate stress experienced by the family appeared to be (1) internal, that is, at least one of the parents was actively experiencing stress due to his/her perceived role in producing the problem or difficulty in making the needed changes, or

(2) external, that is stress created primarily by pressure from the outside, generally the referring professional, but in a few cases the court or the threat of court involvement.

Examples of internal sources of stress are the following:

— a mother requesting removal of a seven-year-old son to foster care because she could not stand his difficult behavior;

— parents almost completely controlled by the very coercive behavior of their preschool child, which they felt powerless to change;

— a couple experiencing great tension because of the husband's unemployment after an accident, his retreat to activities whch he enjoyed and his wife disliked, and their inability to talk with each other about the causes of their hurting.

Examples of external sources of stress are the following:

— school personnel threatening to take a mother to court because of the extremely difficult behavior of her son at school;

— a couple referred by an agency worker because of alleged neglect of their two young children.

Nearly three-fourths of the mothers in the "E" group were rated as evidencing internal stress, while only one-fifth of the "P" group had a similar rating (Table 1). If this rating has validity, this difference suggests that the experience of internal stress is more likely to be associated with a positive response to treatment.

b . A second subjective rating referred to the "degree of stress" evidenced by families at the time of referral. A four-point scale was used: severe, moderate, relatively little, none apparent. Included in the judgment was evidence as to whether the family had sought or welcomed outside help because of their problems, or had resisted such help or shown ambivalence in other ways. The ratings suggest that substantially fewer of the "P" families were experiencing a high degree of stress than those in either of the other groups—20% as compared with 62 and 64% in the "E" and "I" groups. However, when the records of the individual families in the "P" group were examined, it appeared that more than half had problems which would be judged as serious or more serious than those in the "E" group, but that many of them had psychological "defenses" which enabled them to deny the seriousness of the problems. One was a mother with three school-aged sons, each a very serious problem in school, and, in our eyes, very asocial both at school and at home. She had a rigid way of coping with them, and in general had very little interaction with them. Another blamed the school personnel for the difficult behavior of her son. One mother, while under considerable external pressure because of the agency's explicit threats to remove her son, and very angry at the withdrawal of a previous attempt to give her help, was possibly too quickly reassured and made comfortable by the OPT team so that the stress on her was too quickly relieved.

Table 1
Primary Source of Stress in Families at
Time of Referral

	Outcome groups		
Primary source of stress	"E" %	"P" %	"I" %
Internal	72	20	13
Cannot determine	14	—	37
External	14	80	50
	100	100	100
Number of families	14	10	8

Although similar proportions of both the "E" and "I" families were rated as under moderate or severe stress, there is evidence that half the families in the "I" group could be judged more dysfunctional than those in the other two groups, that is, having pervasive problems affecting the family's functioning in many different areas. This is found in ratings made at the beginning of treatment describing the environment each family was providing for its children in terms of (a) physical care, (b) emotional nurturance, (c) cognitive development, and (d) socialization. Families in the "E" group were given significantly higher ratings than those in the "I" group on all four dimensions. One possible explanation of the failure of treatment, then, is that the dysfunctional "I" families had a precarious family "balance," barely maintained, so that any attempt to introduce change would be likely to threaten the entire functioning of the family. Consequently, the treatment would be rejected. Some of the comments made at the time of withdrawal support this interpretation:

It's been a farce; the kids haven't changed.
I just don't want to see you again.
You're upsetting me; I can't take it. Please go; leave me alone.

The data summarized here suggest that some stress must be experienced by the parents if they are to work toward changing, but that there are probably limits to the "breadth" or "depth" of the stress experienced if treatment is to be effective. The dynamics in these families are undoubtedly very complex, and much more research is needed to further the understanding of the relationship among these variables.

Evidence from the Families as to the Effectiveness of Treatment

Tape-recorded interviews were conducted with each family at the end of treatment, always by a staff member who had not been involved in working with them. This meant that only the families who had completed treatment were interviewed; most of those who withdrew were too eager to sever their contacts to permit an interview. From the information obtained in the interviews, the following differences between the "E" and "P" groups were found:

1. When asked what they saw as the "main problems in your family right now," 45% of the "P" group listed only problems very similar to those named in the initial interview,
while none of the "E" group gave such a similar list although they still enumerated problems.

2. Regarding "any change in your family during the period of OPT involvement," a very large majority of both groups mentioned acquiring parenting skills, but considerably more of the "E" than "P" group mentioned that in general things were better, the family happier, or that they had become "more confident" as a parent. In addition, more of the "E" mothers mentioned that they had a "much better personal outlook on life," and referred spontaneously to enjoying their children more than they had previously. These changes suggest that their coping skills had improved.

3. Regarding the ending of treatment, half the "E" group clearly indicated they wished it would continue longer, and none was glad that it was ending. Only 22% of the "P" group would have liked it to continue longer; 45% were ambivalent about its ending, and one-third were glad it was over.

4. Readiness to contact their social worker if seeking help with a problem was greater in the "E" than the "P" group (67% as compared with 28% of those having an on-going worker). Such readiness suggests that these women had greater protection against future severe stress than those who felt ambivalent or negative about seeking help.

In general, the mothers in the "E" families were much more enthusiastic about their work with the OPT staff than those in the "P" families. Clearly the former had developed better rapport with those women. We conjecture that this difference may at least in part be related to the greater internal stress which the "E" families seemed to show as compared with the "P" families. This in turn might be expected to produce a greater desire for help and motivation to work toward change.

Discussion

Evidence has been presented that the kind of intensive in-home intervention described here, limited in duration to a period of 8 to 12 weeks, is more likely to produce positive changes judged to be significant and likely to be maintained in families in which the mother indicates that she has some self-esteem, a fairly satisfactory relationship with her own mother or a desire for a better relationship, and available sources of social support in her environment. These characteristics, taken together, are defined by Cobb (1976) as evidence of "social support," which he indicates can moderate life stresses. In this study two groups of families, those in which treatment was judged effective (E), and those in which it was judged ineffective (I), showed consistent differences with respect to such "social support," while the group for whom treatment was judged partially effective (P) showed greater similarity to the "E" group in "social support." An attempt to understand why treatment was not as effective with the "P" families revealed that: (a) the referring professionals more frequently referred these families in terms of inadequate parenting behavior, while (b) the mothers themselves more often described their problems solely in terms of the child's behavior. There is evidence that the "P" families experienced less internal stress than the "E" families and felt external stress created by an authority outside the family who urged them to accept the training offered by our project. It is also possible that a number of the "P" families had rationalized their problems—even regarding them insoluble—and hence did not feel the kind of stress generally experienced by the "E" families. An example is the "P" mother who acknowledged verbal abuse of her child: "That's just the way I am."

None of these outcome groups is completely homogeneous; in each are some families that do not fit the general pattern. These exceptions have been examined in an attempt to increase understanding of some of the dynamics involved, although it is recognized that many other factors and personality characteristics complicate the picture. Two single mothers in the "E" group showed much less promising "social support" than the rest of the group; neither reported that there were other persons she could count on or go to, and neither had a very good relationship with her own mother. One also showed low self-esteem, while the relatively high self-esteem score of the other was the only promising detail in her picture. In the case of this latter woman, we believe that the degree of support,

skilled counseling, use of community resources, and firm expectations offered by the OPT staff member primarily involved with her accounted for the great improvement shown. The other woman seems, on retrospect, to have been mainly depressed, probably by her husband's recent move out of the home, but did not have as serious problems within her family. She improved her child management skills, and, with help provided from another source, was able to take all the necessary steps to go back to school to learn a skill. Follow-up of these two families will be of particular value in showing whether their gains were maintained.

One single mother in the "P" group provides an exception in that group as she indicated no sources of social support in her environment, and had no stable mother figure when growing up, but had a relatively high self-esteem score. She barely tolerated her children, and although she seemed to make a few significant changes, they were very limited in comparison with all of the changes that would have been desirable for her. The team involved in working with her had no confidence that the changes would be maintained.

Two families in the "I" group, on the other hand, appear to have been reasonably promising in terms of the three dimensions: each mother indicated relatively high self-esteem and a fairly good relationship with her own mother, as well as good social support in her environment. One of these families consisted of a couple with one young child of their own and two older children of the mother's. They presented a very complex situation which only gradually became apparent. Because the entire focus of the referral, however, had been the evidence of delayed development in the youngest child, the team did not have the family's "permission" to work on other problem areas. When an attempt was made to do this, the family withdrew.

The other "I" family with reasonably promising "social support" was a single mother, very upset at her husband's desertion, disorganized, and unable to give her young children adequate care. Her relatives were no longer willing to "rescue" her and she showed considerable stress. Even the strenuous efforts of the staff seemed ineffective, however, and she made virtually no change before withdrawing, merely wanting the staff to discipline and manage her children. Some months after her involvement ended, however, it was learned that her child care had improved greatly when a stable relationship with a live-in mate had developed.

In conclusion, this study represents only a very preliminary effort to understand some of the factors contributing to the degree of stress experienced by families with problems in parent-child interaction and the effectiveness of in-home intervention in helping the parents develop appropriate parenting and coping skills. Much more study of such families is needed in order to unravel the relative contribution of the many pertinent variables and increase the effectiveness of intervention efforts.

REFERENCE NOTES

1. Helfer, R. E. *The diagnostic process and treatment programs*. U.S. Department of Health, Education, and Welfare Publication No. OHD 75-69, 1975.

2. *Home and community treatment programs*. Unpublished manuscript, 1980. (Available from Mendota Mental Health Institute, 301 Troy Drive, Madison, WI 53704).

REFERENCES

Butcher, J. N., & Koss, M. P. Research on brief and crisis-oriented therapies. In S. L. Garfield & A. E. Bergin (Eds.), *Handbook of psychotherapy and behavior change*. New York: Wiley, 1978.

Cautley, P. W. In-home treatment with dysfunctional families. *Social Work*, in press.

Cobb, S. Social support as a moderator of life stress. *Psychosomatic Medicine*, 1976, **38**, 300-314.

Fahl, M. A. Shaping parent-child interaction: A behavioral model in a family context. In M. E. Bryce & J. C. Lloyd (Eds.), *Treating families in the home: An alternative to placement*. Springfield, IL: Charles C. Thomas, 1980. 80.

Fahl, M. A., & Morrissey, D. The Mendota model: Home-community treatment. In S. Maybanks & M. Bryce (Eds.), *Home-based services for children and families: Policy, practice, and research*. Springfield, IL: Charles C. Thomas, 1979.

Lazarus, R. S. *Psychological stress and the coping process*. New York: McGraw-Hill, 1966.

Lazarus, R. S. Cognitive and coping processes in emotion. In A. Monat & R. S. Lazarus (Eds.), *Stress and coping: An anthology*. New York: Columbia University Press, 1977.

Coping With Sudden Infant Death Syndrome: Intervention Strategies and a Case Study

SHARON AADALEN*

Survivors of Sudden Infant Death Syndrome (SIDS) are a population at risk of disorganization and dysfunction. This paper documents their needs and describes a program of identification and intervention in which the public health nurse is a primary but not exclusive interventionist. A brief discussion of relevant theoretical frameworks for working with the family system as client is presented. Documentation of healthful outcomes for the target population which can be correlated with service provision is necessary. Presentation of case study data attempts to address this need.

The sudden, unexpected death of an apparently healthy infant shocks and disorganizes the surviving family system (DeFrain & Ernst, 1978). Sudden Infant Death Syndrome (SIDS) is the most common single cause of death in infants between one week and one year of age, with up to two deaths per 1,000 live births per year (Bergman, 1969; Bergman, 1972; Maeye, Ladis, & Drage, 1976; Valdes-Dapena, Note 1; Weinstein, Note 2).

The occurrence of "crib death" is described in the Old Testament of the Holy Bible (I Kings, 3:19). However, identification of the syndrome as a public health problem did not occur until the 1960s through the efforts of surviving parents. The National Sudden Infant Death Syndrome Foundation and the Guild for Infant Survival promote: (a) medical research; (b) support for family system survivors; and (c) public education related to the syndrome. With the passage of U.S. Senate Bill 206 (Report 92-830, June 7, 1972) federal appropriations to the Department of Health, Education and Welfare have supported basic pathophysiologic and epidemiologic research, as well as the establishment of state and municipal programs providing education, coordination and counseling services (Franciosi, 1977). There is a need for behavioral research on SIDS survivors (Weinstein, Note 2).

In the past, public ignorance of SIDS has contributed to the development of uninformed opinions and judgments about SIDS deaths. For example, survivor parents have been accused of neglecting and/or abusing their dead child. Throughout the United States, SIDS Programs are informing human service professionals (e.g., medical examiners, rescue team members), health care delivery professionals (e.g., physicians, nurses), and lay persons about the syndrome in an effort to sensitize them to the needs of SIDS survivors. Local and state SIDS programs also coordinate care and support services to survivors by: (a) informing them of their right (free of charge) to an autopsy of their dead infant; (b) monitoring autopsy reporting to families; (c) making direct contact with survivors or referral to public health nurses; (d) sponsoring mutual support groups; and (e) evaluating SIDS programs.

The purpose of this paper is to emphasize the surviving family's recognized need for intervention at the time of the death. Family-focused assessment, diagnosis, and interven-

*Sharon Aadalen is Instructor, Program Public Health Nursing, School of Public Health, University of Minnesota, Minneapolis, MN.

(*Family Relations*, 1980, **29**, 584-590.)

tion strategies for practitioners working with survivors in crisis are identified. The SIDS program of social support is discussed with specific reference to the role of public health nurses as primary interveners in the community. The SIDS program assumes that intervention at the time of loss facilitates active, shared grieving among survivors. But what about survivor families for whom this support is not available? What are the outcomes for these families? Can delayed intervention by community mental health workers, such as public health nurses, promote healthful family adaptations? Case study data lend support to the hypothesis that family system oriented intervention with a SIDS family two years post infant death can facilitate unfinished grief work, interrupt patterns of family disorganization, and relieve symptomatology.

SIDS Program

The sudden death of a seemingly healthy child is an unthinkable event in the Twentieth Century. At this time, SIDS is unpredictable and unpreventable. Survivors experience acute grief somato-physically and as intense subjective mental pain. SIDS parents may experience despondency, concentration difficulties, time confusion, loss of appetite, or inability to sleep. Particularly intense may be a dread of being alone and the fear of responsibility for the care of other children (Pomeroy, 1969). Parents feel impotent, angry, and guilty (Bugen, 1977; Hanseli, 1976). These powerful emotions do not go away; they need to be experienced and shared.

The SIDS Program advocates survivor rights to active, unconditional support at the time of the SIDS death; social support; autopsy to determine the cause of death followed by a written report to survivors; instrumental support (counseling) as needed; and mobilization of material, non-human resources. Cobb (1976, p. 300) defines social support as "information which leads one to believe that he is cared for and loved, esteemed, and has membership in a network of mutual obligations." The SIDS Program of intervention is grounded in a growing body of research which affirms that supportive human interactions are protective against the health consequences of life stress (Cobb, 1976).

Anyone who comes in contact with a SIDS family can play a most important role in implementing the specific aspects of the SIDS Program intervention strategies:

1. Unconditional support of survivors

a. attempt to resuscitate the baby

b. when an infant is declared dead, provide active support of and privacy for survivors to say goodbye to their baby and to express their emotions.

c. consider non-family survivors who may have been intimately involved in the dead infant's care such as babysitters

d. leave determinations of the presence or absence of injury or abuse to the medical examiner

2. Accurate information

a. explain to survivors the importance of an autopsy to establish the diagnosis of SIDS (diagnosis is made when death remains unexplained after review of circumstances surrounding death and a complete autopsy) (Valdes-Dapena, 1978; Franciosi, Note 3)

b. inform survivors of right to autopsy and support them in any decision making about autopsy

c. facilitate communication to survivors of clear, interpretive written autopsy findings as quickly as possible (48-hour maximum)

Community health professional (typically, public health nurse) intervention includes:

1. Visiting the survivor family in their home as soon as possible after the death and funeral

a. share specific information about the syndrome

b. establish a relationship with survivors supportive of their needs for acceptance, esteem, and interdependence

2. Facilitating grief response and grief work

a. interpret the experience of extreme grief (physical, psychological, and emotional symptoms) to survivors as normal

b. attempt to link survivors to surrounding community by increasing their awareness of existing human networks and resources such as mutual support groups for SIDS survivors and published materials about SIDS (Bureau of Community Health Services Publications Center, Room 7-A, Fishers Lane, Rockville, MD 20857).

3. Providing advocacy for survivors at the time of death and in the days, weeks,

months and years ahead (Minnesota Department of Health, Note 4).

The SIDS Program provides a model for meeting population and family system needs where they exist through coordination of services and existing community resources and involvement of health care consumers.

Family System Assessment, Diagnosis and Intervention

Given the limits of knowledge at this time and the aura of mystery which continues to surround Sudden Infant Death, a family system has no base of experience with which to cope when a baby dies; it is by definition a crisis for the family system (Aguilera & Messich, 1974; Hill, 1953).

Reuben Hill's ABC = X conceptualization of variables which interrelate to determine family vulnerability (the degree to which a stressful event is experienced as a crisis) provides a model for assessing and intervening with survivors of Sudden Infant Death (Hill, 1958). A stressor event (A), interacting with the family's crisis-meeting resources (B), interacting with the perception of or meaning a family ascribes to an event (C), produces a crisis (X). Hill defines "hardships" as external to the family: "complications in a crisis-precipitating event which demand competencies from the family which the event itself may have temporarily paralyzed or made unavailable" (Hill, 1958, p. 35). The hardships experienced by a family as it tries to assimilate the death may render the period of disorganization more severe, prolonged, or debilitating.

A crisis involves systems of interacting individuals. People in crisis may appear quite fragmented (Haan, 1977). An ecologic perspective on the client system in the community (Auerswald, 1966) incorporates the developmental and situational stressors to which individuals and family systems are subject within the total human and non-human environment.

General systems theory views member dysfunction as a system disturbance rather than a loss of individual functions (von Bertalanffy, 1974). It provides the conceptual base for viewing the family as a social system engaged in complex, multidirectional and multilevel interactions within the family, and between the family system and the surrounding environment. A tension may be observed in any given family between the tendency to close boundaries (seeking stability), and to allow for permeability of boundaries which facilitates adaptation (change).

The circumplex model developed by Olson, Sprenkle, and Russell (1979), provides a measure of the degree to which a family system achieves such a balance. The model identifies major orthogonal (independent) dimensions of family behavior, cohesion and adaptability, and proposes that a balance of these dimensions is the most functional for spouse relationships and family development. Family cohesion is described as "the emotional bonding members have with one another and the degree of individual autonomy a person experiences in the family system" (p. 5). The definition of family adaptability is "the ability of a marital/family system to change its power structure, role relationships, and relationship rules in response to situational and developmental stress" (p. 12). Crisis-prone and multi-problem families share inadequate organization; cohesion and adaptability are impaired (Hill, 1958).

Burr (1973) has reviewed studies related to both vulnerability to stressors and the regenerative power of families. Recent research efforts have attempted to identify the parameters of "coping," defined as strategies for managing stress (McCubbin, in press). Identification of coping strategies could guide the development of intervention procedures aimed at altering the impact of stressor events on family systems through decreasing system vulnerability and increasing family regenerative power.

Family System Intervention: A Case Study

When the C family sought help through a crisis center for Mrs. C's suicidal impulses and anxiety attacks, she and other family members labeled her "sick," i.e., the patient in the family. She was put on medication to "calm her."

Two years earlier, Mr. and Mrs. C had lost their first child, a 2½-month-old baby boy to SIDS. Their experience substantiates the isolating and isolated position of the survivor system; they lacked social supports (family and community), and their perception of the meaning of their son's death was inaccurate and devastating.

During the first home visit by a public health nurse Mrs. C said:

I've been thinking about suicide a lot. I felt I really had to die because it was my fault he died. I put him in a crib when he was crying. And I hadn't taken him to the doctor for his loose stool, because he had been checked the week before.

When the regional SIDS Program opened one and a half years after their son's death, the C's received information about the SIDS Program. The material helped Mrs. C know in her head that her baby's death was not her fault but she couldn't shake the feeling in her gut. Almost two years after her son's death, her impulses to commit suicide remained real and terrifying. Significant was her awareness of the discrepancy between her head and her gut. The ability to make this distinction indicated a firm grasp of reality. This was an important factor in determining the appropriate care for the family. Mr. C had assumed a strong protector role in the family, a role which appears to have prevented his feeling or experiencing his grief at the loss of his son. The C's female child was born fifteen months after the son's death. She appeared to be at risk of emotional distancing from her parents who were preoccupied with the fear of a second SIDS death.

The public health nurse's assessment was corroborated in an interdisciplinary conference involving Mr. and Mrs. C, the mental health consultant for the SIDS Program, the public health nurse, and the social worker from the crisis center. The mutually determined plan for the C family was family-focused care in the home coordinated by the public health nurse.

The public health nurse's ongoing-assessment of the C family drew on the family development conceptual framework (Aldous, 1975; Duvall, 1962; Hill & Hansen, 1960), as well as the circumplex model dimensions of cohesion and adaptability. A review of Mr. and Mrs. C's families of origin suggested both had early-life experiences in demoralized families (i.e., the families' ability to carry out task and role functions was impaired). Both of their parents had problems with chemical de-

pendency which limited their ability to model cooperative, interdependent functioning.

When Mr. and Mrs. C married, they had the goal of moving beyond the control and criticism of their families of origin. They appeared to compromise the development of adaptive skills in order to maintain their boundaries and equilibrium to an even greater degree than expected among the newly married. They did not seem to understand that as they formed their own family unit, they would need to meet the requirements of societal institutions and more importantly that their own unmet needs would continue to make demands on their nuclear family unit. Based on identified patterns of avoidance, withdrawal, detachment, suppression of emotion, and cutting off relationships when conflict or some other stressor arose, very tight boundary maintenance would be expected within the family.

Extreme cohesion (lack of differentiation of self) was suggested in the C family by initial verbal acceptance of the public health nurse; but non-verbal resistance hindered the development of a relationship with her. Another indication of high cohesion was the degree to which Mr. and Mrs. C spoke for one another and made assumptions about one another's feelings with no effort to check out the assumption with the partner.

The C family lacked crisis-meeting resources. Their crisis of SIDS led to premature adaptive closure: "I went back to work and kept busy and tried not to think about it. It doesn't do any good to think about it" (Mr. C). The C family seemed to have short-circuited the important step of mourning; their level of reorganization may have been quite rigidly structured and limited. Two years after the SIDS death, their family system was in great distress.

The public health nurse organized her assessment findings according to Snyder and Wilson's (1977) eclectic approach to psychosocial assessment which includes: response to stress; coping and defense mechanisms; interpersonal relationships; motivation and life-style; thought processes and verbal behavior; non-verbal behavior; awareness and handling of feelings; support systems; talents, strengths, and assets; physical health; and the influence of the self of the nurse.

The intervention strategy employed by the public health nurse reflects concern for all levels of prevention, primary, secondary, and tertiary (Leavell & Clark, 1965). It reflects an ecologic perspective on stressors as they arise from within the client system (intrapersonal and interpersonal), from the external environment, and from the interaction between the family system and the external environment. The intervention reflects a parallel conceptualization of client and family coping as a complex of intrinsic adaptive mechanisms (intrapersonal), learned behaviors (interpersonal), and extrinsic environmental resources and interactive support systems, which can be mobilized and nurtured to promote family system movement to new levels of structural and emotional integrity (Aadalen, 1978; Argyris, 1965; Coleman, 1973; Lazarus, 1966; Mechanic, 1968). From this perspective individuals and families are viewed as variably open systems (von Bertalanffy, 1974). Richman (1979) suggests family therapy as an appropriate if under-utilized approach for suicidal client systems. The use of the family systems approach by nurses has been documented by Smoyak (1975) and Hazzard (1976).

The public health nurse worked with the C family to identify their goals. The goals are stated using Mr. and Mrs. C's words. The public health nurse's identification of objectives follows in parentheses:

1. To get off medication—Mrs. C (develop alternative coping strategies);

2. To feel safe at home (obtain improvements to dwelling to meet housing code safety standards; identify support systems within and beyond the family system);

3. To find health care we can afford (explore available resources; learn health promotion, and disease prevention life style strategies);

4. To feel comfortable and at ease (facilitate grief work; experience feelings; develop communication skills);

5. To be good parents (reflect on their own experience of parenting; learn new parenting skills; develop problem-solving skills).

The intervention strategy incorporated development of a genogram (Bowen, 1966), which identified past history and relationships and the way(s) they can affect current interactions within the family. Use of the genogram also facilitated work on member differentiation of self which was important in this enmeshed family system. The work of Satir (1967) and her techniques for strengthening families was the basis for involving Mr. and Mrs. C in the process of discovering themselves as individuals, their experiences as a family, and their feeling states. The public health nurse also drew on Glasser's (1965) reality therapy, which focuses on present behavior and individual responsibility for behavior. Specific aspects of the nurse's intervention strategy included:

1. Explore family as a system (whole greater than the sum of parts)

   a. differentiate members within the family (feelings, experiences) through empathy, acceptance, respect, and concreteness

   b. identify public health nurse as an individual subsystem interacting with the family system

2. Develop work relationship

   a. identify member and system strengths

   b. identify problems and approaches to problem resolution

   c. identify family system goals and explore possibilities for member growth and health development

   d. identify periods of regression (their meaning and value)

   e. public health nurse as role model for candor, confrontation, and accountability

3. Movement of family system toward interdependence with community (behavior change)

   a. action on housing; identification of health care resources

   b. budgeting time, energy, resources

   c. develop support systems

   d. public health nurse as advocate for family system

4. Analysis and evaluation

   a. new coping and life skills of family

   b. influence of nurse on family system

   c. relationship of C family to extended family

   d. relocation of C family.

Behavioral Outcomes for the C Family

In a report of research conducted among public health nurses to identify criteria for assessing client well-being, Mayers (1972) identified nine client behavioral or situational clues ranked in decreasing order of frequency by practicing public health nurses. They were: ability to act independently, physical condition, congruent feelings or affect, interpersonal ability, verbal ability, ability to meet role expectations, congruent life style, appropriateness of future plans and intellectual ability. During data analysis, Mayers identified four other factors which correlated closely with nurse-perceived coping abilities of patients. These four factors are: ease or difficulty of entree by the nurse, open or closed environment (shades drawn or light sources maximized), ability or inability to focus on conversation, and a positive or negative mood-response pattern (non-verbal aspects of patient's behavior).

The relationship between Mayers' empirically derived criterion categories and Snyder and Wilson's conceptually conceived categories is clear. Using these criteria as guides, documentation is presented of behavioral change noted in the C family over the five-month period of intervention:

1. *Interpersonal relationships.* Mr. and Mrs. C are risking involvement with each other and persons beyond the family system. While still very concerned about their daughter's well-being, they have begun to relax with her. The amount of interpersonal anxiety has diminished in the family system, and the relative amount of interpersonal security has increased. The couple is developing communication skills which help them to work through disagreements before they escalate into fights or flights. They are developing new levels of tolerance and understanding for each other and their child.

2. *Motivation and life-style.* Mrs. C had discovered that she can choose responses as well as reacting impulsively. Mr. C has begun to plan for a future in contrast to earlier efforts to blot out the past (e.g., avoidance, denial). They both evidence aspirations and hope which were lacking before intervention.

3. *Awareness and handling of feelings.* Mrs. C's suicidal feelings and anxiety attacks decreased and then disappeared within the first month of referral. There has been no recurrence of suicidal impulses. This may reflect the family system's new level of organization. They are more realistic in their self assessments and have an improved sense of competency. There is increased congruence between verbalizations and affect for both Mr. and Mrs. C.

4. *Support systems.* Relationships within the extended families have not really improved. The couple has sporadic contact with extended family members which Mrs. C is better able to handle without losing her sense of self. The couple rely less on family contacts and are developing new friends through the work situation. Through one friend, they located a pleasant, affordable apartment in a town beyond the suburban ring, close to their place at work. They are considering a church affiliation in the community to which they have moved. They have reached out to other SIDS families for mutual support.

5. *Physical health.* Mrs. C is off drugs completely. Mr. and Mrs. C identified on-going health maintenance and promotion care for each member of the family. Mrs. C is obtaining some long needed dental care.

Conclusion

Preventive intervention by a public health nurse using a family-centered approach two years after the death of a baby to SIDS appears to have facilitated reorganization, growth and development in the family system. What may have been a permanently defeating crisis has become an opportunity for developing coping skills and strengthening individual family members and the family system as a whole. While such an intervention may be provided by any mental health professional who shares an ecologic developmental family systems perspective, public health nursing's outreach to families in their homes has become a most significant component of the total SIDS Program.

REFERENCE NOTES

1. Valdes-Dapena, M. *Sudden unexplained infant death, 1970 through 1975: An evolution in understanding.* DHEW Publication No. (HSA) 78-5255. Bureau of Community Health Services, 1978.

2. Weinstein, S. (Ed.). *Mental health issues in grief counseling. Summary of proceedings: National conference on mental health issues related to Sudden Infant Death Syndrome,* February 23-27, 1977. DHEW Publication Number (HSA) 79-5264. Rockville, MD: Bureau of Community Health Services, 1979.

3. Franciosi, R. A. *The diagnosis of SIDS*. Presentation at the Fourth National SIDS Conference in Minneapolis, MN, June, 1980.

4. Minnesota Department of Health, Section of Maternal and Child Health, *Guidelines for public health nurses for Sudden Infant Death Syndrome*, 1977. (Available from the Minnesota Department of Health, Minneapolis, MN)

REFERENCES

Aadalen, S. P. *The concept of coping: An inquiry in search of criteria.* Minneapolis: Unpublished Master's thesis, University of Minnesota, 1978.

Aguilera, D. C., & Messich, J. M. *Crisis intervention theory and methodology* (2nd ed.). St. Louis: Mosby, 1974.

Aldous, J. *The developmental approach to family analysis* (Vol. 1). *The conceptual framework*. Athens, GA: University of Georgia, 1975.

Argyris, C. Explorations in interpersonal competence—1. *Journal of Applied Behavioral Science*, 1965, **1**, 58-83.

Auerswald, E. H. The "interdisciplinary" versus the "ecological systems" approach in the field of mental health. Atlantic City, NJ: American Psychiatric Association, 1966.

Bergman, A. B. Psychiatric toll of the Sudden Infant Death Syndrome. *General Practice*, 1969, **40**, 99-105.

Bergman, A. B. Sudden Infant Death. *Nursing Outlook*, 1972, **20**, 775-777.

Bowen, M. The use of family therapy in clinical practice. *Comprehensive Psychiatry*, 1966, **7**, 345-374.

Bugen, L. A. Human grief: A model for prediction and intervention. *American Journal of Orthopsychiatry*, 1977, **47**, 196-206.

Burr, W. R. *Theory construction and the sociology of the family*. New York: Wiley, 1973.

Cobb, S. Social support as a moderator of life stress. *Psychosomatic Medicine*, 1976, **38**, 300-314.

Coleman, J. C. Life stress and maladaptive behavior. *The American Journal of Occupational Therapy*, 1973, **27**, 169-186.

DeFrain, J. D., & Ernst, L. The psychological effects of Sudden Infant Death Syndrome on surviving family members. *The Journal of Family Practice*, 1978, **6**, 985-989.

Duvall, E. M. *Family development*. Philadelphia: Lippincott, 1962.

Franciosi, R. A. Approaching the problem of Sudden Infant Death Syndrome. *Minnesota Medicine*, 1977, **60**(2), 117-119.

Glasser, W. *Reality therapy: A new approach to psychiatry*. New York: Harper & Row, 1965.

Haan, N. *Coping and defending: Processes of self-environment organization*. New York: Academic Press, 1977.

Hansell, N. *The person-in-distress: On the biosocial dynamics of adaptation*. New York: Human Sciences, 1976.

Hazzard, M. E. Family systems therapy: A new way to help families in trouble. *Nursing 76*, 1976, **6**, 22-23.

Hill, R. Social stresses on the family. *Social Casework*, 1958, **39**, 139-150.

Hill, R. & Hansen, D. A. The identification of conceptual frameworks utilized in family study. *Marriage and Family Living*, 1960, **22**, 299-311.

Holy Bible: King James Version. Translated 1611. Cleveland: World Publishing.

Lazarus, R. S. *Psychological stress and the coping process*. New York: McGraw-Hill, 1966.

Leavell, H. R., & Clark, E. G. *Preventive medicine for the doctor and his community* (3rd ed.). New York: McGraw-Hill, 1965.

Mayers, M. G. A search for assessment criteria. *Nursing Outlook*, 1972, **20**, 324-326.

McCubbin, H. I. (Ed.). *Family stress, coping and social support: Theory, research, and practice for family and health professionals*. New York: Springer Publishing, in press.

Mechanic, D. *Medical sociology*. New York: Free Press, 1968.

Naeye, R. L., Ladis, N., & Drage, J. S. Sudden Infant Death Syndrome: A prospective study. *American Journal of Diseases in Children*, 1976, **130**, 1207-1210.

Olson, D. G., Sprenkle, D. H., & Russell, C. S. Circumplex model of marital and family systems: 1. Cohesion and adaptability dimensions, family types, and clinical applications. *Family Process*, 1979, **18**, 3-28.

Pomeroy, M. R. Sudden Death Syndrome. *American Journal of Nursing*, 1969, **69**, 1886-1890.

Richman, J. The family therapy of attempted suicide. *Family Process*, 1979, **18**, 131-142.

Satir, V. *Conjoint family therapy* (Rev. ed.). Palo Alto, CA: Science & Behavior Books, 1967.

Smoyak, S. (Ed) The psychiatric nurse as a family therapist. New York: Wiley, 1975.

Snyder, J. C., & Wilson, M. F. Elements of a psychological assessment. *American Journal of Nursing*, 1977, **77**, 235-239.

von Bertalanffy, L. General systems theory and psychiatry. In S. Arieti (Ed.), *American Handbook of Psychiatry*, (2nd ed). New York: Basic Books, 1974.

Crisis Group Therapy with the Separated and Divorced

EDWARD HASSALL AND DOROTHY MADAR*

This paper examines the use of crisis intervention techniques in a group setting as an effective modality for meeting the social and emotional needs of separated and divorced people and helping them to deal with their relationship loss trauma. The authors have drawn on their own experience with groups of separated and divorced people. The steps in the treatment process begin with cognitive mastery of the normal spectrum of reaction, and continue through the stages of expressing and resolving grief to the restructuring of the individual life situation.

The Problems of the Newly Separated and Divorced

The social and emotional problems of separation and divorce are well documented in the literature. For the newly separated person, feelings of guilt, hostility, depression and failure abound, with loneliness being the most distressing feeling (Hunt, 1966). The potency of these feelings makes separation a time of emotional crisis even if the separation is wanted by both spouses (Price-Bonham & Rose, 1973). A change in marital status usually brings about a change in social relationships, since many of a separated person's previous relationships have been associated with the marital union. In many situations the separated person, experiencing self doubt and questioning his or her own judgment, tends to withdraw from social intimacy, into isolation (Schlesinger, 1977). For their part, friends and relatives are often unsure what behaviors and feelings are appropriate responses to the newly separated, and therefore often diminish their contacts. A sense of rejection and abandonment, which is deeply felt by both partners, is inherent in the separation process (Morris & Prescott, 1975)

and this occurs at a time when the need for emotional support is greatest.

Problems in Finding Appropriate Support

Many separated persons consult physicians and mental health practitioners because of lassitude, insomnia, anxiety, and psychosomatic conditions. Twenty-two percent cf separated and divorced men and 40% of the women have been reported to seek help for personal problems (Gurin & Veroff, 1960). Hunt reported that one-sixth of all family heads who approached family agencies were separated or divorced persons in need of counseling (Hunt, 1966). More recent studies indicate that over 30% of families serviced by child welfare agencies are single parent families (Hassall, Note 1). Despite the large number of the separated seeking professional service, many do not receive the help they need. The problem originates in training programs for marriage and family therapists where emphasis is placed on the goal of improving the marital relationship, and little on understanding divorce processes or defining what is appropriate treatment for the separating client (Brown, 1976). Therapists, agencies and institutions tend to want newly separated persons to involve themselves in an attempt to re-establish the marriage, rather than to assist them in adjusting to the reality of their separation—a step often more appropriate to the needs of the client (Canadian Council on Social Development, Note 2).

*Edward Hassall is Supervisor and Dorothy Madar is a therapist, Family Counselling Centre, Family and Children's Services, St. Catharines, Ontario, Canada.

(*Family Relations*, 1980, **29**, 591-597.)

A Group Approach to Crisis Intervention

The literature suggests that for families or individuals in crisis situations, crisis intervention should be the method of choice. In a number of settings the crisis intervention method is applied in a group context (Golan, 1974). Because many clients suffer rejection, loneliness and social isolation (Hunt, 1966; Morris & Prescott, 1975; Price-Bonham & Rose, 1973; Schlesinger, 1977), an important variable in the helping process is the opportunity to become part of a network of social relationships and the experiencing of a sense of belonging to a group of peers (Goroff, 1972). Group members have the opportunity to share their own experiences and provide immediate mutual feedback—two processes that are advantages of the group milieu over individual therapy in the treatment of relationship loss trauma (Hiltz, 1975). Groups are especially effective with clients immobilized by unresolved grief, since participation in a group is helpful in enabling the resisting client to unburden his grief (Olsen, 1970). These, indeed, have been the observations of the authors; a group approach, using the crisis intervention model of treatment, is our treatment of choice with the newly separated. The following represents a description of treatment interventions in this context.

Selection of Single Parent Group Members

Working in a family agency setting, the authors have noted that often single parents select a child as the identified patient. The symptom-bearer for the family is brought to the therapist as the one in need of professional input. A family diagnostic session is held and parents are referred to the group work program if they meet the following characteristics:

1. Parents are able to identify a recent loss in their life. Either they are in crisis or their recent crisis was not adequately resolved.
2. The therapist is able to demonstrate to the single parent the functional aspect of the identified patient's behavior in helping the parent avoid dealing with his or her own feelings.
3. The parent becomes at least intellectually aware of feelings concerning the loss situation.

4. The parent is able to acknowledge a regression in his or her coping patterns and finally through the help of a therapist is able to recognize the need to become involved in the grief resolution process.

At the group level we have found that the most effectively functioning groups have included a mixture of personality types and social backgrounds. They have also included at least one person who is farther along in the resolution of his or her loss. The element of hope and the introduction of the concept of the time-limited nature of the grieving process is thus included. In our experience, the mixed-sex group seems to be most effective in allowing the challenging of distortions and generalizations about the opposite sex, and in the therapeutic realization that the pain and uncertainties of loss are not sex-specific. A mixed group also allows the members to learn new behaviors toward the opposite sex in a less threatening environment.

The Beginning of Therapy—Cognitive Reorganization

At the first group session, clients are presented with a review of the crisis intervention model (Caplan, 1964). This is an important part of the group program and is aimed at giving clients an intellectual understanding of themselves and of their particular life situations. This is especially helpful with those clients who tend to deny affect and who carry within them very powerful emotions awaiting release. These clients tend to find that their behavior is disorganized and are generally fearful of this. What is wrong with me? Am I going crazy? These are questions and fears that emerge again and again.

I kept it all to myself, but finally it came through and I went to pieces. I was scared I was getting mentally ill. The memories keep coming alive over and over. I found myself getting up at 3 a.m. to clean the house. I really felt frenzied. I was so tired, but I didn't seem able to stop.

It was very supportive to her to learn that she was not becoming mentally ill. Her frenzied activity was interpreted as being an external representation of her inner tensions. The therapist stressed to her that her feelings and behaviors were a normal response to a loss situation which, it was also interpreted, could present an opportunity for growth. Most clients are usually comforted to receive such information, for it places their feelings and actions within the normal limits of expected behavior.

Steps to crisis resolution, shown in Table 1, are presented to the group as are the intentions of the therapists to move each member through the sub-steps of the model. The notion of early-life crisis is introduced as one particular part of the model with the explanation that people who are unable to resolve present hazardous situations are often those who have had an earlier life crisis which was itself not resolved. It is explained that "if grief is not expressed at the time of a loss, the feelings can hang on for years" (Simos, 1977, p. 339). Indeed, past failures at resolution of old conflicts, threats and trauma may well act as additional burdens in attempts at resolution of the present crisis (Rapoport, 1965). Therefore, the importance of exploring areas of previous crisis is presented to the group.

By introducing a model that contains a progression of steps, the notion of movement and progress through the grieving process is established at the outset within a broader context of hopefulness. Hopefulness is a necessary ingredient for action in therapy (Stotland, 1969). Recognizing this, the therapists select at least one person who has made positive gains in crisis resolution to be a member of each group. This person can be influential to those members of the group who are anxious and doubtful about what is before them. Having a peer say, "I know how you feel, I have been that way myself; but, you know, like myself, you will feel better in time," motivates and encourages group members to make a contract to continue with the group in its planned format.

Table 1
Steps to Crisis Resolution

1. Identify the emotionally hazardous situation.
2. Identify defenses you create to avoid grief.
3. Give up these defenses to permit yourself to experience your emotions as intensively as possible—begin to mourn.
4. Obtain new information about your relationship with the lost person, e.g., what were all the reasons for the marital conflict.
5. Learn to manage your feelings by becoming more and more aware of your emotions.
6. Verbalize and experience the feelings which lead to discharge of tension.
7. Identify the early-life crisis in your life you have not resolved.
8. Problem solving—restructure life.

Identification of the Emotionally Hazardous Situation

Following presentation of the model, each participant is helped to unfold his or her own emotionally hazardous situation. For some clients the loss of a meaningful relationship with their spouse may be the most painful part of their reality. For other people it may be the loss of a highly valued role. It is not uncommon to hear a sad or angry woman expressing that,

All I really wanted was to be someone's wife and stay at home with my children. Now I have to go out to work full time. I have no husband and not enough time with my children. I liked things the way they were for me. I don't like where I am. I want to be where I was.

Or the client may experience the loss of children as the most painful loss if there has been relinquishment or denial of custody. Separation involves not only the loss of a partner, but also of a social status, a set of roles, perhaps children, for many people a certain financial position, and often of dreams and expectations of self.

Some clients define their emotionally hazardous situation readily, but those who tend to defend by denial or projection usually have more difficulty. The therapist helps each member identify the object loss situation producing the emotional crisis. Through a series of go-arounds from member to member, and through group discussion, each person in the group is helped to identify the meaningful loss or losses that have occurred recently in his or her life.

I still love her. I want her back. When she left with the kids I felt as though the world

had fallen apart, and then when I found out she was with him, I thought I was going crazy. Now my house is full of ghosts. I come home sometimes and I almost think I hear them all. I'm just so lonely.

Identification and Removal of Defenses to Avoid Grief

As the clients define their emotionally hazardous situations, it becomes evident what their coping patterns have been and what their defensive patterns are. The therapists identify and confront these patterns with each group member. Interpretations are given that these defensive maneuvers themselves cause tension, and the clients are guided into an affective expression of their grief.

Cheryl verbalized her defenses: *I'm so busy all the time* [she showed no tears but was visibly tense] *when I go to bed I just pass out. I didn't want the separation and I try not to think about it. I try to keep my mind off it."* Therapist: *It's over, Cheryl, your marriage is gone."* [Cheryl burst into tears and wept for several moments with the encouragement of the therapist.] *"Let your sadness flow, Cheryl, it's good for you . . . Your denying your sadness only leaves you with more tension. . . . "*

Due to social constraints, the effective expression of loss may be difficult in normal interpersonal contexts. "Because of our cultural emphasis on competence, adequacy and strength, the bereaved are often prevented by family and friends from experiencing the emotions which should follow loss in order to find a healthy resolution" (Simos, 1977, p. 338). In fact, clients who resist experiencing feelings of loss inflict a great deal of additional stress upon themselves. Since the peer group of people shares a relationship loss trauma, the normal constraints are lessened. The group can therefore have a powerful effect in eliminating the resistance to expression of loss. This overcoming of resistance is necessary, for "obsessive review provides a means for gradual acceptance of an unpalatable reality" (Weiss, 1975, p. 80).

Going over and over the loss in private memory and in the group frees a person to experience the grief and accept the loss.

Through group discussion, focusing, labeling, confrontation, and support, the clients are encouraged to give up their defenses and begin the mourning process within the group session.

I've tried to keep busy, I guess, to keep my mind off my personal situation, but it's all coming alive in me now. I find myself going over all the memories and feelings. It's like it was all held back. I have to get it out of my system. I have my children and it's spring, and I can see all the beautiful things and I just think, why do I have to feel so miserable inside? It is just a very deep sadness I have to work out.

Each client is encouraged to begin this ventilation process in the group. Quite often this represents a first for each client, since the clients who come into the group tend to be ones who deny feelings of loss. After having truly begun to experience and express their grief and all the associated feelings of guilt, anger, hostility, etc., and to start the obsessive review in a supportive, accepting group environment, clients usually experience a noticeable relief of tension. This is interpreted to the individual and to the group as a whole as the beginning step in the process of resolving a major loss and thus freeing themselves from an old relationship. The clients' acceptance of their loss enables them to avoid becoming fixated on the grief. They then have more freedom to redefine past and present relationships, and to begin to restructure their lives.

When clients correctively experience their grief for the first time, they leave the group experiencing the beginnings of tension relief. Following this breakthrough, they are given some homework to take with them: instructions to complete the process at home by themselves. Because their group experience has been very positive and has produced a reduction of their tension, clients usually follow through with their assignment. The therapist encourages them to find a half an hour each day to be alone, to get in touch with their feelings, to think of the good times of their marriage, to think about the bad times, to think of their faults, the faults of their spouse, and to think of the many positive experiences they might have had in the marriage—and then to remind themselves that these are now gone. It is important that they allow themselves to experience their grief and to verbalize their feelings. Clients who move into this process subsequently learn to manage their affect through ventilation, and they come to see that verbalization of feelings will lead to a discharge of inner tension and a beginning resolution of the loss.

Obtaining New Information

Most notable with group members are the many "whys" they bring to the group. Clients often do not understand the conflicts within themselves, their spouses, and within the marital system itself which resulted in dissolution of the marriage. The group can be very helpful in providing new information regarding the client's reality. For example, with clients who experience considerable guilt over the breakup of the marriage, the group can be very skillful at helping them to look at the faults of their ex-spouse, often for the first time. These clients will tend to feel a tremendous emotional release from the insights that stem from the realization "it wasn't all me."

I can cope better, be stronger. I can now see that we both had problems. I can see what was his responsibility and what was mine. I hope now I know my problems and my insecurities, I can work on these.

The group is also particularly good at promoting the expression of anger from these clients, and at being able to talk about the frustrations of being let down and left alone by their spouse. For those clients immobilized by guilt, the beginning of the expression of anger in the group is extremely helpful.

For those clients who deal with their situation through projection, the group is also helpful. These are the clients who initially want to relate to the group their spouse's problem behaviors. The group can be quite confronting, however, in turning these projections around and saying, "You know, you seem to have had a role in this, too."

The result of this reality testing in the group is that clients gain new information and knowledge about their marriage, and thus are better able to piece together the many questions about the relationship loss. They are instructed, if possible, to talk to their ex-spouses, to have a session with them outside the group and become aware of the variety of reasons behind the marriage breakdown.

Early Life Crisis

A present crisis, such as a separation or a divorce, "awakens unresolved key problems from both the near and distant past, and revives old feelings of upset and conflict which are linked with previously unresolved crises" (Caplan and Parad, p. 67).

Last year I separated from my wife. That was a little after losing a baby—my youngest one. I was recovering from that part of it, I thought. When this happened it just knocked me flat. I haven't been able to get over it as I should, as I figure I should just feel maybe if I'd been different, able to take control, maybe it wouldn't have happened.

Within the group setting clients are encouraged to rethink important incidents of their past lives and to identify some of their early life crises and the conflicts and feelings surrounding them. Often there is a strong initial resistance to exploring and dealing with powerful and conflict-ridden areas which have been suppressed or repressed. The therapist must be prepared to deal with this feeling, for as the clients go through this process, they will begin resolving some of these conflicts and emotions in the present.

There was one real bad time when I was a kid. I was ten years old and you know how your parents have drawers you can't go into. I went into that drawer and found out that I was adopted. I wanted to say something, but I thought, 'No, they've never said anything so I shouldn't.' I never have and they never have. I don't really let myself think about it. I guess we just didn't talk a lot about feelings. I have always kept my feelings in a drawer.

The therapist challenged Lynn that at present she has an opportunity to finally discuss the adoption issue with her parents. Lynn's response was, "I would not do that, my mother is not well, my father has a weak heart, it would only upset them." After attempts at persuasion, the therapist said,

Lynn, close your eyes, imagine the time when your parents will both be dead. Imagine yourself standing at their grave . . . How will you feel then if you have

never taken the opportunity to discuss this very meaningful situation with your parents? Lynn thought and replied, *Yes . . . I will talk to them.*

With this support of the group Lynn was able to engage her parents in discussion and tell them she was aware of her adoption. Through this process she began to discuss her feelings with her parents, something she had never done before. The trauma of the adoption disclosure was talked about and resolved, with both the parents and Lynn feeling good about it. Lynn began to ask to have her needs met and share her feelings more freely in other contexts as well.

Progress reports back to the group have often been amazing, as group members work in the present at resolving earlier crises in their lives. In some groups, members with families still living in Europe have initiated discussion with them of past traumatic situations that they previously had been afraid to discuss on a feeling basis. Often there followed exchanges of long letters and audiotapes as these issues unfolded and were resolved in the present.

Problem Solving

The final step in the therapists' model is that of problem solving. From the beginning of the group sessions, members have, at times, attempted to avoid dealing with the painful gamut of feelings surrounding their loss and the loss itself by suggesting and attempting specific life changes. Such suggestions as beginning to develop new relationships by getting involved with single-parent groups, keeping busy, going back to school or securing employment are all potentially positive courses of action after the grief process has begun to be resolved. The therapist "must be able to distinguish between a hasty and premature replacement of the loss and the eventual healthy restitution which follows grief, and represents a new sense of self without that which has been lost" (Simos, 1977, p. 342). Until the point when the clients have freed themselves from the old relationships and are emotionally ready to restructure their lives, it is important that the therapist re-focus from problem solving to an expression and working through of loss.

One of the criticisms of crisis intervention as it is practised is that practitioners often tend to focus too quickly on enabling people in loss situations to resume task-oriented behavior as rapidly as possible. "Too often the crisis-intervention practitioners reflect their own socialization into a society where problem-solving takes precedence over emotional expression . . . (thus) the helper himself can become a deterrent to the working through of grief" (Simos, 1977, p. 341).

It is only when the emotional tie to the lost relationship is broken that a person is able to re-invest in other situations or relationships. Problem-solving is encouraged at this point and now the group will help each member to examine the realities of his or her life, examine the needs that are not being met through existing relationships and activities, and encourage the beginning of the restructuring of each member's life situation to better meet these perceived needs.

REFERENCE NOTES

1. Hassall, E. *Groupwork with single parents.* Ontario Association of Children's Aid Societies, 663 Younge St., Suite 501, Toronto, Ontario, Canada, M4Y 2A4, 1971.
2. Canadian Council on Social Development. *The one-parent family: Report of an inquiry on the one-parent families in Canada.* 55 Parkdale, Ottawa, Ontario, Canada, K1Y FG1, 1971.

REFERENCES

Brown, E. M. Divorce Counselling. In D. L. Olson (Ed.), *Treating relationships.* Lake Mills, IA: Graphic, 1976.

Caplan, A., *Principles of preventive psychiatry.* New York: Basic, 1964.

Caplan, H., & Parad, H. A framework for studying families in crisis. In H. Parad (Ed.), *Crisis intervention: Selected readings.* New York: Family Service Association of America, 1965.

Golan, N. Crisis theory. In F. Turner (Ed.), *Social work treatment: Interlocking theoretical approaches.* New York: Free Press, 1974.

Goroff, N. Unique properties of groups: Resources to help people. *Child Welfare,* 1972, **4**, 494-503.

Gurin, A., & Veroff, S. F. *America looks at its mental health.* New York: Basic, 1960.

Hiltz, S. Helping widows: Group discussions as a therapeutic technique. *The Family Coordinator,* 1975, **24**, 331-336.

Hunt, M. M., *The world of the formerly married.* New York: McGraw-Hill, 1966.

Morris, J. D., & Prescott, M. R. Transition groups: An approach to dealing with post-partnership anguish. *The Family Coordinator*, 1975, **24**, 325-330.

Olsen, M. *Group counselling*. New York: Holt Rinehart Winston, 1960.

Price-Bonham, S., & Rose, V. L. Divorce adjustment: A woman's problem. *The Family Coordinator*, 1973, **22**, 291-297.

Rapoport, L. The state of crisis: Some theoretical considerations. In H. Parad (Ed.), *Crisis interventions: Selected readings*. New York: Family Service Association of America, 1965.

Schlesinger, B. One parent families in Great Britain. *The Family Coordinator*, 1977, **26**, 139-141.

Simos, B. Grief therapy to facilitate healthy restitution. *Social Casework*, 1977, **58**, 337-342.

Stotland, E. *The psychology of hope*. San Francisco: Jossey-Bass, 1969.

Weiss, R. *Marital separation*. New York: Basic, 1975.

Application of a Bicultural Assessment Framework to Social Work Practice with Hispanics

JOAN S. VELASQUEZ AND CESAR P. VELASQUEZ*

Considering it essential that cultural factors be taken into account throughout the helping process, project staff developed a bicultural assessment framework for social work practice with Hispanic clients. Case material illustrates its use with families at varying locations on a cultural continuum. Although developed as an aid for assessment, the framework proves useful in treatment and training as well.

Traditionally, mental health and social services to Hispanic[1] clients have been based on an assimilationist model, which assesses and treats the client family from an Anglo-American cultural perspective and views success in Anglo-American terms. This approach is exemplified in most extreme form by White (1971), who presented community center teachers with his interpretation of Mexican cultural characteristics and then explained how understanding of these characteristics could be used to "Americanize" their clients. Within the past decade, numerous authors have pointed to the need for consideration of cultural factors when providing services (Padilla, Note 1). Recognition of this need led to the current legislative mandate that all mental health centers provide culturally and linguistically appropriate services to ethnic populations in their catchment areas (Public Law 94-63). The perspective of cultural pluralism, as opposed to assimilation, is conso-

nant with this mandate and provides the value base for the bicultural assessment framework presented here. Our aim is to increase awareness of the importance of cultural factors and provide a conceptual framework for integrating these factors into service delivery to Hispanic families under stress.

Through a National Institute of Mental Health training grant (NIMH training grant #5-TO1-MH13891), the University of Minnesota School of Social Work, in collaboration with the Ramsey County Mental Health Department, recruited bilingual (Spanish/English) students and trained them through an internship and seminar to provide counseling, advocacy and community development services to the Hispanic community (Benavides, Lynch, & Velasquez, 1980). Field instructors for these students found that, in addition to developing the competencies required for generic social work practice, it was also essential to integrate consideration of cultural variables into all phases of service delivery.[2] The occurrence of intrafamilial culture conflict in several families requesting service provided an additional impetus to

*Joan S. Velasquez is Director of Research and Evaluation, Ramsey County Community Human Services, St. Paul, MN, and Cesar P. Velasquez, student, University of Minnesota, Institute of Technology, St. Paul, MN.

[1]Hispanic refers to individuals of Spanish-speaking origin.

(*Family Relations*, 1980, **29**, 598-603.)

[2]Marilyn Vigil de McClure, Minnesota Commissioner of Human Rights, conceptualized the range of movement continuum and contributed to all aspects of its development. Mental Health Department Latino Program staff carefully refined, modified and applied it.

develop a conceptual framework which incorporates the varying patterns of cultural identification found among Hispanic families.

Through case discussion, examination of literature, and analysis of their own values and role expectations, the students and instructors developed a framework with which to assess degree of biculturalism and locate sources of culture conflict in client families. The framework came to be viewed as a treatment tool as well, and was eventually used as an aid in training other staff and students.

The Framework

The framework rests on the concept of biculturalism, defined here as the capacity to function effectively and comfortably within two distinct cultural contexts. A continuum which has Anglo and Hispanic cultures as its end points is used to illustrate each individual's range of movement between these contexts. The Anglo culture, as discussed here, is that which has evolved from a number of Northern European sources, whereas Hispanic culture includes systems of Spanish and Latin American origin.

There exists, of course, a wide range of individual and group differences within each cultural system; yet, there is a recognizable sharing of values, beliefs, norms, and role expectations which are viewed by members of one cultural group as different from those of the other (Velasquez, McClure, & Benavides, 1979). Anglo Americans function primarily within the context of the dominant culture, and experience minimal press toward learning the language, values or expectations of other groups. Hispanics, on the other hand, have experienced a press toward assimilation into the dominant culture in order to gain access to the goods and services which are controlled primarily by Anglo Americans. Chestang (Note 2), in discussing this experience from a Mexican American viewpoint, asserts that functioning in two cultures can result in the capacity to develop two distinct ways of coping with other's expectations, and to respond with the coping pattern related to the cultural context in which one is operating. The individual who has developed sets of patterns for coping with both Anglo and Hispanic expectations is considered to be bicultural. In

this bicultural person, distinct response patterns do not create a dual personality but, rather, have converged into an integrated whole, enabling the individual to function within both "worlds" (Cruz, 1979).

The bicultural assessment framework assists social workers in examining the extent to which each family member functions in two "worlds" and in determining which cultural values influence the performance of selected roles. Three steps comprise this process: (a) diagram each family member's range of movement across a cultural continuum; (b) locate members on continua which represent specific roles; and (c) compare members to uncover potential areas of culture conflict. Information yielded reduces the risk of misinterpreting clients' perceptions and desired outcomes, of working toward culturally dissonant goals, and of inaccurately assessing family dynamics. Functional behavior and relationships are often assessed as pathological when not viewed within the appropriate cultural context (Mirandi, 1979). The assessment also provides the worker with an expanded view of the family's relationship to external systems.

The worker considers five dimensions in making the assessment. The following list of these dimensions includes examples of questions which the worker may address when exploring that aspect of family members' lives.

1. *Language used*. Under what circumstances does each family member speak Spanish or English? Many Hispanics choose Spanish for expressing tenderness or for prayer, even though they speak English fluently.
2. *Frequency and location of interaction within each cultural context*. Do family members work or attend school primarily with Hispanics or Anglos? With whom do they socialize?
3. *Level of comfort within each context*. Do members *prefer* to use Spanish or English? Are they more at ease with one cultural group than another?
4. *Value base from which relevant roles are performed*. How do family members describe a "good" mother, a "bad" son?

Does the family nurture Hispanic identity?

5. *Specific life style factors*. What type of food is prepared in the home? Do members listen to music of Hispanic or Anglo origin?

The following diagram and discussion illustrate use of the assessment framework with members of three families.

Application to Assessment

Mrs. Vasquez recently moved to the U.S. from Puerto Rico with her family, lives in a Hispanic neighborhood where Spanish is the dominant language and works in a store with other Puerto Ricans. She does not speak English and chooses not to travel beyond her neighborhood. Mrs. Vasquez is located, at this point in time, within the boundaries of Hispanic culture with no range of movement recorded. If all members of her family are located at this point on the range of movement continuum, culture conflict is not an issue: the worker focuses on assessing family dynamics from an Hispanic value base. The worker also considers the impact on this family of being newly identified as minorities in a foreign culture and of the press toward assimilation which they will begin to experience.

At the Anglo end of the continuum, also with no range of movement recorded, is Mr. Puerta, who grew up and lives in an all Anglo suburb, operates a small business which employs no other Hispanics, does not speak Spanish, is married to an Anglo, and does not identify himself as Hispanic. The worker will cautiously assess dynamics in this family from an Anglo value base, remaining open to re-assessment should unrecognized cultural influences become apparent later while exploring Mr. Puerta's family of origin.

The Garcia family, on the other hand, presents the more usual circumstance of family members who have identifiable ranges of movement along the continuum. The variability of ranges within this family creates potential for culture conflict. During the assessment process, the worker located Mr. and Mrs. Garcia and their three children on the continuum illustrated above. The diagram indicates that Mrs. Garcia's coping patterns are predominantly Hispanic but that she draws from "Anglo" patterns under some circumstances. For example, she shops in stores where only English is spoken, and attends an English speaking Catholic church. Mrs. Garcia, having recently moved to St. Paul from a Hispanic barrio in Texas, is in increased contact with Anglo culture; her range of movement may be expected to expand over time. When asked for her description of a good mother or a good wife, Mrs. Garcia responds from a traditional Hispanic value base. In these critical roles, she is located on the right end of the continuum.

Mr. Garcia has a wider range of movement than his wife. Though most comfortable with Spanish, he speaks English well enough to attend classes at a local vocational institute. It is through Mr. Garcia that most of the family's interaction with external systems occurs;

Anglo/white culture Mr. Puerta	Range of Movement	Hispanic culture Mrs. Vasquez
	Mrs. Garcia	
	Mr. Garcia	
	Raul and Racquel Garcia	
	Pablo Garcia	
	Ms. Lopez	

	Parent Role	Mr. Garcia Mrs. Garcia
	Spouse Role	Mr. Garcia Mrs. Garcia
Pablo Garcia	Child Role	Raul Garcia Raquel Garcia

Figure 1. Use of the assessment framework with members of three families.

this representation of the family to the outside world is generally expected of the Hispanic husband (McClure, Note 3). That Mr. Garcia has retained the full range of Hispanic patterns is evident in his extensive contacts with extended family members, activity in a local Chicano organization and, particularly, his description of a good husband or father. His location at the Hispanic end of the parent and spouse role continua reflects the perspective from which he discusses these roles.

Comparison of Pablo Garcia's range of movement to that of his parents illustrates the locus of culture conflict in this family. Pablo speaks both English and Spanish fluently. He attends an all Anglo school and spends most of his time with Anglo teenagers. He says he prefers to be with Anglos and criticizes his parents for being "too Mexican." When asked for his description of what teenagers and parents should expect of each other, he responds with an emphasis on gaining independence, freedom to express opinions which conflict with those of parents, and setting one's own rules. His parents identify these expectations as Anglo. Drawing from Hispanic values, they assert that Pablo should not challenge his father's authority and should strengthen intrafamily ties rather than strive for independence from them. Pablo and his parents are operating from conflicting value bases as they perform their reciprocal roles.

Raul Garcia (age 6) and Raquel Garcia (age 5) attend a school in which they interact primarily with Anglo teachers and students. As neither child attended school prior to this year, and because they spend most of their non-school hours with the extended family, Spanish continues to be their most comfortable language. Raul and Raquel are confused and upset by Pablo's disrespect of their parents; their view of good children is consonant with that of Mr. and Mrs. Garcia. As indicated by their location on the range of movement continuum, they appear to retain age-appropriate Hispanic patterns and are learning Anglo patterns.

The bicultural assessment diagram highlights the varying degrees to which members of the Garcia family function within each of two "worlds," which value system most influences member's performance of crucial roles,

and the locus of conflict in reciprocal roles. Note that all factors considered in the assessment process are subject to change over time. All members of the Garcia family speak English more frequently and have more contact with Anglos since their relocation from Texas to Minnesota. Each member's range of movement is likely to expand, though not at the same rate, particularly since type and frequency of contact with Anglos differ among family members. Culture-based conflict occurs most often where families such as the Garcias relocate in areas with smaller Hispanic populations, or when children have considerably more exposure to the "Anglo world" than their parents.

Ms. Lopez, the Garcia family's social worker, diagrammed herself along with her clients and is presented here to illustrate the range of movement of the fully bicultural individual. Ms. Lopez speaks Spanish and English fluently and with ease. She has frequent contact with her Spanish speaking family as well as with her Anglo husband's family and feels "at home" with both groups. Being bilingual and bicultural, she is able to move across the entire continuum to work with clients within their cultural contexts and thus not exert pressure on them to expand ranges of movement unless that is their choice.

Our examples illustrate that families may be located solely within the boundaries of one cultural system, effectively use a full range of coping patterns relevant to both systems, or function within each context under selected circumstances with varying degrees of comfort. The assessment begins as the worker and family discuss the presenting problem. It may be completed during the first interview or require two to three sessions, depending on family size and the extent of variation in range of movement. The assessment is reconsidered during quarterly case reviews to take into account the changes which occur when families are in a state of transition.

The framework assists in developing a bicultural as opposed to an assimilationist perspective and ensures that cultural content will be incorporated into the assessment process. At this point in its development, the tool provides a beginning method for examining critical concepts and a means for preparing the worker to approach families from a culturally relevant value base.

Application to Treatment

Initially, workers applying the bicultural framework gathered the required information from family members and then completed the diagram apart from the family. Finding the framework useful in identifying areas of culture conflict in the Garcia family, Ms. Lopez decided to discuss her diagram with them and found it useful as a treatment technique. Additional information regarding the Garcias illustrates the application of the framework in treatment.

Mrs. Garcia telephoned the agency, requesting counseling for her family. Pablo, age 15, was refusing to attend school, smoking marijuana and consistently disobeying his father. Mr. Garcia punished Pablo by not speaking to him and threatened to send him to reform school where he would be "taught to respect his father" and to become a "gentleman not a punk." Mrs. Garcia complained of gastro-intestinal discomfort and "nervios." She was fearful that her husband would either leave the family or send their son away.

Prior to moving to St. Paul, the Garcias lived with Mrs. Garcia's family in Texas. Mr. Garcia had been an over-the-road trucker since shortly after Pablo's birth until a back injury forced him to resign and seek other employment. The family moved to Minnesota to live near his brothers who promised to help support them and find work for Mr. Garcia. Pablo remained with his grandparents in Texas for several months to complete the school year and then joined his parents in Minnesota.

During her first contact with the family, the worker, Ms. Lopez, obtained information required to diagram the continuum and discuss member's perceptions of current difficulties. Recognition that Mr. and Mrs. Garcia performed their roles as parents from a Hispanic value base resulted in Ms. Lopez' accurate assessment of the intensity of conflict within the family. That Mrs. Garcia had requested help without her husband's knowledge violated expected patterns where the husband

initiates contact with the outside world and is the primary decision maker in the family. Mrs. Garcia confided later that she circumvented her husband from a sense of desperation. Mr. Garcia demonstrated flat affect and communicated only his distress that his son had no respect for him. From a traditional Hispanic viewpoint, to challenge or openly disagree with parents signals lack of respect and unwillingness to acknowledge or accept their legitimate authority. Pablo's disrespect for his father at a time when Mr. Garcia was particularly vulnerable (under stress from physical discomfort and loss of work) triggered Mr. Garcia's sense of having lost his rightful position in the family and the resulting depression. Both parents experienced an intense sense of shame.

The worker recognized the importance of two Hispanic cultural values for the Garcias: that the father be seen as the authority figure in the family and that respect, meaning not challenging or openly disagreeing with that authority, is essential (Thorpe, Meadow, Lennhoff, & Satterfield, 1968). She also recognized Pablo's exposure to the value placed by many Anglo Americans on negotiation of rules, increased independence for adolescents, and consideration of children's opinions in a family discussion. Ms. Lopez explained the concept of biculturalism to the family and asked members to locate themselves on several continua. Neither the Garcias nor any other Hispanic family with whom this framework has been used had difficulty understanding or placing themselves on a continuum. Direct use of the framework with the Garcias served to open communication between Mr. Garcia and Pablo, who talked to each other for the first time in several weeks, as they determined ranges and locations. The diagram clearly illustrated cultural differences, allowing the worker to focus immediately on the area of conflict. Increased awareness of the cultural basis for their differences enabled Mr. Garcia and Pablo to move away from viewing each other as totally unreasonable and rejecting and toward more benign interpretations of the other's behavior.

Though not developed for use as a treatment technique, discussion of the framework often facilitates positive communication among family members. It also encourages active participation in counseling by providing the family with a relevant, concrete task to complete. Relationship development between worker and family is enhanced as the worker demonstrates awareness and acceptance of the range of cultural values within the family and instills confidence that differences do not preclude resolution of conflict.

Application to Training

Finding the framework useful in both assessment and treatment, program field instructors applied it to training other staff and students. Explanation of the bicultural continuum with extensive case illustrations can be used to sensitize human services professionals to the need to consider cultural factors in all aspects of service delivery and provides a base from which to teach culture-specific content. Training sessions begin with a didactic presentation of the continuum, then focus on discussion of participant's backgrounds to increase worker's understanding of the influence of cultural values on their own behavior. Having examined their heritages and noted the diversity within all cultural systems, staff are better prepared to recognize cultural influences within Hispanic families. Case materials introduce specific values and role expectations. Since avoidance of stereotyping is a major concern, instructors draw examples from several locations on the continuum as well as from different Hispanic backgrounds.

Summary

Cultural factors must be considered in all aspects of the helping process if clients are to be served appropriately. The bicultural framework integrates the client's value base into assessment, while avoiding a stereotyped approach and reducing the press toward assimilation. Direct examination of location and range of movement with family members has led to improved communication and re-interpretation of each other's behavior. The framework also aids in sensitizing staff to the importance of considering cultural factors when working with Latino clients and in recognizing their own need for consultation when unable to interpret these factors. Current work toward refining the framework focuses on identifying specific cultural values and developing a scale which measures biculturalism.

REFERENCE NOTES

1. Padilla, A. M., & Ruiz, R. A. *Latino Mental Health*, DHEW Publication #(HSM) 73-9143, 1976.
2. Chestang, L. W. *Character development in a hostile environment*. Paper presented at the American Group Psychotherapy Association Meeting, San Antonio, 1975.
3. Vigil de McClure, M. E. *Counseling with the Spanish speaking*. Paper presented at the Minnesota Social Service Association Conference, March, 1976.

REFERENCES

Benavides, E., Lynch, M., & Velasquez, J. Toward a culturally relevant field work model, *Journal of Social Work Education*, in press.

Cruz, A. M. *Research Bulletin*, Spanish Speaking Mental Health Research Center, Los Angeles, Jan.-Feb., 1979.

Mirandi, A. A reinterpretation of male dominance in the Chicano family. *The Family Coordinator*, 1979, **28**, 473-479.

Thorpe, R., Meadow, A., Lennhoff, S. G., & Satterfield, D. Changes in marriage roles accompanying the acculturation of the Mexican American wife. *Journal of Marriage and the Family*, 1968, **30**, 404-412.

Velasquez, J. Vigil McClure, M. E., & Benavides, E. A framework for establishing social work relationships across racial/ethnic lines. In Compton, B. R., & Galloway, B. (Eds.),*Social Work Processes*. Dorsey Press, Homewood, Ill., 1979.

White, A. E. *The apperceptive mass of foreigners as applied to Americanization; the Mexican group*. R. & E. Research Associates, San Francisco, 1971.

Index to Volume 29, 1980

Authors

Titles

Inexpressive Males or Overexpressive Females? A Reply to Balswick, *L. L'Abate*, 2:229.

Integrating Attitudinal and Behavioral Change in Marital Enrichment, *L. Hof, N. Epstein, and W. R. Miller*, 2:241.

Male Friendship and Intimacy Across the Span, *J. Tognoli*, 3:273.

Managerial Behavior and Stress in Families Headed by Divorced Women: A Proposed Framework, *C. A. Buehler and M. J. Hogan*, 4:525.

Marriage Experiences of Family Life Specialists, *P. C. Glick*, 1:111.

Mother-Daughter Communication About Sex, *G. L. Fox and J. K. Inazu*, 3:347.

Normal Stresses During the Transition to Parenthood, *B. C. Miller and D. L. Sollie*, 4:459.

Normative Family Stress: Family Boundary Changes Across the Life-Span, *P. G. Boss*, 4:445.

Normative Stress and Young Families: Adaptation and Development, *C. S. Bell, J. E. Johnson, A. V. McGillicuddy-DeLisi, and I. E. Sigel*, 4:453.

"Palimony": The Impact of Marvin v. Marvin, *N. Myricks*, 2:210.

Parent Education: A Classroom Program on Social Learning Principles, *R. A. Dubanoski and G. Tanabe*, 1:15.

Parent Satisfactions, Concerns, and Goals for Their Children, *C. S. Chilman*, 3:339.

Participation in and Enjoyment of Family Maintenance Activities by Elderly Women, *G. J. Hildreth, G. Van Laanen, E. Kelley, and T. Durant*, 3:386.

Patterns of Coping in Divorce and Some Implications for Clinical Practice, *K. Kressel*, 2:234.

Premarital Sexual Experience Among College Females, 1958, 1968, and 1978, *R. R. Bell and K. Coughey*, 3:353.

Rapid Changes in Household Composition Among Low-Income Mothers, *D. P. Slesinger*, 2:221.

Reactions and Adjustments to Divorce: Differences in the Experiences of Males and Females, *S. L. Albrecht*, 1:59.

Review of Theories and Research Concerning Sex-Role Development and Androgyny with Suggestions for Teachers, *C. Flake-Hobson, P. Skeen and B. E. Robinson*, 2:155.

Role-Sharing Couples: A Study of Egalitarian Marriages, *L. Haas*, 3:289.

Role Strain and Depression in Two-Job Families, *P. M. Keith and R. B. Schafer*, 4:483.

Rural Plant Closures: The Coping Behavior of Filipinos in Hawaii, *R. N. Anderson*, 4:511.

Satisfaction with Family Relations Among the Elderly, *W. C. Seelbach and C. J. Hansen*, 1:91.

Self-Disclosure and Satisfaction in Marriage: The Relation Examined, *S. R. Jorgensen and J. C. Gaudy*, 3:281.

Supporting Families under Stress: The Role of Social Networks, *D. G. Unger and D. R. Powell*, 4:566.

The "Home Treatment": The First Steps in Trying to Cope With An Alcoholic Husband, *J. P. Wiseman*, 4:541.

The Hyperactive Child as a Source of Stress in the Family: Consequences and Suggestions for Intervention, *C. Balkwell and C. F. Halverson, Jr.*, 4:550.

The Impact of the Environment on the Coping Efforts of Low-Income Mothers, *D. Dill, E. Feld, J. Martin, S. Beukema, and D. Belle*, 4:503.

The Mother-Adolescent Daughter Relationship as a Sexual Socialization Structure: A Research Review, *G. L. Fox*, 1:21.

The Only Child Grows Up: A Look at Some Characteristics of Adult Only Children, *D. F. Polit, R. L. Nuttall, and E. V. Nuttall*, 1:99.

The Purchase of Contraceptives by College Students, *D. J. Kallen and J. J. Stephenson*, 3:358.

The Role of Parental Beliefs in the Family as a System of Mutual Influences, *A. V. McGillicuddy-DeLisi*, 3:317.

The Social Consequences of Single Parenthood: A Longitudinal Perspective, *M. J. Smith*, 1:75.

The Vital Marriage: A Closer Look, *P. Ammons and N. Stinnett*, 1:37.

The Widowed, Black, Older Adult in the Rural South: Implications for Policy, *J. P. Scott and J. R. Kivett*, 1:83.

Trends Affecting Adolescent Views of Sexuality, Employment, Marriage, and Childrearing, *J. Walters and L. H. Walters*, 2:191.

Trends in Marriage and the Family—The 1980's, *D. Knox*, 2:145.

Unemployment and Family Stress: A Reassessment, *L. E. Thomas, E. McCabe, and J. E. Berry*, 4:517.

Using Kohlberg's Moral Developmental Framework in Family Life Education, *C. L. Englund*, 1:7.

Value Reasoning: An Approach to Values Education, *M. E. Arcus*, 2:163.

Voluntary Childlessness, Involuntary Childlessness, and Having Children: A Study of Social Perceptions, *L. G. Calhoun and J. W. Selby*, 2:181.

Women and Retirement: A Study and Implications, *C. K. Johnson and S. Price-Bonham*, 3:380.

Working with Defensive Projections in Conjoint Marriage Counseling, *J. F. Sunbury*, 1:107.

Work Roles as Stressors in Corporate Families, *P. Voydanoff*, 4:489.

Contemporary Family Materials

Adolescent Coping, *A. E. Moriarty and P. W. Toussieng*, 2:255. (R) J. H. Curtis.

Aging: A Guide to Reference Sources, Journals and Government Publications, *B. McIlvanie and M. Mundkun; with L. Yurchyshyn and L. DeLuca*, 2:263. (R) W. H. Quinn.

Aging Parents, *P. K. Ragan*, 2:255. (R) J. H. Curtis.

All Our Children: The American Family Under Pressure, *K. Keniston*, 1:131. (R) J. A. Mancini.

And Say What He Is: The Life of a Special Child, *J. B. Murray and E. Murray*, 2:256. (R) J. H. Curtis.

Authors Guide to Journals in Sociology and Related Fields, *M. B. Sussman*, 1:133. (R) J. Walters.

Battered Women: A Psychological Study of Domestic Violence, *M. Roy (Ed.)*, 2:259. (R) J. H. Curtis.

Birth of a Family: The Role of the Father in Childbirth, *N. C. Hale*, 3:414. (R) P. Morris.

Child Abuser: A Study of Child Abusers in Self-Help Group Therapy, *M. C. Collins*, 2:256. (R) J. H. Curtis.

Children of Parting Parents, *L. H. Tessman*, 2:257. (R) J. H. Curtis.

Conflict and Power in Marriage: Expecting the First Child, *R. LaRossa*, 1:134. (R) M. S. Herrman.

Counseling in Correctional Environments, *L. A. Bennett, T. S. Rosenbaum, and W. R. McCullough*, 3:417. (R) D. A. Dosser.

Daddy Doesn't Live Here Anymore, *R. Turow*, 3:421. (R) C. A. Everett.

Divorce in the United States, Canada and Great Britain: A Guide to Information Services, K. D. Sell and B. H. Sell, 2:256. (R) J. H. Curtis.

Dr. Block's Do-It-Yourself Illustrated Human Sexuality Book for Kids, W. A. Block, 3:422. (R) L. A. Klein.

Enhancing Self-Concept in Early Childhood, S. C. Samuels, 1:132. (R) L. A. Kirkendall.

Exploring Intimate Life Styles, B. I. Murstein (Ed.), 2:258. (R) J. H. Curtis.

Exploring Marriage and the Family, D. Knox, 3:415. (R) K. L. Christman.

Family-focused Care, J. R. Miller and E. H. Janosik (Eds.), 3:420. (R) D. R. Tate.

Family Therapy: An Interactional Approach, M. Andolf, 2:263. (R) K.S. Wampler.

Family Therapy: Full Length Case Studies, P. Papp (Ed.), 2:259. (R) J. H. Curtis.

Family Therapy: Theory and Practice, P. J. Guerin, Jr. (Ed.), 1:134. (R) B. B. Ingoldsby.

Finding Intimacy, H. G. Zerof, 1:137. (R) K. Young-Kerr.

Flying Solo, K. Wydro, 3:410. (R) H. D. Le Blanc.

Group Counseling and Group Psychotherapy with Rehabilitation Clients, M. Seligman, 1:137. (R) D. Logan.

Handbook of Sexology (5 volumes), J. Money and H. Mursaph (Eds.), 2:260. (R) J. H. Curtis.

Healthy Sexuality, D. A. Read, 2:260. (R) J. H. Curtis.

How to Have a Happy Marriage, D. Mace and V. Mace, 2:258. (R) J. H. Curtis.

Inventory of Marriage and Family Literature, D. H. Olson (Ed.), 2:258. (R) J. H. Curtis.

Kiss Daddy Goodnight, L. Armstrong, 1:130. (R) B. E. James.

Leisure and the Family Life Cycle, R. Rapoport and R. N. Rapoport, 2:257. (R) J. H. Curtis.

Living and Loving after Divorce, C. Napolitane and V. Pellegrino, 1:136. (R) S. L. Halperin.

Love, L. Buscaglia, 2.257. (R) J. H. Curtis.

Marital and Family Therapy, I. D. Glick and D. R. Kessler, 2:258. (R) J. H. Curtis.

Marriage and Marital Therapy; Psychoanalytic, Behavioral and Systems Perspectives, T. J. Paoline, Jr., and B. S. McCrady (Eds.) 1:136. (R) W. C. Nichols, Jr.

Marriage and the Family, C. B. Boderick, 2:258. (R) J. H. Curtis.

Maternal-infant bonding, M. H. Klaus and J. H. Kennell, 1:132. (R) B. Davidson.

Military Families: Adaptation to Change, E. J. Hunter and D. S. Nice, 2:257. (R) J. H. Curtis.

Naked Nomads, G. Gilder, 3:410. (R) H. D. LeBlanc.

National Directory of Children and Youth Services, CPR Directory Services Co., 2:265. (R) E. E. Neubaum.

Normal Psychology of the Aging Process, N. E. Zinberg and I. Kaufman (Eds.), 3:422. (R) C. Balkwell.

Parent-child Relations, J. Bigner, 3:413. (R) J. R. Blair.

Parents' Yellow Pages, F. Caplan (Ed.), 1:130. (R) V. de Lissovoy.

Sex and the Liberated Man, A. Ellis, 3:417. (R) S. A. Terry.

Sex Research: Bibliographies From the Institute for Sex Research, J. S. Brewer and R. W. Wright, 2:260. (R) J. H. Curtis.

Sex Research: Bibliographies from the Institute for Sex Research, J. S. Brewer (Ed.), 3:413. (R) J. H. Curtis.

Sexually Victimized Children, D. Finkelhor, 3:414. (R) G. L. Schilmoeller.

Single, P. J. Stein, 3:410. (R) H. D. Le Blanc.

Single Blessedness, M. Adams, 3:410. (R) H. D. Le Blanc.

Tantrums, Toads, and Teddy Bears, S. Cragg, 2:265. (R) C. Balkwell.

Teenage Pregnancy: A New Beginning, L. Barr, C. Monscrrat, C. Gaston, and T. Berg, 1:130. (R) C. Walters.

The American Family: A Demographic History, R. R. Seward, 3:416. (R) L. A. Kirkendall.

The American Family in Social-Historical Perspective (2nd ed.), M. Gordon (Ed.), 2:262. (R) L. A. Kirkendall.

The American Family: Variety and Change, E. Dyer, 2:262. (R) S. B. Gruber.

The Broken Taboo: Sex in the Family, B. Justice and R. Justice, 2:260. (R) J. H. Curtis.

The Challenge of Being Single, M. Edwards and E. Hoover, 3:410. (R) H. D. Le Blanc.

The Challenge of Daycare, S. Provence, A. Naylor, and J. Patterson, 3:415. (R) P. M. Lobdell.

The Child in His Family: Children and Their Parents in a Changing World, E. J. Anthony and C. Chiland (Eds.), 2:261. (R) P. Richards.

The Child in His Family: Vulnerable Children, E. J. Anthony, C. Koupernick, and C. Chiland (Eds.), 1:129. (R) J. V. Davis.

The Family Crucible, A. Y. Napier and C. A. Whitaker, 1:135. (R) J. Kropp.

The Family Handbook of Adolescence, J. E. Schowalter and W. R. Anyan, 3:421. (R) C. A. Brennan.

The Intimate Hours (Female Questionnaire), R. F. Kaufman, 3:419. (R) J. Walters.

Theory and Practice of Counseling and Psychotherapy, G. Corey, 1:133. (R) L. H. Walters.

The Police Marriage, 1:137. (R) J. H. Curtis. (film)

The Psychology of Adolescence (3rd ed.), A. T. Jersild, J. S. Brook, and D. W. Brook, 3:414. (R) M. D. Baranowski.

The Regulation of Psychotherapists (Vol. 1): A Study in the Philosophy and Practice of Professional Regulation, D. B. Hagan, 3:418. (R) W. C. Nichols.

The Regulation of Psychotherapists (Vol. 2): A Handbook of State Licensure Laws, D. B. Hogan, 3:418. (R) W. C. Nichols.

The Regulation of Psychotherapists (Vol. 3); A Review of Malpractice Suits in the United States, D. B. Hogan, 3:418. (R) W. C. Nichols.

The Regulation of Psychotherapists (Vol. 4): Bibliography, D. B. Hogan, 3:418. (R) W. C. Nichols.

The Runaways: Children, Husbands, Wives, and Parents, M. Brenton, 2:264. (R) C. Edelbrock.

The Sex Atlas: A New Illustrated Guide, E. J. Haeberle, 1:134. (R) J. H. Curtis.

The Sex Offender, B. Delin, 2:256. (R) J. H. Curtis.

To Be A Therapist, J. M. Lewis, 1:135. (R) N. L. Gaylin.

Turning Points: Historical and Sociological Essays on the Family, J. Demos and S. Spence (Eds.), 2:261. (R) J. W. Dykstra.

Understanding Human Sexuality, J. S. Hyde, 2:260. (R) J. H. Curtis.

Unplanned Parenthood: The Social Consequences of Teenage Childbearing, F. F. Furstenberg, 1:131. (R) V. B. Harvey.

Women, Work and Family, L. A. Tilly and J. W. Scott, 2:259. (R) J. H. Curtis.

Working Couples, R. N. Rapoport and R. Rapoport (Eds.), 2:258. (R) J. H. Curtis.

You and Your Child: A Common Sense Approach to Successful Parenting, B. R. Wagonseller and R. L. McDowell, 3:416. (R) B. B. Ingoldsby.